JAPANESE VEGETARIAN COOKERY

JAPANESE VEGETARIAN COOKERY

Lesley Downer

JONATHAN CAPE
THIRTY-TWO BEDFORD SQUARE LONDON

Illustrated by John Shelley

First published 1986
Copyright © 1986 by Lesley Downer
Jonathan Cape Ltd, 32 Bedford Square, London WC1B 3EL

British Library Cataloguing in Publication Data
Downer, Lesley
Japanese vegetarian cookery.
1. Vegetarian cookery   2. Cookery,
Japanese
I. Title
641.5'636'0952   TX837

ISBN 0–224–02811–1
ISBN 0–224–02862–6 Pbk

Phototypeset by Falcon Graphic Art Ltd
Wallington, Surrey
Printed in Great Britain by
The Camelot Press Ltd, Southampton

To my 'mothers', 'older sisters' and friends in Japan – origatou

Contents

Introduction   1
The Vegetarian in Japan   7
Tea and Sake   11
Planning Your Menu   15
Some Unfamiliar Ingredients   21
Some Useful Japanese Utensils   34
Cooking Techniques   39

PART ONE: VEGETABLES

Aubergines   45
Broccoli   53
Cabbage and Chinese Cabbage   57
Carrots   64
Cauliflower   71
Chestnuts   73
Cucumbers   80
Daikon Radish   86
Leeks and Spring Onions   93
Mushrooms   95
Onions   105
Peppers   107
Potatoes   110
Pumpkin   116
Spinach   120
Sweetcorn   127
Sweet Potatoes   129
Turnips   133
Seaweeds   140
Mixed Vegetable Dishes   150
Pickles   171

PART TWO: BEANS, SOYA BEAN PRODUCTS AND EGGS

Beans   179
Tofu   187
Deep-fried Tofu   204
Yuba   210
Okara   222
Miso   224
Natto   234
Eggs   242

PART THREE: GRAINS

Rice   257
Mochi (Rice Cakes)   277
Soba (Buckwheat Noodles)   283

Japanese Food Suppliers in the United Kingdom   295
Japanese Food Suppliers in Australia   300
Index   302

Introduction

Since I first became a vegetarian, I have been aware of the strange and exotic foods of Japan. Investigating the mysteries of my local health-food shop I would discover little bags of dark, salty bean paste, stringy dried seaweeds and soft, custardy blocks of tofu. Gradually I began to experiment with these new foods in my own cooking. But I could never discover how these ingredients were used in traditional Japanese cookery, for the only Japanese restaurants were in London and, as to-day, they were prohibitively expensive. I prepared miso soup, enjoyed the chewy sweetness of hiziki, and even made tempura, with no idea of how the traditional Japanese version tasted.

Over the years Japan and its culture seemed to take a greater and greater hold on me. I learnt about the qualities of Japanese pottery, which had inspired Bernard Leach, the great English potter; I became interested in the austerity of Zen Buddhism and its poetry and art; and eventually I persuaded a friend to teach me spoken Japanese, practising my week's new words on the dog during our daily walk.

When the chance arose for me to work in Japan, I snapped it up. I prepared for the land of samurai, Mount Fuji and cherry blossom, poohpoohing the warnings of my Japanese friends that behind every temple was a factory. I asked to be sent to the countryside of Japan.

Finally, in 1978, I found myself in Gifu, a small provincial town set on a plain between steep, pine-covered mountains a little north of the main bullet-train route from Tokyo to Osaka. Every town in Japan has a famous local product and delicacy; Gifu is known for its paper lanterns and oiled paper umbrellas such as we see in woodblock prints, and for the small ayu, the sweetfish, which is caught by cormorants on the Nagara river. This much every Japanese knows about Gifu; but most Japanese have never actually been there, and indeed pitied me my exile in this most old-fashioned of towns, renowned mainly for being a good thirty years behind the rest of Japan. However, this provinciality suited me very well; I had come to Japan to be in Japan, not in some throbbing cosmopolitan metropolis. Gradually I came to know Gifu, and was a familiar face myself in this city with its population of only six Westerners.

Japanese society is polarised: women mix with women and men mix with men, and the two worlds are very different. One reads accounts of Japan written by men, who mention among other things how rare it is to be invited into Japanese homes, and who can only suggest that one stay in a Japanese-style hotel in order to get a glimpse of something approximating to them. Guests are entertained in a restaurant, not in the home; most Western men of my acquaintance knew a lot about bars and clubs, but not much about Japanese family life.

As a woman, nearly all my Japanese friends were women. A main point of contact between us, transcending culture and language, was our mutual interest in food, its preparation and consumption. My friends frequently invited me not just to dine but to stay in their homes, entertaining me with tea ceremony, and laying out their softest bedding on the thick, fragrant straw matting in the best room. In theory guests are not encouraged to enter the kitchen; but I spent hours helping to prepare meals, and chatting about the differences between life in Japan and in the West, in tiny inconvenient kitchens with very little chopping space and only two gas rings on which to cook, designed, my friends insisted, by men to be used by women. The men I encountered were mainly the fathers and husbands of my friends, although I never met the husbands of some of my closest friends because they were always at work.

Once Mrs Ishikawa, whose husband incidentally had taken her name instead of vice versa to ensure the continuance of her family name, promised me a meal served in traditional Japanese fashion. In all innocence I arrived at her house to visit her, and was greeted by her husband and father, who entertained me in the guest room while she and her mother brought in a succession of beautifully prepared dishes, kneeling down to serve us, and speaking only to inquire whether the food was to our satisfaction or whether we needed any more. They themselves ate in the kitchen, which, in that traditional household, neither the menfolk nor the guests ever entered.

Naturally my friends wanted to prepare their most delicious dishes and specialities for me, but at first they were rather bemused to discover that I was vegetarian. Most of them had never met a Westerner before, and were expecting a meat-eating, coffee-drinking, blue-eyed giant (in spite of my diminutive size, gifts of clothing were invariably Extra Large). They had been all prepared to cook up steaks and hamburgers to suit my supposed Western tastes, just as they assumed that, as a long-legged Westerner, I would be unable to sit, let alone sleep, on the floor. But with a little thought they realised that the traditional Japanese dishes which they had enjoyed as children before the advent of Western fast foods were largely vegetarian. Indeed it is only since the end of the Second World War that meat has become at all common in Japan, and most older people still prefer a largely meatfree diet. Harassed housewives often have to prepare two evening meals, traditional dishes of fish and vegetables for the grandparents and maybe even the husband, and hamburgers for the children. Before the Meiji restoration in the last century the Japanese ate no meat at all, and were shocked and disgusted when the Western newcomers demanded beef.

As far as I could I repaid all this hospitality in the Japanese fashion. Whenever I visited my friends I took gifts of exotic foods, fruit and cakes; and I often invited them to dine with me. I would scour the local supermarket, a treasure house filled with shelf upon shelf of different varieties of miso, dark and light soy sauces, seaweeds, and big freezers containing every imaginable transformation of tofu – sheer paradise for the vegetarian cook. I used these traditional ingredients to produce concoctions that my friends had never dreamt of cooking, but ate with relish.

During my four years I wandered extensively around Japan, staying with friends and friends of friends, in temples which doubled as hostels, or in homely little inns. Inevitably my travels tended to be a cook's tour. I sampled the great cuisines of Japan, which incidentally are all vegetarian, savouring the varieties of fine temple cuisine in the great temples of Kyoto

and Kamakura, and sampling the speciality tofu dishes of
Tokyo's famous tofu restaurants; I discovered that the little
temples hidden deep in the countryside of my own Gifu region
offered the finest tofu preparations of all. In the spring I tasted
wild vegetable dishes and learnt how to cook horsetail shoots,
which I gathered myself along the riverbanks. I even had the
chance to try Japan's *haute cuisine*, delicate morsels exquisitely
arranged on tiny plates which are served as part of the extended
tea ceremony, although, as my Japanese friends warned, the
appearance really is more important than the taste.

Again and again the talk would return to food and to cooking. To the Japanese, as to the French, food and eating are of
prime importance. During the whole time I was in Japan, the
only party I ever attended where a meal failed to materialise
was at not a Japanese but an English gathering at the British
Consulate in Osaka. Unfortunately, well trained by a few
years' residence in Japan, I arrived with a healthy appetite, only
to spend the entire evening politely refusing potato crisps and
sausage rolls.

In Japan, as in most Asian countries, food and eating have a
deep ritual and ceremonial significance, and are an integral part
of the complex social fabric of Japanese society. In spite of
Japan's superficial Westernisation, the traditions of hospitality
remain very strong. A guest will always be offered a meal.
Thus it would be quite impolite simply to drop in on a friend.
A Japanese will telephone to pre-arrange the date and time of
the visit so that the hostess can clean the house and make
preparations. And, as with so much of Japanese social inter-
action, the forms of behaviour appropriate to paying a visit or
to receiving guests are to a considerable extent prescribed.

The guest arrives with a gift, usually a gift of food, a flawless
melon tied with a ribbon, laid like an Easter egg in a presentation box, and beautifully wrapped in the paper of the
high-class department store from which it was bought; or a
box of the expensive little cakes for tea ceremony from a
famous local shop. It took me a long time to work out the
subtle rules of gift giving so that I could select something
exactly appropriate; for if the gift is too valuable it puts the
recipient under a heavy obligation to shower the giver with
even more valuable gifts, and so on *ad infinitum*.

The guest presents the gift, apologising for its inadequacy;

the hostess sets it aside without opening it and invites the guest to come in, apologising for the smallness and dinginess of her home, which is probably large and certainly spotless. She immediately sets a cup of green tea before the guest. Many are the tales of Japanese abroad who are quite bewildered by the many choices confronting the innocent guest, offered tea or coffee, with or without milk or sugar, or maybe a cold drink. In Japan there are no choices to be made. The tea is accompanied by a cake, with a tiny fork or stick with which to eat it.

After this comes the meal. In a traditional home like Mrs Ishikawa's the hostess will not participate in the meal, but will serve the guests and the male members of the family, although this custom is dying out in modern Japan. First the diners are given steaming hot towels with which to wipe face and hands. Each person's place is already set, the tiny dishes carefully laid out according to the prescribed rules. The diners say a word of thanks to the deities for providing another day's food before eating, usually in silence, for it is traditionally considered bad form to speak during a meal.

Afterwards the hostess offers fruit, peeled and cut into segments, ready to eat. When I was new to Japan and still ignorant of the niceties of Japanese etiquette, I offered some guests a bowl of fruit, leaving them to select and peel their own. One husband, who had clearly never before been called upon to exercise such culinary skills, picked a tangerine and handed it to his wife, who opened it up like a flower, separated the segments and removed the pith before returning it to him.

Finally guests and host once again thank the deities, and departures are made amidst much bowing.

Any invitation, no matter what the time of day or the

apparent purpose, is bound to include a meal. Many a time
before I had fully absorbed this essential fact of Japanese life, I
would make the foolish mistake of assuming that, for example,
a purported visit to a local paper mill to watch handmade paper
being produced, at two o'clock, would not include a meal, and
would therefore have lunch, only to be whisked from the mill
into a restaurant at two-thirty and confronted with a vast
spread. As in any other Asian country, it is considered most
impolite to refuse food. When I came to leave Japan, I was only
able to bid farewell to one friend a day, for each would have
been most upset if I had refused the enormous Farewell Feast
which she had spent days preparing, and one feast a day was
quite enough. It took me weeks to say goodbye to everyone.

The rituals of eating are also bound up with the social
stratification of Japanese society. Everyone you meet is likely
to be either your superior or your inferior. On first meeting,
the Japanese exchange namecards which show their occupa-
tion, thus indicating their relative status; they then know
whether to use polite forms of speech or to be more casual.

All Westerners are automatically honoured guests for the
entire duration of their stay in Japan, no matter how long. I
was also a teacher, the most highly honoured profession in
Japan. I was thus the sometimes reluctant recipient of much
respect and hospitality. Hospitality frequently involves being
taken to a restaurant rather than being invited home. When I
was new to Japan, a group of elderly teachers from my
university, unable to believe that a Westerner could be vegetarian, took me out to a steak restaurant. I was asked what I
wanted, and cast my eye down the menu, aghast at the long list
of steaks. At last I spotted 'Salad', and ordered one. The head
professor immediately ordered twenty salads. I realised too late
that the hosts must honour the guest by eating the same dish,
and watched in embarrassment as these elderly gentlemen
toyed with their lettuce leaves, having missed a fine chance to
enjoy a juicy steak.

The Vegetarian in Japan

There can be few countries in the world – maybe none – where it is easier and more pleasurable to be vegetarian than Japan. Every type of raw ingredient is of the highest quality and perfectly fresh. Simply to look at the vegetables, be it in a small local market or a big supermarket, is a pleasure. They are brought in fresh every day from the countryside or from the big Tsukiji market in Tokyo, and are laid out almost like an English vegetable show, row upon row, gleaming and flawless. Young shopboys are hired to splash cold water over them to keep them sparkling fresh.

No matter what the season, there are always vegetables in abundance; and the variety is quite spectacular. Most of our Western leaf vegetables are available, plus many more, such as perilla with its clean fresh taste, chrysanthemum leaves, trefoil, and many different varieties of spinach. Japanese women living in England frequently complain about how difficult it is to plan a meal here with such a dearth of green vegetables, and I myself have been tempted to smuggle out seeds.

Potatoes in Japan are but one representative of a whole family of tubers, which includes the small, brown, hairy taro, several varieties of sweet potato, long hairy yams, and a large, smooth, hand-shaped yam whose gooey flesh is eaten raw. There are big and small fungi of every description, from clumps of tiny mushrooms in shades of brown, gold, white or grey, to the ever-popular, chewy, brown shiitake mushroom. Even our rather characterless Western mushrooms have recently become available. Matsutake mushrooms, the subject of much mystique, appear briefly in the autumn, picked at great risk to life and limb on steep mountain slopes, or imported from Canada, where the naïve Canadians do not appreciate the subtlety of taste that makes this mushroom quite outrageously expensive in Japan. In what other country in the world would a mere mushroom be so celebrated as to be sold for a small fortune, nestling grandly in a bed of pine needles in a gleaming presentation box?

Wild vegetables are available in markets and supermarkets in season; the culling and eating of wild foods has never declined as it has in the West, and everyone knows and can cook burdock root, or the white fleshy horsetail shoots which spring up by the riverside in March, and many other roots, stalks, leaves and fruits which we are just beginning to rediscover. Gifu, like much of Japan, stands on a completely flat plain, hemmed in by mountains too steep to grow crops or build on, and covered in dense scrub and trees. Wild vegetables proliferate in this dense uncultivated woodland, which is not much more than a bicycle ride from anyone's home. It is not unusual to see a young mother helped by a couple of children picking horsetails or coltsfoot to prepare for supper. A husband off on a business trip to a far corner of Japan will not forget to bring his wife back some famed local wild delicacy.

This wealth of vegetables is by no means the end of the story. The Japanese have explored and developed the possibilities of a meat-free cuisine, perhaps more than any other people in the world. We in the West are just beginning to be aware of the potential of the sea as a source of food. Sea vegetables, which we lump together as mere 'seaweed', have been an essential part of the Japanese diet for a thousand years; kombu, our kelp, is mentioned with reverence in the classic tenth-century collection of poetry known as the *Manyoshu*. Seaweeds offer almost as much variety as vegetables in appearance, texture and taste. No Japanese cook would be without kombu, the essential ingredient in dashi, the Japanese stock which is used for cooking vegetables and making soup. And the traditional Japanese breakfast would be impossible without dark green silky fronds of wakame for the miso soup and crisp toasted nori in which to roll the rice.

Japan's soya bean products are justly famous. In fact, Japan's particular contribution to world cuisine is perhaps not so much a characteristic style of cooking as the development and production of a considerable variety of different cooking materials, for Japanese cooking, as we will see, tends to be deliberately simple, treating the basic ingredients with reverence. Some soya bean products are now well known in the West, although not available in anything like the variety that can be found in the most remote corner of Japan. Supermarkets offer a bewildering range even of soy sauces, dark and light, naturally fermented, or, more commonly, synthetic. There are big barrels of misos – a salty soya bean paste – at least twenty different varieties including misos for each season of the year, dark red and salty for winter, white and sweeter for summer, and fancy misos brought down from mountain districts, containing ginger, kombu or barley, and enough of a delicacy to be eaten just as they are, spread on a slice of cucumber. The range of tofus and tofu products is seemingly endless. Tofu, soya bean curd, comes in various types, not only standard 'cotton' tofu, but also 'silken' tofu, a real challenge to the novice chopstick user; the smallest corner shop will also sell lightly grilled tofu, golden deep-fried tofu (both thick and thin) in triangles, rectangles or balls, as well as tofu speckled with slivers of vegetables and even dried tofu.

A varied cuisine with many vegetarian dishes has grown up employing this wealth of raw materials, from simple, every-day, household cookery and robust country dishes to the refinements of temple cookery and the cuisine which accompanies the tea ceremony.

Many of the recipes in this book are simple ones which are usually served at home, although I have also included dishes from the largely vegetarian temple and restaurant cuisines and from different parts of Japan. The traditional Japanese recipes have been adapted to some extent so that they can be made with ingredients easily available in England. Also I have been unorthodox in using some wholefood ingredients. Although still not nearly as widespread as in England, more and more wholefoods are becoming available in Japan, and young people are cooking traditional dishes using wholefood ingredients. The Zen cookery of the temples is traditionally based on brown rice, although sadly most temples seem to use white rice nowadays. I have found that wholefood ingredients work well in traditional Japanese recipes; the resulting dishes are a little nuttier or crunchier but just as tasty as the originals.

All too many Japanese kitchens still contain little buckets of those three dire substances, salt, sugar and monosodium glutamate, which are ladled into sweet and savoury dishes alike. These I have omitted, or replaced with small quantities of salt (I suggest you use sea salt) or soy sauce, and a little sugar or honey, on the principle that well-cooked vegetables do not need much extra seasoning at all.

Tea and Sake

A Japanese meal is accompanied by tea, sake, beer, whisky or wine. Some varieties of beer, whisky and wine are home produced, although the Japanese generally prefer Scotch whisky and European wine.

Tea

Like the English, the Japanese are great tea drinkers; it is drunk throughout the day, both before and after meals, and a guest is always greeted with a cup of tea. Japanese tea is green, made with green, unfermented leaves. The deliciously sweet scent of fresh green tea, rather like the smell of new-mown grass, wafts from the old-fashioned tea shops in the back streets of every town. The tea shop is usually set discreetly back from the road, and is distinguished by its tea grinder, with an enormous funnel. Within the shop the teas are stored in barrels, graded according to type and quality. Having spent much time sniffing and tasting the different leaves, you select your teas, which are packaged in neat round tins with a tightly fitting lid, although you can of course buy ready packaged tea in a supermarket.

Tea is grown throughout central and southern Japan. If you ride the bullet train from Tokyo to Osaka, you will pass hillsides covered with row upon row of round tea bushes, around Shizuoka, almost in the shadow of Mount Fuji. The finest tea is said to come from Uji, near Kyoto. There are many grades of tea. Bancha is the coarsest, containing stems as well as leaves, and is served in big handleless mugs free of charge in restaurants. Standard everyday tea is somewhat finer. The finest and sweetest tea for everyday use is shincha, 'new tea', which is made from the young leaves of the tea plant in spring.

Sencha is a particularly fine grade of leaf tea, saved for special occasions and special guests and served in small porcelain cups; it has its own rather esoteric tea ceremony. Macha is the tea used for the usual tea ceremony; it is a brilliant green powder which is whisked to a foam with a small bamboo whisk and served in a large bowl according to a set of extremely specific rules, to be drunk in exactly three and a half sips. Japanese shops in England stock a variety of Japanese teas, as do some health-food shops specialising in Japanese goods; they can also be found in specialist tea shops. However, if you have difficulty finding them, Chinese teas can be used instead.

Japanese tea is made not with boiling water but with water just a little hotter than drinking temperature. Connoisseurs pour boiling water into a wide-mouthed bowl with a spout, and allow it to cool to just the right temperature before pouring it into the warmed teapot. To make Japanese tea, allow one teaspoonful of tea per cup. Put the leaves into the warmed pot and pour water which has boiled and been allowed to cool slightly on to the leaves. Cover the pot and steep for only a minute or two; if left any longer the tea will become bitter.

Both teapot and teacups are tiny and usually made of porcelain. The cup is filled only two-thirds full so that the rim may be held without burning one's fingers. Drink it holding the cup with the right hand while supporting it on the left.

In summer the most refreshing drink is iced barley tea (mugicha). Barley tea is not strictly a tea, but simply barley grains roasted until dark brown. Roasted barley is sold in

Japanese and some health-food shops. If unavailable, you can roast your own: place whole barley grains in a dry frying pan or a very low oven (about 200°F, 100°C), stirring occasionally, until the grains are dark brown and fragrant. To make barley tea, put 2 tbsps (30 ml) roasted barley in a saucepan with 4 cups water. Bring to the boil and simmer for 5 minutes. Strain the tea, allow to cool, and refrigerate. Serve in glasses with ice cubes.

Sake (Rice Wine)

Sake is celebrated as the national drink of Japan, and has been popular since mythological times. The deities are said even now to be extremely fond of it, and Shinto shrines are ringed with enormous casks donated by local merchants and business-men to ensure a favourable response to their prayers. It plays an important part in Shinto ceremonies; at a wedding, the marriage is sealed by the exchange of cups of sake.

It is made by fermenting freshly steamed white rice. Once fermentation has finished, it can be drunk immediately; it does not need to mature. There are numerous types and grades from different parts of Japan, the most important distinction being between sweet and dry. Sweet sake is considered to be better and more natural than dry. Sake is also used a great deal in cooking, and is usually sold in huge bottles. It should be stored in a cool dry place, and be drunk quite quickly once opened. It can be found in Japanese and Chinese shops and some off-licences in England.

Sake is served in small pottery flasks, sometimes cold but usually heated; warming it seems to bring out the delicate flavour. To heat sake, pour it from the bottle into a small flask, and put the flask into a saucepan of very hot water. Allow it to heat through slowly until the sake is a little hotter than blood heat; never heat over a direct flame.

In Japan sake is drunk from very small ceramic cups. The etiquette of sake drinking demands that you fill your neighbour's cup, never your own. He will then fill yours. When receiving sake, hold the cup in both hands. The toast is 'Campai!' and the sake should be downed in one.

Planning Your Menu

A Western meal follows a definite pattern, a main course of meat or a vegetarian savoury, with a couple of side vegetables or a salad. The Japanese approach is quite different, and can give us a new perspective on menu planning, making a vegetarian meal not just a reproduction of a meat meal with a savoury to replace the meat, but a different experience. It is of course perfectly possible to include Japanese dishes in a Western meal, or to compose a meal combining Western and Japanese dishes. Japanese dishes are generally simple in flavour and quick to prepare, and fit very well with Western food. It may be best to begin your experiments by including some Japanese dishes in a Western-style meal.

A Japanese meal has no main course preceded by an *hors d'œuvre* and followed by a dessert, and consists, not of a heaped plateful of food as in the West, but of tiny portions of various foods, each on its own plate. At each place there are several small dishes (traditionally an odd number, from three to nine). The menu is basically structured around the actual cooking methods used. A typical family meal might consist of a soup and three dishes, each cooked by a different method, usually a grilled or fried dish, a simmered dish, and perhaps a salad or a steamed dish. When a large dish such as a one-pot dish or tempura is served, small quantities of other dishes are served as side dishes.

For a more formal meal in a restaurant or temple, the dishes are served one by one, in a particular order determined by cooking method. First come tiny appetisers and a clear soup, then a succession of dishes each in a set order, with grilled and simmered foods preceding steamed and deep-fried dishes and salads. A sweet dish may be included in the meal, and will be served with, not after the other dishes.

Apart from the occasional meal of noodles, all Japanese meals, both family and formal, end with rice, an assortment of finely sliced pickles, and soup. Dessert, if served at all, consists of fresh fruit, artistically cut.

In planning a Japanese meal, the cook does not think in terms of protein and carbohydrate as we might. While Japanese cuisine is undoubtedly one of the healthiest in the world, this is almost accidental; nutritional considerations have not traditionally carried much weight. Variety and balance are key considerations; but what makes a Japanese meal really distinctive is the aesthetic element, for a Japanese meal is an aesthetic adventure, designed to nourish the spirit as well as the body.

Below are a number of headings which may help you to plan a Japanese-style meal, followed by sample menus.

Season

The various ingredients which make up a Japanese meal are chosen not simply because they are the freshest, but to instil a pleasing awareness of the season, pointed up by a seasonal garnish such as a pine cone or a maple leaf, or even a large and beautiful autumn leaf used as a plate. Particular dishes and types of cuisine are suited to particular seasons, such as one-pot dishes in winter and chilled dishes in summer.

The cook provides both eye and palate with plenty of variety. The traditional structure of the meal ensures variety of cooking techniques.

Variety of Ingredient

Vegetarians in Japan enjoy a wide range of ingredients, including soya-based foods like tofu and natto, seaweeds, nuts and seeds, eggs, grains, and preserved foods like pickles, as well as vegetables. The meal might also include a variety of types of vegetable, perhaps a root vegetable, a stalk vegetable and a leaf vegetable.

Variety of Texture

The meal should also include a variety of textures: soft foods, crisp foods, chewy foods, crunchy foods and liquids. The soft rice, crunchy pickles and soup that end the meal provide a perfect example of balanced textures.

Variety of Taste

There are said to be five tastes: hot, bitter, sweet, salty and sour. In theory, all five should be present to make a balanced meal, with the blandness of rice as a background. In practice, however many are included, the tastes of the different dishes should at least balance each other, a strong-flavoured dish using miso with a bland tofu dish, or a salty dish with a sweet vegetable dish. Many Japanese dishes contain a balance of tastes within the dish itself. A sweet vegetable may be served with a salty dressing, such as aubergine with miso. A sour lemon-based dipping sauce often accompanies the unseasoned 'sweet' vegetables in one-pot dishes, and a salty dipping sauce is served with tempura ('sweet'). The hot sour pickles served at the end of the meal also provide balance, as does the extremely sweet cake served before the bitter tea ceremony tea; we sweeten tea, whereas the Japanese provide the two tastes separately so that each can be savoured.

Visual Effect

Japanese cooks choose ingredients for their visual quality, colour and shape, as well as for their flavour, selecting contrasting bowls and plates on which to serve them. The

simplest family meal is planned with an eye to the total visual effect, combining for example crescent-shaped pumpkin slices with whole dark purple aubergines, or floating a ribbon of yuba tied into a bow in a bowl of clear soup. Some dishes are served primarily for their auspicious colour, such as red rice and red and white salad, which are eaten on every festive occasion.

The food is always carefully arranged within the dish, in much smaller quantities than in the West. Foods do not fill the whole dish, but are artistically placed in the centre, and should not usually touch the edges of the dish. When several chunks of food are served together, the largest should be at the back of the dish, furthest away from the guest.

The various dishes making up an individual meal are traditionally arranged with the rice on the left and the soup on the right, with the other dishes behind them.

Sample Menus
Here are some menu suggestions using recipes from this book, to give some idea of how a complete Japanese meal is built up. Each meal ends with green tea.

Breakfast
One or two simmered seasonal vegetable dishes
Plain natto
Umeboshi (pickled plums)
Rice
Raw egg
Toasted nori seaweed
Assorted pickles
Miso soup with leeks, tofu and wakame

Family Meals for Each Season

SPRING

Clear soup with yuba
Tempura
Spinach roots with walnut
   dressing
Cucumber and tofu salad
Rice, pickles

Tofu dengaku (tofu with sweet
   miso)
Spinach with sesame dressing
Aubergine stuffed with sesame
Daikon salad with kombu and
   orange
Mrs Fujii's nori rolls
Miso soup with bamboo shoots
   and wakame

SUMMER

Summer tofu
Unohana (okara simmered with
   vegetables)
Salad nori rolls
Rice, pickles
Clear soup with spinach and egg

Five-colour soba
Cucumber with walnut miso
Tamago dofu (egg 'tofu')
Iced barley tea

AUTUMN

Sweet potatoes with hijiki
Aubergines with sweet miso
Chawan mushi (savoury
   vegetable custard)
Five-colour tofu pouches
Deep-fried chestnut cakes

Daikon rounds with hot sesame
   sauce
Temple tofu
Autumn salad
Chestnut rice
Miso soup with Chinese cabbage
   and deep-fried tofu

WINTER

Casserole of tofu and vegetables
Winter carrot mix
Broccoli with golden dressing
Rice, pickles

Sushi party
Simmered whole shiitake
   mushrooms
Marinaded turnip and apricot
   rolls
Kaminari jiru (thick vegetable
   soup with tofu)

Some Dishes for New Year

New Year's Eve: Winter soba

New Year's breakfast: Ozoni: New Year's soup

New Year's dinner: Kombu rolls
                                Five-colour soya beans
                                Yuba and natto tempura
                                Turnip chawan mushi (steamed
                                   custard)
                                Red and white salad (carrot and
                                   daikon radish salad)
                                Kuri kinton (chestnuts and sweet
                                   potatoes)
                                Red rice (rice with aduki beans)
                                Pickles

A Special Dinner

Sesame tofu
Clear soup
Fresh yuba
Whole simmered aubergines
Mrs Misono's special tempura
Marinated tofu Tatsuta style
Mount Koya chawan mushi
Cucumber with walnut miso
Coloured rice
Pickles
Miso soup

Some Unfamiliar Ingredients

There are many fascinating Japanese ingredients which can widen any cook's repertoire and which are of particular interest to the vegetarian cook; most of them are listed below. Japanese ingredients are becoming more and more widely available in England, and can be found not only in Japanese food shops, but in health-food shops, and Chinese, Indian or West Indian shops (for a list of stockists see pages 295–301). You are bound to be able to find some Japanese ingredients wherever you live, and you will enjoy experimenting with them. Others, such as tofu and yuba, you can make, although it is quite easy to find tofu. There are usually substitutes for ingredients which you cannot find, or you may simply omit them. Although some of them may be difficult to find, particularly outside London, the ingredients used in the recipes in this book are all available in England.

Aduki Beans
Aduki beans are small red beans related to soya beans, which are used to make festive red rice, and, boiled, mashed and sweetened, as the basis for many Japanese cakes. Soaking overnight speeds up the cooking time but is not essential. Aduki beans can be found in health-food, Chinese and Japanese shops and some supermarkets.

Agar (Kanten)
Agar is a jelling agent produced from a seaweed. It is a very useful addition to the vegetarian kitchen, producing a firm clear jelly which can be used as a base for jellied salads, fruit salads and moulds. In Japan it is used to make sweets and sweet dishes to serve with tea. It is sold in health-food shops,

Japanese and Chinese shops as feather-light bars or flakes. Before use, agar bars need to be torn into small pieces, washed and squeezed. The bars or flakes are then combined with water, usually in the proportion ¼ bar agar or ½ tbsp agar flakes to 8 fl oz (240 ml) water, and brought slowly to the boil to dissolve. Agar sets at room temperature.

Bamboo Shoots (Takenoko)
The shoots of the young bamboo, which grow at an amazing rate, are a symbol of spring in Japan, and are widely used throughout the East. They are enjoyed for their crunchy texture and delicate taste. Tinned bamboo shoots, a rather poor substitute, are available in Chinese and Japanese food shops. Once opened, store refrigerated in fresh water.

Burdock (Gobo)
Burdock, a long, slender, brown, root vegetable with a chewy texture and pleasantly earthy taste, is much used in Japanese cookery in simmered and fried dishes, soups and pickles, and makes a tasty ingredient in nori rolls. Fresh burdock may sometimes be found in Japanese shops and health-food shops carrying Japanese foods; tinned burdock is more readily available. Fresh burdock should be scrubbed or very lightly scraped and immediately immersed in cold water to prevent discoloration.

Chrysanthemum Leaves (Shungiku)
This delicious leaf vegetable is much used in one-pot dishes, and should be cooked for only a short time. Fresh chrysanthemum leaves can be found in oriental and Chinese food shops. However, they are not the same as the leaves of the English chrysanthemum. Look for bright green leaves and springy stalks; leaves with buds are too old. Spinach is a possible substitute but the flavour will be different. In Japan you can also find edible chrysanthemum flowers.

Daikon Radish
The daikon is a long white root vegetable which has a multitude of uses in Japanese cookery. Raw grated daikon is used as a condiment with many dishes. Daikon can be found in ordinary markets and supermarkets as well as Chinese and

Indian shops, and is sold as mooli, daikon or white radish. Select fresh, firm, unwrinkled roots.

Dashi

Dashi is the basic stock of the Japanese kitchen. Classic Japanese vegetarian dashi is made from kombu; any light vegetable stock or even water may be used instead to save time or if kombu is unavailable. For the recipe see page 143.

Ginger (Shoga)

Fresh root ginger has a distinctive, sweetly tangy flavour and is an essential seasoning and condiment in Japanese cookery. It is widely available in England; dried ginger is not a substitute. Choose firm, unwrinkled ginger roots, peel the required amount, and grate with a Japanese grater (see page 36) or any very fine-toothed grater. Squeeze freshly grated ginger to obtain ginger juice. Red pickled ginger can be made or bought in Japanese shops, and is used as a garnish.

Gingko Nuts (Ginnan)

Gingko nuts have a delicate flavour and texture and an attractive pale green colour when cooked. They are used sparingly in many types of dishes, particularly chawan mushi (steamed vegetable custard). Fresh gingko nuts can occasionally be found in the autumn. To prepare, crack the outer shell and

remove; then soak in hot water for a few minutes and rub away the inner skin. Tinned gingko nuts are a rather poor substitute; and cooked chestnuts would be a delicious substitute, but the flavour would be quite different.

Gourd Ribbon (Kampyo)

Gourd ribbon is a kind of vegetable string, used for tying up tofu pouches and kombu rolls; it is also delicious in its own right, simmered in seasoned stock, used in nori rolls and vegetable mixtures. It is peeled from a large white gourd and sold in dried form, and can be found in Japanese shops. The best gourd ribbon is white and of uniform thickness. Gourd ribbon should be kneaded with salt and soaked in water to soften. Store in an airtight tin.

Harusame Noodles

Harusame, which romantically translates as 'spring rain', are very fine translucent white noodles made from rice or potato flour, and available in Japanese food shops.

Hijiki

This black, stringy seaweed with its sweet flavour and pleasantly chewy texture is reputed to be extremely beneficial to health. It softens very quickly in water, and is usually served simmered in vegetable mixtures. Available in all health-food shops as well as Japanese shops.

Katakuriko (Potato Starch)

A thickening agent, katakuriko is often used in Japan as a cheaper alternative to kuzu. It is available in Japanese and Chinese shops.

Koji

Koji is made from rice, barley or soya beans, cooked and mixed with koji spores, which ferment rather like yeast and develop a white mould. Koji is an essential ingredient in miso making and is also used for pickling. Koji spores (tiny packets of grey powder) and ready-made rice or barley koji are available in some health-food shops.

Kombu

Kombu, dried kelp, is the basic ingredient for dashi, and a delicious vegetable on its own. It is sold in Japanese and health-food shops in long dried strips, which should be lightly wiped, not washed, as the flavour is on the surface. The best kombu is a glossy dark green, quite thick. Store in an airtight container.

Konnyaku (Arum Root)

Konnyaku is a sort of vegetable jelly made from arum root, a relative of the potato. It is sold in dark and light slabs, and can be found refrigerated in all Japanese shops. It has a distinctive, slightly fishy taste and jelly-like texture, not immediately appealing to Westerners; but it is a taste worth acquiring. The freshest konnyaku is a delicacy to be savoured uncooked with a dab of wasabi horseradish and a little soy sauce. Konnyaku may be sliced, slivered or cut into decorative knots, and used in mixed vegetable dishes and salads; it is a popular ingredient in one-pot dishes. It should be dry roasted or parboiled before using. Konnyaku will keep for two weeks refrigerated in fresh water; change the water daily. It is reputed to have no calories and to very good for the digestion. To make decorative knots, cut a ¼in (½cm) slice of konnyaku, and cut a slit down the centre of the slice; thread one end of the slice through the slit.

Kuzu

An essential ingredient in the vegetarian or any kitchen, kuzu is a delicate flour produced from the root of the kuzu vine. It is a traditional Japanese thickener; a little gives a particularly light and translucent quality to sauces and soups, and somewhat more makes a solid custard which may be flavoured to make dishes such as sesame tofu. It also makes a light and crisp coating for fried foods. It is reputed to be extremely good for the digestion, and a perfect food for invalids. Kuzu can be found in health-food shops as well as Japanese shops. Arrowroot and cornflour are possible substitutes.

Leeks (Negi)

The Japanese leek comes in several varieties, but all are smaller, sweeter and finer than the English. It is widely used as an ingredient in soups, simmered dishes and grilled dishes, and, finely sliced, is a very common garnish and condiment. Use long slender leeks or large spring onions.

Lotus Root (Renkon)

Fresh lotus root is used in Japanese cooking to give a crunch to mixed vegetable dishes, such as tempura, and for its decorative appearance. In cross-section it makes an attractive flower-like garnish. Lotus root is sometimes available fresh in Chinese shops; choose a firm white root and store in a cool dark place. Tinned lotus root is an acceptable substitute.

Mangetout Peas (Kinusaya)

Mangetout peas are small flat peas which are eaten complete with pod. They are used whole as a decorative garnish, and served in simmered dishes and as salad. They are widely available in the winter in England, and are sometimes sold as snow peas. Substitute French beans if unavailable.

Mirin

Mirin, a sweet, golden cooking wine with a very low alcohol content, is an essential item in the Japanese kitchen, giving a distinctive mild sweetness to simmering stocks, glazes and dipping sauces. It is available in all Japanese food shops. If unobtainable, simply omit, or use a very little honey (½ tsp for 1 tbsp mirin) as a substitute.

Miso

Miso is a rich and savoury paste produced by the fermenting action of koji, a yeast-like mould, on cooked soya beans, which are often mixed with rice or other grains. It takes at least six months and up to three years to mature. Miso is a peculiarly Japanese food; indeed, as miso soup, it is probably eaten by every Japanese every day. It is much used in Japanese cookery as a basic flavouring, as a dressing for simmered and grilled foods and even as a pickling medium. There are many different varieties and colours: basically the lighter white miso is used for sauces and light miso soups, and the thicker red miso for richer soups and general cooking purposes. Miso is available in health-food shops as well as Japanese shops. An extremely nutritious food containing living enzymes, it should be kept under refrigeration.

Mushrooms

Many different varieties of fresh mushroom, both wild and cultivated, are used in Japan: some Japanese mushrooms are available fresh in delicatessens and tinned in Japanese food shops. Ordinary flat or button mushrooms may be used as a substitute, but the taste and texture are rather different. The shiitake mushroom, the most common, is also used in dried form, and dried mushrooms can be found in Japanese, Chinese and some health-food shops. Soak for at least 30 minutes in warm water before use and trim away the hard stem; the soaking water may be used for stock.

Natto
Natto is made from fermented cooked soya beans; it has a strong rather musty taste and sticky texture, and is a traditional breakfast food. Natto is available frozen in Japanese shops and some health-food shops.

Nigari
Nigari is distilled from sea-water, and is the natural coagulant used to make tofu. It is sold as small grey crystals rather like very coarse sea salt.

Nori
Nori is perhaps the most frequently used seaweed. It is sold in large 7 × 8 in (18 × 20 cm) paper-thin sheets in Japanese shops and some health-food shops; Chinese nori is much coarser. Before use, nori needs to be lightly toasted over a hot flame for a few seconds until it changes colour and becomes fragrant. Store in an airtight tin.

Oils
Any pure, neutrally flavoured vegetable oil may be used for Japanese cooking. The Japanese use rapeseed oil; a general purpose oil such as sunflower or safflower oil (preferably cold pressed) is appropriate. Heavy flavoured oils such as olive oil or corn oil should be avoided. A little sesame oil is often added to the basic oil as a flavouring.

Okara
Okara is the soya-bean husks which remain after making soya milk, tofu or yuba.

Perilla (Shiso)
Perilla (also known as beefsteak plant) is related to mint, and is a common plant in Japan. Fresh green perilla leaves have a delicate tangy flavour, and are used in tempura, as a garnish or shredded and mixed with rice. Red perilla leaves are used in the

making of umeboshi (pickled plums). Fresh perilla leaves can sometimes be found in Japanese food shops. Perilla can also be grown from seed. Dried or pickled perilla, to be sprinkled on rice, can be found in Japanese food shops.

Pickles (Tsukemono)

No Japanese meal is complete without a dish of thinly sliced pickles of assorted types, colours and shapes. Many different vegetables can be pickled; the commonest and most popular include daikon radish, Chinese cabbage, cucumber and aubergine. The pickling medium can be rice bran, salt, vinegar or miso. A selection of ready-made pickles is available in every Japanese food shop. Buy several varieties and arrange a few slices of each on a small plate to serve with rice. The opened packets should be kept in the refrigerator.

Poppy Seeds

Poppy seeds are used as a garnish, and should be lightly toasted in the same way as sesame seeds. Poppy seeds are one of the ingredients used to make seven-spice pepper. They are widely available in grocery shops and delicatessens.

Quails' Eggs (Uzura No Tamago)

Small, brown, speckled quails' eggs are hardboiled and make an attractive ingredient in one-pot dishes and soups. In taste they are quite similar to hens' eggs. Fresh quails' eggs can be found in Chinese shops; tins of quails' eggs, hardboiled and ready shelled, can be found in some delicatessens.

Rice (Okome)
Short-grain white or brown rice is used in Japanese cooking; see page 257.

Rice Cakes (Mochi)
Rice cakes are made by pounding rice, traditionally in big tubs, to produce a chewy cake, which is shaped into balls or squares. They are not to be confused with the round, flat, light, Rice-Krispie-like 'rice cakes' which are now widely available. Rice cakes are often simply grilled; they are an essential ingredient in ozoni, the soup which is traditionally served at New Year. Commercially produced rice cakes in a variety of flavours, including a green rice cake coloured with spinach, are sold in Japanese food shops. Brown rice cakes can be found in some health-food shops.

Sake (Rice Wine)
Cooked rice is fermented to make sake, which comes in many different types and grades from the different parts of Japan. It is much used, for cooking as well as for drinking, and is usually sold in huge bottles, in Japanese and Chinese shops and some off-licences. Sake is used in only small quantities in cookery, and if unavailable can be omitted.

Seitan
Seitan is a chewy, very savoury food with a texture akin to meat, which is sometimes included in mixed vegetable dishes. It is made from wheat gluten (see page 33) sautéed and simmered in soy sauce.

Sesame Oil (Goma Abra)
Sesame oil is thick and golden with a deliciously nutty flavour. It is added in small quantities to vegetable oil for deep-frying, and is used to flavour vegetable dishes. If possible, Japanese sesame oil should be used in preference to Chinese, which is somewhat less pure. Available in some health-food shops as well as Japanese shops.

Sesame Seeds (Goma)
Every Japanese kitchen contains a store of sesame seeds, which are used as frequently as salt and pepper to add a nutty flavour

to practically any dish. Sesame seeds need to be toasted to bring out the flavour. Toast in a frying pan or a medium oven, shaking the pan occasionally to ensure even cooking, until the seeds give off a nutty aroma, become golden and start to jump. The Japanese toast sesame seeds in a little pan with a fine meshed lid to stop them jumping out, a very useful utensil. After toasting, they may be used ground or unground. A suribachi (see page 38) is by far the best tool for grinding them, reducing them not just to a powder but to a paste; however, an electric grinder or a mortar and pestle may be used if you do not have a suribachi. Sesame seeds are used whole as a garnish or ground in sauces and dressings. White sesame seeds are available in oriental food shops, health-food shops and delicatessens. Black sesame seeds are basically used for their colour, and can be found in Japanese food shops; substitute white sesame seeds or poppy seeds if unavailable. There are a wide variety of ready-ground sesame pastes available, which can be used for convenience although the flavour is inferior; choose an unseasoned, additive-free sesame paste. Middle Eastern sesame paste, known as tahini, is particularly easy to find.

Seven-spice Pepper (Shichimi Togarashi)

This spicy condiment is a blend of hot red pepper, sansho pepper, ground orange peel, sesame seeds, hemp seeds, poppy seeds and ground nori seaweed, precisely seven ingredients to make a tasty and complex flavour. It is used as a seasoning and condiment, particularly for noodle and one-pot dishes, and is available in Japanese food shops. If unavailable it is possible to grind one's own, using a blend of the above ingredients in roughly equal quantities by volume; substitute cayenne pepper for red pepper, peppercorns for sansho, and include mustard seeds as an optional extra. Grind the ingredients lightly in a suribachi or mortar, or crush with a rolling pin, and store in a shaker to use like pepper.

Shirataki

Shirataki ('white waterfall') is strings of white konnyaku (see page 25), and is often included in one-pot dishes or served raw in salads. It is sold in water packs in Japanese food shops. Parboil in lightly salted boiling water for 1–2 minutes before using.

Somen

A very thin, white noodle, made from wheat flour, which cooks in only 2–3 minutes. It is served chilled with ice cubes in the summer, and is used in temple cuisine to make crisp tempura fans.

Soya Flour, Roasted (Kinako)

Roasted soya flour is made by grinding roasted soya beans, and has a sweet and nutty flavour. It is sweetened and used as a coating for many traditional sweets. Roasted soya flour is sold in Japanese shops and health-food shops.

Soy Sauce (Shoyu)

Soy sauce, made from fermented soya beans, wheat and salt, needs no introduction and is one of the primary seasonings of Japanese cookery. Japanese soy sauce should be used in preference to Chinese – it is sweeter and lighter. Japanese soy sauces are graded into light and dark: the one used for general cooking purposes is dark in colour and easier to obtain. Light soy sauce is saltier and thinner than dark, and is used for aesthetic purposes, to avoid darkening a light dish. In some recipes I have specified light soy sauce, but dark may be used if light is unavailable.

Tamari

Tamari is a thick, dark soy sauce made mainly from soya beans, without the wheat which is used in standard soy sauce. It is fermented like miso and used in dishes where the flavour of the soy sauce is important, such as dipping sauces and marinades. Available in health-food shops.

Tofu

Tofu is one of the most common ingredients in Japanese cooking, used in a wide variety of dishes, and is made by coagulating soya milk. The best tofu is made fresh every day and is sold in large 1½lb (685g) blocks in Chinese supermarkets and Japanese shops. Various types of long-life tofu are also available, as are packs of instant tofu mix. Stored in the refrigerator under water, with the water changed every day, it will keep for 5–6 days. (For more on tofu see pages 187–92.)

Tofu, Deep-fried (Aburage, Usuage)

Deep-fried tofu is made by slowly deep-frying thin slices of tofu. It is available frozen in Japanese shops. Before using, dip into a bowl of boiling water or pour boiling water over it to remove the oil.

Tofu, Dried (Koya Dofu)

Dried tofu is actually freeze-dried to make thin, very light, beige cakes, with a more chewy texture than tofu and a sponge-like capacity to absorb flavour. To use, soak in hot water for a few minutes, then gently squeeze and rinse several times until the water is clear. Dried tofu may be simmered whole in seasoned stock, or cut into strips and mixed with vegetables. It can be found in some health-food shops as well as Japanese shops.

Umeboshi (Pickled Plums)

Often served as a pickle, particularly at breakfast time, umeboshi have a very piquant and refreshing taste. One a day is supposed to ensure good health; they are said to do wonders for the digestion and to be full of vitamin C. Umeboshi are made from unripe Japanese plums (actually closer to our apricot than to our plums), left in salt to mature and mixed with red perilla leaves. Umeboshi can be found in some health-food shops and all Japanese shops.

Vinegar (Su)

The Japanese use rice vinegar, a light, mild vinegar, which can be found in Chinese as well as Japanese shops, and in some delicatessens. Japanese rice vinegar should be used in preference to Chinese. If unobtainable, cider vinegar diluted with a little water is an acceptable substitute.

Wakame

Wakame, a nutritious seaweed with long green fronds and a silky texture, is commonly used in soups and salads. As a soup ingredient it needs very little cooking. To use in salads, scald with boiling water and immediately dip into cold water; or simply soak. Wakame sometimes has a tough spine which should be trimmed away after soaking.

Wasabi Horseradish

Horseradish is rather a misnomer for wasabi, the root of a riverside plant native to Japan. Fresh wasabi, grated on a Japanese grater, makes a brilliant green, extremely sharp condiment, which is used in dipping sauces and to accompany very fresh foods, such as freshly made uncooked tofu, yuba or gluten. It is sold in Japanese food shops ready-made in tubes, and in powder form, to be mixed up as required with a little water to a smooth paste like mustard. Use sparingly.

Wheat Gluten (Fu)

Gluten is the protein in wheat, which is obtained by kneading and rinsing a dough of wheat flour under water until all the starch is washed out. Gluten can be made at home, and freshly made gluten with a dab of wasabi is a delicacy in the same class as fresh yuba. Small pieces of gluten, coloured and shaped into maple leaves, snow flakes, and so on, are often used as a decorative garnish. Dried gluten can be found in various different shapes in Japanese shops and health-food shops. It quickly softens in water and is often added to soups as an instant ingredient. Long strips of gluten may be softened in water and stuffed.

Yuba

Yuba is the skin which forms naturally when soya milk is simmered, and can be made at home (see pages 210–13). Dried yuba can be found in Japanese shops and a few health-food shops. A much thicker, chewier form of yuba is sold in Chinese shops as 'bean curd sheets' or 'bean curd skin'.

Some Useful Japanese Utensils

All the recipes in this book can be prepared using utensils available in any reasonably well-equipped Western kitchen, with just a little improvisation. However, Japanese utensils are beautiful and a pleasure to use, so it is well worth seeking them out and investing in them. Heavy cast-iron saucepans with wooden lids, earthenware casseroles and the famous Japanese knives make marvellous additions to your kitchen. Japanese kitchens are full of utensils and gadgets carefully designed to perform specific tasks, and some of these are extremely useful. They are available in Japanese and Chinese shops; many can also be found in health-food and wholefood shops, and are, generally speaking, long-lasting and not particularly expensive.

Bamboo Rolling Mat (Sudare)
A bamboo rolling mat, made from thin strips of bamboo tied together with string, is useful for shaping and rolling foods such as nori rolls and rolled omelette. Nori rolls may be rolled by hand, but will be less firmly and evenly packed.

Cast-iron Saucepan (Tetsu Nabe)
Black cast-iron saucepans used to hang over the fire in the central hearth of the main room in traditional Japanese houses; they have a handle to hang them by, a slightly curved base and a wooden lid, and are used for deep-frying and simmering. Like any cast-iron equipment, they should be seasoned before use and wiped clean or washed without detergent.

Chawan Mushi Cups (Chawan Mushi no Chawan)
Small, handleless ceramic cups with loosely fitting lids are used both to make and serve chawan mushi, a savoury steamed

custard. They are sold in sets of five in Japanese stores (such as Mitsukiku) and make an attractive addition to the kitchen. Although less aesthetically pleasing, ordinary mugs or ramekins, tightly lidded with foil, make a serviceable substitute.

Chopsticks (Hashi)

Chopsticks are essential in the Japanese kitchen as well as at table. Japanese cooks use far fewer tools than we do, and long, pointed, cooking chopsticks made of bamboo and tied together at one end, perform many of the functions of all our different spoons, spatulas, forks and whisks. They are used for every cooking process, from stirring batter to deep-frying, and are the ideal implement for arranging the completed foods delicately on the dish. It is well worth mastering the art of cooking with chopsticks. Table chopsticks are usually more decorative, made of bamboo or lacquered wood.

Drop Lid (Otoshi Buta)

A drop lid made of cypress or cedar with a small handle is used for simmering. It floats on the simmering stock, ensuring that the foods are completely submerged and cook evenly, and prevents them from being tossed around. Always moisten the drop lid before use. A flat light lid or bamboo plate is a possible substitute, as is a circle of greaseproof paper. You can simply cover the pan with a standard lid to retain the heat, although this does not have the same effect as a drop lid.

Earthenware Casserole (Do Nabe)

One-pot dishes are traditionally made in a heavy, lidded earthenware casserole, which is ideal for the purpose. It can be placed over a direct flame if the outside surface is completely dry, and is an even distributor of heat. It also looks most attractive on the table. A flameproof ceramic casserole is a good substitute.

Grater (Oroshi Gane)

The Japanese grater is ceramic or metal, and extremely fine toothed; it often has a sill to collect the juices. It is ideal for grating daikon radish, fresh ginger and wasabi horseradish, and I have also found it very useful for grating nutmeg. Daikon can be grated with the finest tooth of a Western grater, but for ginger and wasabi a Japanese grater is practically an essential. It is not expensive and is available in most Japanese shops.

Knives (Hocho)

Japanese knives are justly famous. They come directly from a tradition of fine forging, which culminated in the perfect samurai sword, combining the apparently incompatible virtues of strength and flexibility. While any good sharp knife will do for Japanese cookery, a heavy, sharp Japanese knife is a real investment, and a pleasure to work with. The most useful Japanese knife to buy is the vegetable knife (nakiri bocho), which performs all manner of delicate vegetable-cutting operations, from chopping and slicing to fine paring, with efficiency and speed. Using the knife is quite an art: the secret is to move the food rather than the knife, keeping the point stationary and letting the weight of the knife do most of the cutting as you slide the food under it.

Rectangular Omelette Pan (Makiyaki Nabe)

Every Japanese kitchen contains small rectangular omelette pans in a variety of sizes, for making rectangular rolled omelettes. Omelette pans tend to be aluminium; the best are copper, coated with tin. Use an ordinary omelette pan as a substitute.

Rice Paddle (Shamoji)

The rice paddle is made of smooth varnished wood or bamboo, with a wide flat surface ideal for mixing and serving rice. It is

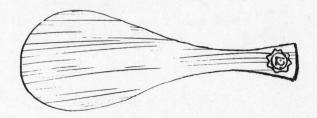

particularly useful for tossing the rice when making sushi rice. A large, flattish wooden spoon is the nearest equivalent, although a rice paddle is inexpensive and well worth buying.

Skewers (Gushi)

Japanese kitchens contain an assortment of bamboo skewers of varying lengths for grilling vegetables, and forked skewers for tofu. Packets of bamboo skewers, like long cocktail sticks, can be bought very cheaply in Chinese and Japanese shops; metal barbecue skewers are a possible substitute. Soak bamboo skewers in water before using. They are also used instead of a fork to test cooking foods.

Steamer (Mushiki)

Flat steamers, both metal and bamboo, are used in Japan. Stacking bamboo steamers are sold in Chinese shops and are most efficient; bamboo makes a better insulator than metal, ensuring that more heat is retained. A steamer can be simply improvised using a large lidded saucepan, in which is set a rack to support the dish above the level of the water. A cloth stretched under the lid will absorb excess moisture.

Suribachi

A big Japanese suribachi is a beautiful piece of equipment to own and use and can be found in most Japanese shops. The suribachi is a heavy ceramic mortar with an unglazed serrated interior; the wooden pestle is also heavy and is rather like a rounded rolling pin. To use, hold the mortar against your body

with the left arm, and grind with the right hand in a clockwise circular motion. The suribachi grinds much more effectively than a wooden or glass mortar and pestle, and although its job can be done by an electric grinder, only the best grinders can grind sesame seeds to a paste.

Tofu Pressing Box

To make small rectangular blocks of tofu, a wooden pressing box is ideal; it is perforated so that the whey can drain away and has a pressing lid that fits inside the box. If you cannot find one in an oriental or health-food shop, it is quite simple to make your own. Tofu can be made in a strainer topped with a plate, which will result in a rounded block of tofu.

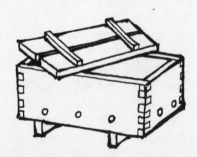

Cooking Techniques

A Japanese meal takes very little time to cook. Food is cooked quickly and lightly to conserve as much goodness and flavour as possible, and is never overcooked.

Parboiling

Vegetables to be served as salad are usually parboiled and rapidly cooled. Hard vegetables like potatoes are often parboiled before being briefly simmered in seasoned stock. To parboil, bring lightly salted water to a rolling boil and plunge in the vegetable; boil hard for a minute or two until the vegetable is just becoming tender. Leaf vegetables are usually immediately drained and then plunged into cold water, to stop further cooking and to seal in the green colour. Other vegetables are simply drained and left to cool. Some vegetables are best if left to cool in the parboiling water.

Simmering

Simmering is the most common Japanese technique for cooking vegetables. Vegetables in small, often decoratively cut, pieces are briefly parboiled or occasionally fried and then simmered in dashi seasoned with soy sauce, mirin, sake, or a sweetener such as sugar or honey for a few minutes until tender. The simmering process is intended to impart flavour rather than to cook the food, and simmering times are usually quite short; simmered foods are well cooked but never overcooked. Vegetables are frequently cooled in the simmering stock, and a little stock is poured over the vegetable before serving. The Japanese do not usually cook vegetable mixtures; vegetables are served separately, and when several types of vegetable are served, each type may be simmered separately in

seasoned stock before being combined. Japanese cooks use a
wooden drop lid (see page 35) for simmering, to ensure that
foods are completely submerged in the simmering liquid and
cooked evenly.

Grilling

Grilling (cooking over a direct flame) has a long history in
Japan. Vegetables and tofu, cut into small pieces and skewered
on bamboo or metal skewers, are often grilled and served with
a sweet rich sauce. Japanese chefs prefer to grill over charcoal,
and in Japan a smokeless and very hot charcoal has been
developed. As the aim is heat, not smoke, a preheated hot grill
or even an improvised 'barbecue' over a gas burner is perfectly
adequate. Shallow frying is considered to be an extension of
grilling.

Steaming

Steaming is an excellent way to cook vegetables because it
keeps the food moist and tender and conserves its natural
flavour and goodness, as well as heightening the colour.
Vegetables are steamed without seasoning and served with a
thick seasoned sauce or a rich topping. The Japanese use flat
steamers which can be stacked like the Chinese bamboo ones; a
folding steamer cannot be used for Japanese steamed dishes. To
improvise a steamer use a large saucepan and place a rack in it
which will support the dish above the level of the water. Lay a
cloth over the top of the pan, under the lid, to absorb excess
moisture. Foods should always be put into a hot steamer full of
steam. Vegetables are steamed over high heat for as short a
time as possible, but classic steamed egg dishes such as savoury
vegetable custard need to be steamed more gently so that the
egg will not bubble or become rubbery.

Deep-frying

Japanese deep-fried foods are light and crisp without a trace of
oiliness; the foods are cooked in just a few seconds, so that all
the freshness and flavour is conserved. The secret of perfect
deep-frying lies in the oil. Pure vegetable oil with a little
sesame oil added for flavour gives the best results. The oil must
be kept at a high and even temperature; you can check this with
a deep-frying thermometer, or use the following test: drop a

little batter or a tiny piece of bread into the hot oil; at 340°F (170°C), the usual deep-frying temperature, it will sink slightly then rise quickly to the surface; if it sizzles on the surface of the oil without sinking, the oil temperature is about 360°F (180°C), too hot for deep-frying; if it sinks to the bottom and does not rise, the oil is about 300°F (150°C). Always deep-fry in plenty of oil and cook only a few items at a time, so that the temperature remains constant. Japanese cooks deep-fry in a small heavy saucepan, fitted with a rack so that the oil from the cooked foods can drain back into the pan, and use only long cooking chopsticks and a skimmer to clear the oil. Deep-fried foods should be briefly drained on absorbent paper and then served immediately.

Note
Each recipe serves four people unless otherwise stated. I have assumed that 1 tablespoon is the equivalent of 15 ml and 1 teaspoon the equivalent of 5 ml.

Part One

VEGETABLES

Aubergines

In the summer and early autumn Japanese markets are heaped with small, gleaming, purple aubergines, sold not singly but in fives and tens or even basketsful. However, in spite of their availability and cheapness, they are still quite a special vegetable, as in England; according to an old saying which was repeated to me many a time, autumn aubergines are too delicious to be wasted on one's daughter-in-law! Japanese aubergines are smaller than those available in England, generally about 4 in (10 cm) long, and gourd-shaped rather than round. Many different varieties are available, including tiny 1½ in (4 cm) aubergines, which are always served whole, and large, imported 'American' aubergines.

Aubergines are usually not mixed with other vegetables as in England, but are served alone, with just a little piquant dressing to accentuate the rich flavour. They may be simmered, grilled or deep-fried, and make delicious tempura; they are often served whole, complete with stem, on small contrasting dishes, to display their attractive colour and shape. It takes a little practice to eat whole aubergines elegantly with chopsticks: insert the points into the aubergine and gently ease it into small pieces.

Aubergines can be cut in a variety of different ways. They are often halved lengthwise and scored deeply in a crisscross pattern through either the cut side or the skin. Large aubergines may be sliced lengthwise or crosswise, or halved and hollowed out for stuffing. Cut thickly so that the fleshy texture and taste can be fully appreciated. To make decorative aubergine 'fans', remove the stems of small aubergines and cut the aubergines in half, then cut lengthwise into quarters. Taking a piece at a time, make lengthwise, evenly spaced cuts very close together, leaving ½in (1 cm) uncut at one end to make the base of the 'fan'. Gently press the base and spread into a fan.

Choose firm, dark purple aubergines. You may be able to find small ones in Indian or Chinese shops; otherwise use large ones and slice them. If there is time, large aubergines should be salted, pressed and rinsed to drain away the bitter juices. In Japan they are soaked in water for 30 minutes to remove bitterness, or briefly parboiled and drained.

GRILLED AUBERGINE

During the heat of summer, many people in Japan retreat from the towns to the cool of their family homes in the mountains. I spent a few days one summer with Mrs Misono and her family in a big airy farmhouse overlooking fields and distant mountains; on a clear day you could see Mount Fuji far away. In front of the house were aubergine plants; we would go out with bamboo trays to pick them, then grill them straight away over charcoal, peel them, and serve them very simply, with just a taste of ginger to bring out the sweetness. Small sweet Japanese aubergines are grilled and served whole, and large aubergines are sliced and grilled, as below.

1 large or 4 small aubergines (about 8 oz, 225 g)
vegetable oil
soy sauce
1 tbsp ginger juice
1 tbsp freshly grated root ginger

Wash and dry the aubergines. For small aubergines: pierce the skin in a few places with a toothpick or fork and brush with oil. For large aubergines: cut into ½ in (1 cm) slices either across or lengthwise, and salt or soak in cold water to remove bitterness. Drain, pat dry, and brush both sides lightly with oil.

Lay the aubergines or aubergine slices on a piece of greased foil and grill under a preheated very hot grill, turning occasionally. Whole small aubergines will take about 15–20 minutes. When the skin is charred and has loosened from the flesh, put the aubergine into cold water and peel away the skin. Large aubergine slices will need 4–5 minutes on each side to become very soft.

Allowing 1 whole small aubergine or 2–3 aubergine slices for each person, arrange them on 4 small plates, and sprinkle with a little soy sauce and ginger juice. Garnish with a small mound of freshly grated ginger.

WHOLE SIMMERED AUBERGINES

Aubergines are at their best at the height of summer, and small, beautifully shaped aubergines are often simply simmered and served whole. You will need the smallest possible aubergines.

4 very small aubergines, with stems intact
8 fl oz (240 ml) dashi (page 143)
2 tbsps soy sauce
2 tsps sugar or honey
1 tbsp sake or mirin

Wash the aubergines and pat dry. Make 3 or 4 lengthwise cuts evenly spaced around each aubergine, almost to the centre, but leaving the top and bottom intact. Put the aubergines into a small saucepan in which they fit neatly side by side, and pour over the remaining ingredients. Cover, preferably with a drop lid, and bring to a boil. Simmer over low to medium heat for 10–15 minutes until the aubergines are very soft. Carefully lift the aubergines from the pan, and make a crosswise cut just above the stem to make them easier to eat with chopsticks. Lay each aubergine in a small dish, spoon over a little of the cooking liquid and serve hot or at room temperature.

AUBERGINES WITH SWEET MISO

Small Japanese aubergines complete with stems are often halved lengthwise to make two boat-shaped pieces, which are carefully fried to preserve the shape, and then spread with a dark red or golden sweet miso. Large aubergines are cut into fat slices which fit snugly into small deep dishes, and prepared in the same way. The quantity of ingredients for the sweet miso depends very much on the miso; you may want to add more sugar or honey if the miso is particularly salty and more dashi if it is thick.

1 large or 2 small aubergines (about 8 oz, 225 g)
vegetable oil

sweet miso
4 tbsps red or white miso
2 tbsps sugar or honey
2–3 tbsps dashi (page 143)
1 tbsp sake or mirin
1 tbsp sesame or poppy seeds, toasted

Wash the aubergines. For the small aubergines: cut them in half lengthwise, through the stems. With a sharp knife, score the cut face deeply, making parallel cuts ½ in (1 cm) apart to within ½ in (1 cm) of the skin; repeat, cutting at right angles, to make a crisscross pattern. For large aubergine: cut the aubergine across into 1 in (2½ cm) slices. Salt and drain the aubergine or soak in cold water to remove bitterness. Drain and pat dry.

Pour enough oil into a heavy frying pan with a lid to cover the bottom and heat. Add the aubergine and cook over low to medium heat for 10–15 minutes until it is very soft. Small aubergine halves should be cooked face down to preserve the shape; turn large aubergine slices to cook both sides. Carefully remove the cooked aubergine, leaving the juices in the pan, and lay on absorbent paper to drain.

To make sweet miso stir the miso and sugar or honey and sake or mirin into the oil and juices remaining in the pan,

adding enough dashi to make a thick, smooth paste; bring just to a simmer over low heat, stirring continuously, and remove from heat immediately. Fit 2 small aubergine halves or 1 thick aubergine slice into each individual dish and spread with sweet miso. Scatter with toasted sesame seeds or poppy seeds and serve hot or at room temperature.

SESAME AUBERGINE, AFTER SEN NO RIKYU

I was sometimes invited to tea ceremony parties in Gifu. After the ceremony we would be served with square lacquer trays holding tiny portions of various simply prepared dishes, such as this light and subtle dish of aubergines and sesame seeds, which is named after Sen no Rikyu, the famous seventeenth-century tea master.

2 small or 1 large aubergine (about 8oz, 225g)
vegetable oil
4 fl oz (120 ml) dashi (page 143)
1 tbsp sake or mirin
1 tbsp white miso
1 tsp sugar or honey
1 oz (30 g) white sesame seeds

Wash the aubergines and cut into ½in (1 cm) cubes. Salt and drain the cubes or soak in cold water to remove bitterness. Drain and pat dry.

Heat a little oil in a saucepan and sauté the aubergine for 2–3 minutes. Add the dashi and sake or mirin, bring to a simmer, and simmer for 3 minutes; the aubergine should be nearly tender. Combine the miso and sugar or honey and stir into the aubergine mixture; continue to simmer, covered, until the aubergine is very soft, and the liquid greatly reduced.

Toast the sesame seeds, reserve some for garnish, and grind the rest in a suribachi, or simply crush them with a rolling pin to make them powdery and fragrant. Stir the sesame seeds into the aubergine mixture. Mix well and remove from heat.

Mound small portions in the centre of individual dishes and serve hot or at room temperature, garnished with the remaining sesame seeds.

STUFFED AUBERGINE TEMPURA

There are several different ways of preparing aubergines for stuffing, depending on their shape and size. Small Japanese aubergines are cut nearly to the stem to divide them into four quarters which open like scissors (this technique is actually called 'scissor frying') so that the stuffing can be pushed into the centre. Large 'American aubergines' are cut into slices and the stuffing is sandwiched between them. The stuffed aubergines are then coated in batter and deep-fried like tempura. The following recipe is for large aubergines.

1 large aubergine (about 8 oz, 225 g)

stuffing
6 dried mushrooms, soaked
4 oz (115 g) tofu, well drained
1 tsp soy sauce
pinch salt
1 tsp sake

dipping sauce
8 fl oz (240 ml) dashi (page 143)
3 tbsps soy sauce
2 tsps sugar or honey

condiments
4 tbsps grated daikon radish
2 tsps grated root ginger

batter
1 egg yolk
4 fl oz (120 ml) iced water
2 oz (60 g) plain white or wholemeal flour
¼ tsp salt

extra flour for dusting
vegetable oil for deep-frying

Wash the aubergine, remove the stem, and cut across into 8 slices, about ½ in (1 cm) thick. Salt and drain the aubergine or soak in cold water to remove bitterness.

Trim away the stems of the dried mushrooms and chop the caps very finely. Mash the tofu in a suribachi or with a fork and mix in the chopped mushrooms and other stuffing ingredients.

Combine the dipping-sauce ingredients in a small saucepan and bring just to the boil; keep warm. Prepare and drain the grated daikon and ginger.

Drain the aubergine slices and pat dry. Dust both sides of each slice with flour and gently tap to remove excess flour. Divide the stuffing into 4 and sandwich the slices in pairs with a thin layer of stuffing. The stuffing should be evenly spread and extend to the edges of the slices.

Half-fill a small saucepan with oil to a depth of 3 in (8 cm) and heat slowly to 340°F (170°C). Prepare the batter while the oil is heating: mix the ingredients together very lightly and rapidly to give a rather lumpy batter.

Dip the slices into batter and slide them gently one by one into the oil; deep-fry, turning, for 1–2 minutes, until the batter is golden. Drain on absorbent paper. Cook the remaining slices.

Fit each stuffed aubergine slice into a small deep bowl; ladle over a little warm dipping sauce, top with a mound of grated daikon and a little ginger, and serve immediately.

AUBERGINES STUFFED WITH SESAME

This unusual aubergine dish combines several traditional Japanese elements in a rather unorthodox way. Aubergines are hollowed out, brushed with sweet miso and filled with sesame tofu to make a rich and subtle combination of tastes. This dish was suggested to me by a young chef from one of Tokyo's most famous and traditional restaurants, where unfortunately such innovative ideas were not encouraged.

1 large or 2 small aubergines (about 8 oz, 225 g)
vegetable oil
2 tbsps red or white miso
2–3 tsps sugar or honey
1–2 tbsps dashi (page 143)
2 tbsps sesame seeds, or 1 tbsp sesame paste
4 tsps kuzu
pinch of salt
8 fl oz (240 ml) water
tiny sprigs of coriander leaf or parsley to garnish

Wash the aubergines and halve lengthwise, leaving the stems

intact. Scoop out the flesh, leaving a shell ¼in (½cm) thick; reserve the flesh to use in another dish. Salt and drain the shells or soak in cold water to remove bitterness; rinse well and dry carefully.

Heat a little oil in a saucepan large enough to hold the shells side by side. Put in the shells with the skin upwards and cook, covered, over low heat until tender; the shells are tender when they can be easily pierced with a fork.

Meanwhile prepare the sweet miso. Combine the miso and sugar or honey in a small saucepan, adding enough dashi to make a spreadable paste. Bring to a simmer. Prepare sesame tofu (page 202) using the sesame seeds or paste, kuzu, salt and water.

Fit the aubergine shells neatly side by side in a small dish so that the sides support each other. Brush the inside of each shell with sweet miso. Pour the sesame tofu into the shells and smooth off the top. Garnish each aubergine half with a sprig of coriander leaf or parsley.

Leave the halves to cool to room temperature so that the sesame tofu sets. Very gently lift each half on to a separate plate for serving. If using a large aubergine, halve each piece with a sharp knife, before carefully placing the halves on separate plates.

Broccoli

Broccoli is a winter vegetable that flourishes in the cold climate of Japan, and is appreciated as much for its rich dark colour and attractive shape as for its fine flavour. In Japan the green broccoli heads are usually served quite simply at room temperature, very lightly cooked, with a scattering of golden sesame seeds or a little pale dressing.

Japanese broccoli is a little different from English broccoli or calabrese; it is slightly crisper and rather less sweet. It can sometimes be found in Chinese shops; otherwise use English broccoli or calabrese. Choose firm unblemished heads. Wash well and cut into flowerettes, cutting a cross in the base of each stem. The stems and leaves are also delicious. Peel the stems if tough or stringy and slice.

Broccoli should never be overcooked. Steam or parboil in a little rapidly boiling water for 2–3 minutes until just tender; then rinse immediately in cold water to seal in the brilliant green colour and prevent further cooking.

BROCCOLI SAUTÉED WITH SESAME

Broccoli is usually served very simply. It can be parboiled
before the meal, and lightly sautéed with sesame oil just before
serving, to give a subtly nutty flavour.

8 oz (225 g) broccoli
salt
1 tbsp white sesame seeds
1 tbsp sesame oil
soy sauce

Break the broccoli into flowerettes and parboil in lightly salted
boiling water for 2–3 minutes until just tender; the stems
should still be a little crisp. Drain, then immerse in cold water
to prevent further cooking. Drain again and pat dry. Lightly
toast the sesame seeds.

   Heat the sesame oil over high heat in a heavy frying pan and
sauté the broccoli for a few seconds to heat through. Turn on
to individual serving plates, sprinkle with sesame seeds and a
little soy sauce and serve immediately.

BROCCOLI WITH GOLDEN DRESSING

Golden dressing is a classic Japanese vinegar dressing thickened
with egg yolks, making a rich and creamy dressing which
complements the crisp sweetness of broccoli.

8 oz (225 g) broccoli
salt

golden dressing
2 tbsps rice vinegar
3 tbsps dashi (page 143)
¼ tsp light soy sauce or salt
2 tsps honey or mirin
2 egg yolks

toasted white sesame seeds

Break the broccoli into flowerettes, and parboil in lightly salted boiling water for 2–3 minutes until just tender; the stem should still be a little crisp. Drain immediately (keep the cooking water to use as stock), and put into a bowl of cold water. Drain again and set aside.

Combine the dressing ingredients in the top of a double boiler and heat gradually, stirring continuously, until the mixture thickens and becomes creamy. Cool to room temperature.

Pat the broccoli dry with absorbent paper and arrange attractively in 4 small bowls. Spoon over the golden dressing, garnish with sesame seeds, and serve.

BROCCOLI WITH TOFU

Tofu gives this dish a rich creamy taste without the fattiness of dairy products, and complements the crispness of the broccoli. Serve in attractive bowls to set off the contrast of white and green.

8 oz (225 g) broccoli
salt

tofu dressing
2 tbsps white sesame seeds
8 oz (225 g) tofu, drained
1 tbsp fresh lemon juice
½ tsp each salt and honey or mirin

a few walnuts to garnish

Break the broccoli into flowerettes, and parboil in lightly salted boiling water for 2–3 minutes until just tender; the stem should still be a little crisp. Drain immediately and rinse in cold water. Drain well.

Lightly toast the sesame seeds; tip into a suribachi or grinder and grind to a paste. Blend in the tofu, lemon juice, salt and honey or mirin, mixing well to make a smooth, creamy dressing.

Pat the broccoli with absorbent paper to make it perfectly dry, and divide the flowerettes between 4 small bowls. Spoon a little tofu dressing over each portion. Crumble or coarsely chop a few walnuts and sprinkle over to garnish.

CLEAR SOUP WITH BROCCOLI

Broccoli flowerettes, button mushrooms, curls of daikon radish and lemon rind all float in a clear soup, making a colourful picture.

4 broccoli flowerettes
4 small broccoli leaves
salt
8 button mushrooms
1 tbsp kuzu or cornflour
1 2in (5 cm) length daikon radish
8 slivers lemon rind
1½pts (900 ml) water
1 4in (10 cm) square kombu seaweed (about ¼oz, 7 g)
2 tsps soy sauce
¼ tsp salt

Parboil the broccoli flowerettes and leaves in a little lightly salted boiling water for 1 minute until bright green; the broccoli will be just tender and still crisp. Rinse immediately in cold water, drain and pat dry.

Wipe the mushrooms and dust with kuzu or cornflour. Drop into boiling water and boil for 2 minutes; drain.

Peel the daikon and pare into a thin sheet; cut off 4 'curls' (page 87) and immerse in cold water. Prepare paper-thin shreds of lemon rind.

Combine the cold water and kombu in a small saucepan and bring slowly to the boil. Remove the kombu just before the water boils and season this very light dashi with soy sauce and salt; taste and adjust the seasoning.

Warm 4 soup bowls with hot water; discard the water and dry the bowls. Arrange 1 broccoli flowerette and leaf and 2 mushrooms in each bowl. Ladle in the hot dashi to fill the bowls ¾ full. Float a daikon 'curl' and 2 slivers of lemon rind on each bowl and serve immediately.

Cabbage and Chinese Cabbage

Japan, like England, is a cold country, and cabbages of many varieties flourish in the fields and feature in a great many classic dishes. Cabbage or Chinese cabbage invariably appears in the one-pot dishes which add such warmth to winter evenings, and in okonomiyaki, the popular, thick, vegetable-filled pancakes. In the summer finely slivered raw cabbage served without any dressing is used as a garnish for many dishes. Chinese cabbage is a favourite vegetable for pickles and may be pickled in salt, rice vinegar or rice bran. In the open markets in Japan you can buy whole pickled cabbages straight out of the pickling barrel, still speckled with yellow, sandy rice bran.

Several varieties of cabbage are used in Japanese cookery. Firm round cabbage, both red and white, is widely available. Chinese cabbage is particularly popular; it has a more delicate flavour than round cabbage, and frequently appears in one-pot dishes.

To retain its sweetness and crispness, cabbage should never be overcooked. It is usually steamed or parboiled for 1–2 minutes, then drained and left to cool.

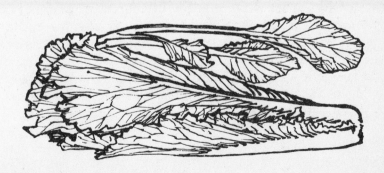

CHINESE CABBAGE AND DEEP-FRIED TOFU

Golden deep-fried tofu provides a contrast of colour, texture and flavour to the crisp, lightly cooked Chinese cabbage in this classic country dish.

4 leaves Chinese cabbage
2 sheets deep-fried tofu
4 fl oz (120 ml) dashi (page 143)
1 tbsp soy sauce
dash sake or mirin (optional)
1 tsp sugar or honey
½ tsp freshly grated root ginger

Wash and trim the Chinese cabbage leaves and cut across into 1 in (2½ cm) slices. Rinse the deep-fried tofu in boiling water to remove excess oil and cut into julienne strips. Pat with absorbent paper to dry.

Combine the dashi, soy sauce, sake or mirin and sugar or honey in a saucepan and bring to the boil. Add the Chinese cabbage and deep-fried tofu and simmer for 2 minutes, ladling over the simmering stock.

Remove the cabbage and tofu with chopsticks or a slotted spoon and arrange in mounds in 4 small deep bowls; pour over a little of the cooking liquid and sprinkle with a very little grated ginger. Serve hot or at room temperature.

CHINESE CABBAGE SHINODA ROLLS

There are many stories relating to foxes in Japan; Ennosuke the great Kabuki actor is famous for his portrayal of foxes who take human form. In one Kabuki play, a fox who has become a beautiful woman and married has to return to her fox life; she tells her human child to come to her in the forest of Shinoda. Shinoda is known as the haunt of foxes, and apparently foxes love deep-fried tofu. Thus long slender rolls incorporating deep-fried tofu have come to be known as Shinoda rolls.

4 leaves Chinese cabbage
salt
2 sheets deep-fried tofu

stuffing
2 dried mushrooms, softened in water
½ young leek
½ carrot
4oz (115g) tofu, drained
½ tsp salt
½ tsp sugar or honey
1 egg yolk

4 12in (30cm) strips gourd ribbon (kampyo)

simmering stock
8 floz (240ml) dashi (page 143)
2 tsps soy sauce
1 tsp honey or mirin
½ tsp salt

a few slivers of lemon rind

Carefully separate the Chinese cabbage leaves, cutting them off at the stem. Boil hard in plenty of rapidly boiling salted water for 2–3 minutes until the leaves and stem are pliable. Remove and drain. With a sharp knife, slit each sheet of tofu around 3 sides and ease open to form a larger single flat sheet. Rinse with boiling water to remove excess oil; drain well.

Make the stuffing. Discard the stems of the dried mushrooms and chop the caps very finely. Wash and trim the leek and carrot and then shred them. Mix the vegetables together and mash in the tofu; season with the salt and sugar or honey and stir in the egg yolk, mixing so that the ingredients are well blended.

Rinse the gourd ribbon to soften, and squeeze lightly.

Pat the Chinese cabbage and deep-fried tofu with absorbent paper to dry. Lay the Chinese cabbage leaves in pairs with the edges overlapping and the stems side by side. Spread a little of the stuffing mixture over the leaves to within ½in (1cm) of the edge. Lay 1 sheet deep-fried tofu on each pair of leaves and spread the remaining stuffing over the tofu. Roll up tightly starting from the tip of the leaves to make 2 rolls, and tie each roll securely at each end with gourd ribbon; trim the ends of the gourd ribbon.

Combine the simmering ingredients in a saucepan large enough to hold the rolls in a single layer and bring to the boil. Lay the rolls in the pan, cover, preferably with a drop lid, and simmer gently for 15 minutes, turning occasionally. Either serve immediately or leave the rolls to cool in the simmering stock and serve at room temperature.

Remove the rolls carefully from the pan with chopsticks or a slotted spoon. With a sharp knife cut each roll into 1–2 in (2½–5 cm) slices. Arrange a few slices in 4 small bowls and spoon over a little of the remaining simmering stock. Garnish with the lemon rind and serve.

SPINACH AND CABBAGE ROLLS

Spinach and cabbage leaves, lightly parboiled and rolled together, make an attractive combination of pale and dark green. These rolls are often included in one-pot dishes.

4 leaves Chinese cabbage
8 oz (225 g) spinach
salt
soy sauce

Separate the Chinese cabbage leaves carefully. Parboil in rapidly boiling salted water for 2–3 minutes until pliable. Drain and pat dry with absorbent paper. Wash and dry the spinach leaves and make into 2 rolls (see page 122).

Lay 2 Chinese cabbage leaves on a bamboo rolling mat with the edges overlapping and the stems pointing in opposite directions. Lay 1 spinach roll lengthwise along the centre of

1 cabbage leaf. Roll the cabbage leaves firmly around the spinach to form a neat cylinder.

Leave in the bamboo mat for a few minutes, then unroll and cut into 1 in (2½ cm) lengths.

Arrange 2 or 3 rolls on plates. Serve with soy sauce to dip.

GYOZU: JAPANESE 'PANCAKES'

Gyozu are small pancakes stuffed with cabbage, with a crisp brown base and soft glossy top. The making of gyozu tends to be a family affair, with the smallest children stuffing the little pancakes and learning how to fold the edge over neatly to shape each gyozu into a crescent. The crescents are then fitted as tightly as possible into the frying pan in neat concentric rows. The cooking process looks dramatic: the pancakes are first rapidly fried over high heat, then a little water is poured into the pan, creating lots of steam, and within a couple of minutes the gyozu are on the table, ready to be eaten piping hot. Gyozu are the kind of food that children love. Many small cafés in Japan specialise in them. Ready-made gyozu 'skins', like small spring-roll 'skins', can be bought in any Japanese supermarket; they are also sold in Japanese shops in London. The gyozu skin is usually made with white flour; wholemeal flour gives a nuttier taste and firmer texture.

gyozu 'skin'
8 oz (225 g) wholemeal or plain white flour
½ tsp salt
6–8 fl oz (180–240 ml) hot water (see recipe)

stuffing
4 oz (115 g) firm white cabbage
2 spring onions or young leeks
4 oz (115 g) mushrooms
½ medium carrot
4 oz (115 g) tofu, well drained
2 oz (60 g) walnuts
salt

vegetable oil for frying

First make the gyozu skins: combine the flour and salt in a large bowl, and mix in enough very hot water to make a stretchy dough that is soft but not sticky. Turn out on to a lightly floured working surface and knead well. Put into an oiled bowl, cover with a damp cloth or cling film, and leave at room temperature for at least half an hour.

Wash and trim the vegetables for the stuffing and pat dry. Shred the cabbage and finely chop the spring onions or leeks and the mushrooms. Grate the carrot. Put the drained tofu into a mixing bowl and mash roughly with a fork. Mix in the vegetables and chopped walnuts, and season to taste with salt. Knead lightly to bind the mixture together.

Turn the dough for the gyozu skins on to a lightly floured surface and pinch off 20–5 walnut sized balls. Roll each ball out as thinly as possible into rounds 2½–3 in (60–70 cm) across, or press into rounds with your fingers. Heap 1 tbsp filling towards the front of each round. Fold the dough over the filling to make a semi-circle and pinch the edges together firmly to seal. Bring the two points slightly towards each other to make a crescent. Continue in this way until all the dough and filling is used.

Brush a large, heavy-lidded frying pan with oil, and heat for a few minutes over moderate heat. Fit in the gyozu snugly in concentric circles until the pan is full, and fry for 3–4 minutes, occasionally shaking the pan a little to prevent sticking, until the gyozu are brown and firm underneath; lift one to check. Pour in just enough hot water to cover the bottom of the pan and cover immediately with a tightly fitting lid; there will be a lot of steam. Turn the heat down, and leave to steam, covered, for 5–6 minutes until all the water has evaporated and the top of the gyozu feels firm and not sticky. Serve immediately.

The dough need not all be used at once. Any leftovers can be returned to the bowl, covered with cling film and kept overnight; the gyozu skin will be slightly tougher the second day.

JAPANESE CABBAGE SALAD

Raw vegetables do not feature much in the traditional Japanese diet, and are considered hard to digest. Plain, raw, shredded cabbage is often served as a garnish, or may appear with a slice of tomato and a decorative squirl of mayonnaise as 'Western salad', but the older generation will probably regard it with disdain and push it to the edge of the plate. However, cooked vegetable salads have an honourable pedigree in Japan. In this salad, lightly poached vegetables are served with a classic tofu dressing. Most everyday family cookery in Japan takes very little time, and this salad is no exception.

4 oz (115 g) cabbage
4 oz (115 g) carrots
4 oz (115 g) French beans
salt

tofu dressing
2 tbsps white sesame seeds or 1 tbsp sesame paste
8 oz (225 g) tofu, drained
2 tsps honey or mirin
½ tsp salt

toasted sesame seeds

Wash and trim the vegetables. Shred the cabbage and cut the carrots into fine julienne strips. Cut the French beans diagonally into thin strips. Parboil the cabbage for a few seconds in lightly salted, rapidly boiling water; remove and immediately rinse in cold water. Drain and pat dry with absorbent paper. Parboil the carrot and French beans separately in the same way, rinse in cold water and pat dry.

Lightly toast the sesame seeds for the dressing and grind to a paste in a suribachi, or use ready-made sesame paste. Cream in the tofu and honey or mirin and season to taste with a little salt.

Just before serving, fold the vegetables into the dressing. Serve small mounds of salad in deep pottery bowls of a contrasting colour, and sprinkle over a few sesame seeds to garnish.

Carrots

In Japan, as in England, carrots are to be found in abundance, and are much appreciated for their sweet flavour. Because of their colour and texture they are ideal for decorative cutting, and carrot 'plum blossoms', 'maple leaves', even the occasional carrot 'prawn', make attractive and tasty garnishes. In Japan red symbolises happiness and good luck, and carrots are always used in auspicious dishes for festive occasions, such as red and white salad (pages 90–1), which is served at New Year. Shredded and mixed with other winter vegetables, carrots are a staple winter food in Japan, and are particularly popular combined with the earthy flavour of burdock root.

Choose firm, bright orange carrots; young small carrots are best if you can find them. Top and tail and wash well. Young carrots do not need to be peeled; older carrots should be scraped.

Carrots may be cut into a wide variety of different shapes, depending on the cooking method to be used. They may be sliced thickly or thinly, and the slices halved to make 'half moons' or quartered to make 'gingko leaves'. Chunks of carrot may be sliced lengthwise and then trimmed to make rectangles named after the New Year poem cards. They are often cut into julienne strips; cut a few slices at a time from the carrot and sliver to make matchsticks. For simmering, they are cut into diagonal wedges or big chunks.

Carrots may be cut into many decorative forms, of which the most popular are carrot flowers (known in Japanese as plum blossoms). Cut the carrots into 2–3 in (5–7 cm) sections. Taking one section at a time, carefully cut out 5 or 6 thin, wedge-shaped slivers, about ⅛ in (½ cm) deep, all the way down the carrot, evenly spaced around the edge. You can trim the carrot to make the petal shapes smooth and round. Then cut slices of the desired thickness; thick slices are used for simmering and thin slices for garnishes. Carrots can also be cut into twists like lemons (see page 221). In Japan you can buy vegetable cutters in a variety of different shapes, so that you can simply stamp out plum blossoms or maple leaves from carrot slices.

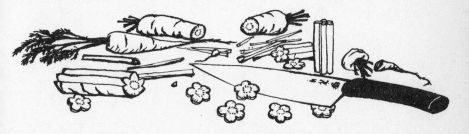

In Japan carrots are frequently simmered, but may also be sautéed, deep-fried or even brushed with a sweet and salty coating and grilled on bamboo skewers (page 111). Like all vegetables they should not be overcooked, and need only a few minutes. They are usually cut into small pieces or parboiled before cooking, and cooking times kept as short as possible. They should be served soft but still a little crisp.

CARROTS SIMMERED IN DASHI

Carrots carefully cut and just simmered to bring out their natural sweetness make a popular winter dish. Japanese cooks often sweeten their vegetables; add a little honey for extra sweetness if you like.

2 medium carrots

simmering stock
8 fl oz (240 ml) dashi (page 143)
½ tsp salt
1 tsp light soy sauce
1–2 tsps honey or mirin (optional)
1 tbsp sesame seeds, toasted

Wash and trim the carrots and cut into flowers or half moons.

Combine with the simmering stock ingredients in a small saucepan and bring to the boil. Cover, preferably with a drop lid, and simmer 3–4 minutes until the carrots are just tender. Uncover and simmer for a few more minutes until the cooking liquid is slightly reduced.

Serve hot or at room temperature. Remove the carrots from the stock with chopsticks or a slotted spoon and arrange in 4 small bowls. Spoon over a little of the cooking liquid, scatter with sesame seeds and serve.

KIMPIRA

Sakata Kimpira is a legendary Japanese folk hero, whose feats of strength, including his wrestling match with a bear, are recorded in a long epic poem. This popular dish of carrots simmered in soy sauce is named after him; perhaps its powerful flavour is reminiscent of his strength. Kimpira may be made with burdock root, slivered and cooked in the same way; it will take slightly longer to cook. Slivered lotus root and konnyaku are also often added to kimpira. Using sake instead of dashi gives a very rich flavour.

4 medium carrots
2 tbsps vegetable oil
2 tbsps dashi (page 143) or sake
2 tbsps light soy sauce
1 tsp sugar or honey
seven-spice pepper

Wash and trim the carrots and cut into fine julienne strips. Heat the oil in a small saucepan, add the carrots, and sauté for 1 minute until they begin to soften. Reduce the heat a little, mix in the dashi or sake, soy sauce and sugar or honey, and simmer uncovered until the liquid is much reduced and the carrots are tender; this will take 3–4 minutes. Leave to cool in the cooking liquid.

Serve the carrots heaped in 4 small, deep bowls; spoon over the remaining cooking liquid and sprinkle with a little seven-spice pepper.

DEEP-FRIED CARROT CAKES

These crisp, deep-fried cakes with a sweet and moist filling of grated carrot are made in special moulds in Japan to give an auspicious or decorative shape, and served up to the crowds that gather for the festivals at the great Shinto shrines. Make each cake in a shallow ladle with a long handle to help keep the shape.

batter
2 oz (60 g) plain white or wholemeal flour
½ oz (15 g) cornflour
½ tsp baking powder
1 egg yolk
¼ tsp salt
2 tbsps vegetable oil
4–5 fl oz (120–50 ml) water

4 oz (115 g) carrots
¼ tsp salt
vegetable oil

sauce
8 fl oz (240 ml) dashi (page 143)
1 tbsp kuzu
1 tbsp soy sauce
1 tsp each sugar or honey, shredded orange peel and fresh orange
  juice

shredded orange peel to garnish

First make the batter. Mix the flour, cornflour and baking powder in a bowl. Make a well in the centre and add the remaining batter ingredients, stirring well to blend. The batter should be runny but not too thin. Set aside.

Grate the carrot, and put into a piece of muslin. Squeeze gently to expel excess moisture. Put the carrot into a bowl and mix with the salt.

Half-fill a small saucepan with oil, and heat to 340°F (170°C). Put a long-handled shallow ladle into the oil to heat for 2–3 minutes; then drain the oil from the ladle and pour in 1 tbsp of batter, swirling it around to coat the inside of the ladle. Put a spoonful of grated carrot in the centre of the ladle, and pour another tbsp batter over the carrot to cover it completely.

Lower the ladle into the hot oil, and adjust the temperature so that the oil is bubbling around the ladle but not spitting. After 2–3 minutes gently remove the ladle, leaving the cake in the oil. Turn the cake so that both sides are well cooked. After a total of about 6 minutes, when both sides are golden brown, remove the cake from the oil and drain on absorbent paper. Make 3 more cakes with the remaining ingredients.

While the cakes are cooking, combine the sauce ingredients in a small saucepan and heat over a low flame, stirring continuously, until the sauce thickens.

Put each cake into a small deep bowl, ladle over a little of the sauce and garnish with a few shreds of orange peel. Serve immediately.

WINTER CARROT MIX

The wide range of dried vegetables, seaweeds and prepared foods like tofu available in Japan means that in the winter, when there are fewer fresh vegetables, the Japanese cook still has plenty of choice. One of the dishes I was most often served in Japanese homes was a colourful, sweet mixture of carrots combined with deep-fried tofu, hijiki seaweed and gourd ribbon, all simmered in seasoned stock until very soft. Fresh burdock root, a winter staple in Japan, makes a delicious addition to this dish if you can find it.

1 medium carrot
1 oz (30 g) fresh burdock root (optional)
1 sheet deep-fried tofu
¼ oz (7 g) hijiki seaweed
¼ oz (7 g) dried gourd ribbon (kampyo)
6–8 fl oz (180–240 ml) dashi (page 143)
1 tbsp light soy sauce
1 tbsp sake (optional)
1 tsp honey or mirin
¼ tsp freshly grated root ginger
1 tbsp sesame seeds, toasted

Wash and trim the carrot; peel the burdock if used and put into cold water to prevent discoloration. Rinse the deep-fried tofu in boiling water to remove oil, and drain. Rinse the hijiki and gourd ribbon. Cut all the above into very small pieces of approximately the same size.

Put all the vegetables into a saucepan and add enough dashi to cover. Bring to the boil, cover, preferably with a drop lid, and simmer for 5 minutes until the carrots are semi-cooked. Add the soy sauce, sake, honey or mirin and ginger and simmer uncovered, stirring occasionally, for 30–40 minutes, until well flavoured and nearly dry.

Arrange in neat mounds in the centre of small deep bowls of a contrasting colour, and scatter over a few sesame seeds. Serve hot or at room temperature.

WHITE SALAD: CARROT SALAD WITH TOFU DRESSING

Cooked vegetable salad with a creamy, tofu-based dressing is very popular in Japan and is known as 'white salad'. The ingredients and quantities for the dressing vary according to the cook, who may add white miso, sugar or a little vinegar or mirin (sweet cooking wine) to the basic drained tofu. This version is rather less sweet than the standard Japanese one. The freshly toasted sesame seeds are usually ground by hand in a big ceramic suribachi with a wooden pestle, and all the other ingredients are then mixed in with long cooking

chopsticks. Many different cooked vegetables may be served with this dressing; carrots and konnyaku are a particularly popular combination.

3 large dried mushrooms, softened in water
2 tsps soy sauce
1 tsp sugar or honey
2 medium carrots (4–5 oz, 115–40 g)
salt
¼ cake konnyaku

tofu dressing
1 oz (30 g) white sesame seeds
8 oz (225 g) tofu, drained
1 tbsp sugar or honey
1 tsp white miso

toasted white sesame seeds

Drain the mushrooms, reserving the soaking water; remove the stems, and slice the caps thinly. Put into a saucepan with enough of the reserved soaking water to cover. Add the soy sauce and sugar or honey, bring to the boil, and simmer uncovered over very low heat for 15–20 minutes until the mushrooms are tender and well flavoured and the simmering liquid is nearly all absorbed. Leave to cool in the cooking liquid, then drain.

Wash and trim the carrots and cut into fine julienne strips. Parboil in a little lightly salted, rapidly boiling water for 2–3 minutes until just tender; rinse in cold water, drain and pat dry.

Cut the konnyaku into fine julienne strips. Parboil for 2–3 minutes, then sauté in a dry pan over medium heat for 3–4 minutes until glossy and dry. Combine the carrots, mushroom and konnyaku and set aside.

Lightly toast the sesame seeds for the tofu dressing; tip into a suribachi and grind until oily (this is a long job). Blend in the tofu, sugar or honey and miso to make a thick dressing with the consistency of mayonnaise. Taste and add a little more sugar, honey or miso if required.

Just before serving, make sure that the vegetables are all perfectly dry, and fold them into the dressing. Serve in small mounds in individual dishes, and garnish with sesame seeds.

Cauliflower

The cauliflower, with its crisp white head, is one of the most visually appealing of vegetables. In Japan the small white flowerettes are served simply, with a light dressing, as tempura, or in vegetable mixtures.

Choose a white cauliflower, free from blemishes. Remove the leaves, which may be reserved to make stock; trim away any discoloured parts. Separate the cauliflower into flowerettes, cut a cross in the base of each stem, and wash thoroughly.

Japanese cooks sometimes soak cauliflower in cold water for 30 minutes to reduce bitterness before cooking. Cauliflower should be cooked for as short a time as possible to retain its crispness. Put the flowerettes into 1 in (2½ cm) of rapidly boiling salted water, cover, and cook over medium heat for 4–5 minutes until the stems are just tender and can be pierced with a fork. Drain immediately.

SAUTÉED CAULIFLOWER WITH MISO

Miso gives a rich flavour to the crisp sautéed cauliflower.

1 lb (450 g) cauliflower (about ½ cauliflower)
2 tbsps white miso
2 tsps sugar or honey
1 tbsp sake or water
vegetable oil

Wash the cauliflower and cut into small flowerettes. Blend the miso and sugar or honey, diluting with the sake or water; set aside.

Put a little oil into a frying pan and heat over medium heat. Add the cauliflower and sauté for 2–3 minutes until tender. Stir in the miso mixture and cook for a few seconds, stirring to coat the cauliflower evenly with miso.

Arrange in 4 small bowls and serve hot.

CAULIFLOWER AND FRENCH BEANS WITH SESAME DRESSING

Cauliflower and French beans, lightly cooked so that they are still crisp, are topped with a golden sesame dressing to make a colourful dish.

8 oz (225 g) cauliflower
4 oz (115 g) French beans
salt

sesame dressing
1 oz (30 g) white sesame seeds
1 tbsp sake or mirin
1 tbsp dashi (page 143)
½ tsp light soy sauce
½ tsp sugar or honey

Wash the cauliflower and cut into flowerettes; cut a cross in the base of each stem. Wash the beans; top and tail, and cut on the diagonal into 1 in (2½ cm) slices. Parboil the cauliflower and beans separately in lightly salted water until just tender. Drain well and set aside to cool to room temperature.

Make the dressing. Toast the sesame seeds lightly, reserving a few for the garnish. Tip the remaining seeds into a suribachi or grinder and grind until pasty. Stir in the sake or mirin, dashi, soy sauce and sugar or honey, blending to make a smooth paste.

Arrange the cauliflower flowerettes in 4 small deep bowls together with some French bean slices. Spoon over a little sesame dressing and garnish with the reserved sesame seeds.

Chestnuts

When autumn comes in Japan with its clear blue skies and tiny red and orange maple leaves, chestnuts appear on street charcoal braziers and in the shops. As always, the cuisine mirrors the fleeting seasons. Small beige tea ceremony cakes made of mashed and sweetened chestnuts, carefully reshaped to look like untouched chestnuts and served on dainty plates set off by a single maple leaf, appear for a tantalisingly short time. In the fine cookery of the temples, whole chestnuts, peeled and cooked in sweetened broth, are served in a nest of needle-fine noodles deep-fried until crisp and brown and arranged to look like the chestnut's spiky outer shell, a dish so attractive that it seems a shame to eat it.

Choose firm, shiny chestnuts. There are at least three ways of removing the hard outer shell. The English way is to nick the shell with a sharp knife, boil the chestnuts for 8–10 minutes, and then peel; or nick the shell and bake the chestnut in a medium-hot oven for 30 minutes. The Japanese insist that the chestnut should be completely peeled and skinned before cooking. For myself, I favour the Japanese way. First soak the chestnuts overnight. Then peel with a sharp knife, scraping off the inner skin. It is best to soak the chestnuts in fresh water for a few more hours, changing the water several times. Whichever way you choose, make sure that all the stringy skin is removed and discard any that are dark or strange-smelling. Simmer the chestnuts for 15–20 minutes until tender, and purée or use whole according to the recipe. 1 lb (450 g) of chestnuts should give about 14 oz (400 g) of purée.

Peeling chestnuts is hard work. Enlist a friend, or several, to help you. But it is definitely worth the effort; tinned chestnut purée is no substitute.

If fresh chestnuts are not available, you can use dried ones. Soak in water overnight and simmer them in fresh water for 2–3 hours until soft. The taste is a little different from fresh chestnuts. Unsweetened bottled chestnuts, which are available in Chinese and Japanese shops, may also be used as a substitute.

CHESTNUT RICE

Chestnuts lend their subtly sweet flavour to rice in this classic autumn dish; the nutty flavour of brown rice marries particularly well with chestnuts. Chestnut rice is served instead of plain rice at the end of a meal. The recipe below is for the simplest version; to make a more festive dish, replace 4 of the chestnuts with 8 shelled and peeled gingko nuts, and add some sake to the cooking water.

16 large fresh chestnuts (4–6oz, 115–70g)
2 leaves spinach
10oz (285g) short-grain white or brown rice
16 floz (480ml) water
2 tsps soy sauce

Soak the chestnuts overnight in cold water. With a sharp knife, pare away the shell and scrape off the inner skin. Soak in fresh water for another 3–4 hours, changing the water several times. Drain and cut neatly into quarters.

Parboil the spinach leaves until just tender, and dip into cold water. Drain, pat dry with absorbent paper and cut into 1in (2½cm) lengths. Set aside.

Wash the rice thoroughly and combine with the measured water and soy sauce in a heavy saucepan with a closely fitting lid. Leave to soak for 1 hour. Add the chestnuts, bring to the boil, and simmer over very low heat for 15–20 minutes for white rice and 40–50 minutes for brown, until the rice is cooked. Turn off the heat and allow to stand for 10 minutes.

Mix the chestnuts into the rice with a wooden rice paddle or with a spoon, and serve hot in rice bowls, distributing the chestnuts evenly. Garnish each bowl with 3 or 4 lengths of spinach.

KURI KINTON: CHESTNUTS AND SWEET POTATOES

At New Year the wife and mother of the household has her annual three-day holiday. Before the festival begins she prepares enough dishes for the whole holiday. For each meal, she arranges small portions of every dish in a stack of square lacquer boxes, artistically arranging the portions with a sprig of green here and there for decoration. Chestnuts and sweet potatoes (kuri kinton is a much more mellifluous name and full of wonderful wintry associations) invariably appears, and is a perennial favourite. Add more sugar or honey to make a sweeter dish if required.

4 oz (115 g) chestnuts
8 oz (225 g) sweet potatoes, washed and trimmed
1 tbsp sake or mirin (optional)
1 tbsp sugar or honey
½ tsp salt
1 tbsp black sesame seeds

Peel the chestnuts (see page 73) and simmer until soft. Drain well and pat dry with absorbent paper. Cube the sweet potatoes and soak in cold water for at least 30 minutes. Simmer in fresh water for 15–20 minutes until tender. Drain well, season with sake or mirin (if used), sugar or honey and salt, and mash. Crumble the chestnuts and stir into the sweet potato mixture. Taste and add a little more salt or sugar and honey if required. Allow to cool to room temperature.

Mould into chestnut shapes and arrange in dainty mounds on small individual plates. Lightly toast the sesame seeds and sprinkle over to garnish.

Kuri kinton will keep 4–5 days in the refrigerator.

CHESTNUTS IN BURRS

One of Gifu's claims to fame is Gifu Castle, perched on the very top of a steep craggy hill, approached only by cable-car or a perilous climb up a nearly vertical flight of stone steps. Halfway up, and somewhat off the main track, is a tiny temple renowned for its fine cookery, where, one day, we went for a meal. A room had been prepared for us, and while we were waiting we stood at the window, admiring the view of the winding Nagara river and the occasional skyscrapers jutting out amongst the hills. After a few cups of sake, the old priest who served us was quite relaxed, and regaled us, as all Japanese priests are expected to do, with some rather risqué jokes. One of the dishes consisted of brown chestnuts in little spiky cases, like natural chestnuts in their burrs. After many efforts, I managed to make a less beautiful but still very tasty imitation. Serve this dish on small leaves, perhaps even real chestnut leaves, to complete the illusion.

12 large chestnuts (3–4 oz, 85–115 g)
1 egg white
1–2 oz (30–60 g) somen noodles
vegetable oil for deep-frying
1 oz (30 g) plain white or wholemeal flour

Peel the chestnuts (see page 73) and simmer until soft. Drain well, pat dry with absorbent paper and set aside. Beat the egg white very lightly with a fork; 5–10 strokes are enough. Break the noodles into ¼–½in (½–1 cm) lengths.

Pour oil to a depth of 3in (8cm) into a small saucepan and heat to 340°F (170°C) (to test see pages 40–1). Line up the chestnuts, flour, egg white and noodles in bowls near the cooker.

Prepare 2 or 3 chestnuts at a time. Dust with flour, making sure that the chestnuts are completely covered; gently shake off the excess. Dip into the egg white, and finally roll in noodles so that the chestnuts are well coated. Place gently in the hot oil. The noodles will make a golden 'burr'. Cook for just 30 seconds to 1 minute, then remove and drain on absorbent paper. Repeat until all the chestnuts are cooked.

STEAMED CHESTNUT CAKES

These little round cakes, made of chestnuts coated in aduki bean paste, may be served as part of a Japanese meal or, sweetened, as a cake with tea before the meal. The Japanese like to sweeten chestnuts, but I prefer not to because chestnuts are naturally very sweet.

12 chestnuts (about 3oz, 85g)
15 floz (450ml) aduki bean paste (see page 183)
good pinch salt
1–2 tbsps sugar or honey (optional)
1oz (30g) plain white or wholemeal flour

Peel the chestnuts (see page 73) and simmer until soft. Drain well and pat dry with absorbent paper. Season the aduki bean paste with salt and sugar or honey to taste.

Wrap each chestnut in aduki bean paste to make neat balls and roll in flour. Set the cakes on a napkin or thin towel in a preheated steamer and steam over high heat for 15 minutes until the flour coating is shiny. Remove and cool immediately; the Japanese use a paper fan to accelerate the cooling process.

Serve 2 or 3 cakes on small individual plates.

DEEP-FRIED CHESTNUT CAKES

Each week in Tokyo's Meguro district a few women gather in a small room above the health-food shop to prepare a meal together, under the instruction of a bright-eyed, lively lady of about seventy-five. On one occasion we made deep-fried chestnut cakes to serve as the dessert course. Japanese 'cakes' are very different from our idea of a cake; perhaps 'sweetmeat' would be a better word. This deep-fried chestnut cake is actually not very sweet, and is a sort of extended variation on Ohagi (see page 185), using chestnuts, rice and aduki beans, three favourite ingredients of Japanese cakes. Japanese cooks use white glutinous rice to make cakes; I have found that short-grain brown rice, cooked until it is very soft, also works well.

8 chestnuts (about 2 oz, 60 g)
10 fl oz (300 ml) aduki bean paste (see page 183)
salt
2–3 tsps sugar or honey (optional)
13½ fl oz (400 ml) well-cooked white or brown rice
1 egg white
4–6 tbsps lightly toasted sesame seeds
vegetable oil for deep-frying

Peel the chestnuts (see page 73) and simmer until soft. Drain well and pat dry with absorbent paper (the cooking water may be reserved to use as stock). Season the aduki bean paste with a little salt and sugar or honey to taste. Mash the cooked rice in a suribachi or food processor, and knead, adding a very little water to make a stiff paste; season with a little salt. Beat the egg white until it forms stiff peaks. Line up the chestnuts, aduki bean paste, rice, egg white and sesame seeds near the cooker.

Pour oil to a depth of 3 in (8 cm) into a small saucepan and heat to 340°F (170°C) (to test see pages 40–1).

Prepare 2 or 3 chestnuts at a time. Enclose each chestnut in aduki bean paste. Take about 4 tbsps rice, knead, and press into a flat round in the palm of your hand. Place one bean-paste-covered chestnut in the centre and close the rice around it to cover it completely. You will have quite a large ball by now. Coat the ball in stiffly beaten egg white, and finally roll in sesame seeds.

Gently place in the hot oil and deep-fry for 2–3 minutes until the cake is brown and crisp.

Serve on small individual plates. Unsweetened, the cakes can be served as part of the main meal. Serve the sweetened version with tea, preferably Japanese green tea. In Japan cakes are eaten with a tiny fork or a wooden stick.

Cucumbers

Japanese cucumbers are half the size of Western ones and, like all Japanese vegetables, quite perfect. In fact they are grown in sheaths to make them perfectly straight. They are the basis for many popular summer salads and used in soups and pickles.

Select small firm cucumbers. In Japan cucumber is not simply sliced and served, but is first treated in some way to make it crisper and to reduce bitterness. While it is not essential to follow the painstaking Japanese methods, they do produce a more authentic taste. First cut off both tips of the cucumber and rub the tips against the cut ends until a white foam appears. Rinse and cut the cucumber according to the recipe. Then either soak in lightly salted water for 20 minutes, or sprinkle with salt and press or lightly knead. Finally rinse the cucumber, gently squeezing out as much moisture as possible, and drain and pat dry with absorbent paper.

Japanese cucumbers are seldom peeled, for the contrast of dark-green skin and pale flesh opens up many artistic possibilities. A cucumber is the ideal material on which Japanese chefs can demonstrate their virtuoso knifework. I once watched in amazement as a chef in Kyoto sliced a 6 in (15 cm) cucumber all along into paper-thin slices, his knife moving at lightning speed, leaving the slices attached at the base. He then turned the cucumber, sliced it again, and with a flourish opened it out like an accordion 3 ft (90 cm) long.

Cucumbers for salad are generally sliced paper thin. Use a very sharp knife and rest on the point, moving the knife rapidly up and down while you slide the cucumber under it, rather like an old-fashioned bacon-slicer. Cut decoratively, cucumbers make most attractive garnishes; for example, they can be cut into 'fans' in the same way as aubergines (see pages 45–6).

CLEAR SOUP WITH CUCUMBER

Cucumber makes a refreshing, light, clear soup for summer.

1½in (4cm) chunk cucumber
½ sheet nori seaweed
1½pts (900ml) dashi (page 143)
2 tsps soy sauce
½ tsp salt
1 tsp sugar or honey
4 sprigs fresh coriander

Cut the cucumber into paper-thin slices and plunge into boiling water to parboil for just a few seconds. Rinse in cold water, pat dry with absorbent paper, and arrange in 4 soup bowls. Lightly toast the nori and cut with scissors into 1in (2½cm) squares; put some squares into each bowl. Bring the dashi to the boil and season carefully with soy sauce, salt and sugar or honey; taste and adjust the seasoning. Ladle the hot dashi into the bowls, and float a sprig of coriander on each just before serving. This soup may be served hot or chilled.

EGG-DROP SOUP WITH CUCUMBER

This delicate clear soup with its filaments of beaten egg is very popular in Japan.

1½in (4cm) chunk cucumber
1¼pts (800ml) dashi (page 143)
1 tbsp soy sauce
1 tbsp sugar or honey
1 tbsp kuzu or arrowroot
2 eggs
1 tsp finely grated root ginger

Slice the cucumber paper thin and combine with the dashi, reserving 2 tbsps dashi. Bring to the boil and simmer for 1 minute. Remove from heat and season with soy sauce and sugar or honey, adjusting quantities to taste. Dissolve the kuzu in the reserved dashi and stir into the soup off the heat. Return to the heat and bring back to a simmer, stirring occasionally. In a small bowl, beat the eggs and pour slowly over the simmering dashi; the eggs will set almost immediately. Ladle into soup bowls, distributing the cucumber evenly. Sprinkle a little grated ginger on each bowl and serve.

CUCUMBER AND TOFU SALAD

Cucumber is combined with tofu, sautéed to make it crisp and golden, in a light vinegar dressing.

½ cucumber
½ tsp salt
1 tbsp vegetable oil
6 oz (170 g) tofu, well drained

dressing
3 tbsps rice vinegar
2 tbsps dashi (page 143)
1 tbsp sugar or honey
¼ tsp soy sauce

lightly toasted sesame seeds

Slice the cucumber into very fine julienne strips; salt lightly, then place in a colander and cover with a plate and small jar of water to act as a weight. Set aside for 10 minutes to drain; then knead lightly, rinse and pat dry with absorbent paper. Cut the tofu into 1 in (2½ cm) cubes. Brush a small frying pan with the oil, heat over medium heat, and sauté the tofu for 5 minutes until golden. Allow to cool and combine with the cucumber. Combine the dressing ingredients in a small saucepan and heat to blend; bring just to the boil, then cool to room temperature. Toss the salad in the dressing just before serving and heap in small mounds in the centre of 4 deep bowls. Sprinkle over a few sesame seeds to garnish.

CUCUMBER WITH WALNUT MISO

Cucumber ovals topped with a rich, sweet miso dressing are often served as a pre-meal snack or a side dish.

1 small cucumber
salt

walnut miso
2oz (60g) walnuts
2 tbsps (30ml) white miso
1 tbsp sugar or honey
1–2 tbsps dashi (page 143)

Slice the cucumber on the diagonal to form ovals. Soak for 20 minutes in lightly salted water, then squeeze lightly, rinse and pat dry with absorbent paper. Sauté the walnuts in a dry frying pan for 2–3 minutes until fragrant. Chop coarsely and combine with the remaining ingredients in a small saucepan. Heat gently for a few minutes, then set aside to cool. Top each cucumber slice with a little walnut miso and serve.

THREE-COLOUR SALAD

Chilled noodles are a feature of Japanese summer salads, and this salad includes shirataki – fine noodle-like filaments of konnyaku (arum root). Shirataki is either soaked for a few minutes or parboiled to accentuate its whiteness. If shirataki is unavailable, any vegetable of a contrasting colour may be used to provide the third colour. Carrots in fine julienne strips, parboiled, are often included.

½ small cucumber
salt
egg strands using 1 egg (see page 247)
½ pkt (3½oz, 100g) shirataki

dressing
2 tbsps rice vinegar
3 tbsps dashi (page 143)
2 tsps soy sauce
2 tsps sugar or honey

½oz (14g) white sesame seeds

Cut the cucumber into fine julienne strips. Salt, knead lightly, and set aside for 20 minutes to drain. Rinse and pat dry with absorbent paper. Prepare the egg strands and set aside to cool. Parboil the shirataki in lightly salted water for 1–2 minutes and drain; pat with absorbent paper to dry. Combine the dressing ingredients and bring just to the boil; cool to room temperature. Lightly toast the sesame seeds and grind in a suribachi until flaky and paste-like. Combine the cooled dressing with the sesame seeds. Arrange the cucumber, egg strands and shirataki separately on a large platter, and serve the dressing separately.

KAPPA ROLLS

Crunchy cucumber rolled in sushi rice and nori makes a refreshing nori roll which is much loved in Japan, and which goes under the name of kappa roll. The kappa is a lovable but mischievous frog-like creature, a little like Toad of Toad Hall, who features in Japanese fairy-tales and folklore, and who is said to love cucumbers.

sushi rice prepared from 10 oz (285 g) uncooked rice (pages 260–1)
½ cucumber
salt
½ tsp freshly made wasabi horseradish
1 tbsp white sesame seeds
4 sheets nori seaweed
rice vinegar
soy sauce

Prepare the sushi rice. Peel and deseed the cucumber and slice into julienne strips. Either use raw, or soak in lightly salted water for 20 minutes, gently squeeze, rinse and pat dry on absorbent paper. Prepare the wasabi (see page 33). Lightly toast the sesame seeds. Toast the nori and halve each sheet with scissors.

Lay one half-sheet of nori on a bamboo rolling mat or on a working surface. Spread 1–2 oz (30–60 g) prepared sushi rice over the front half of the nori and, with wet hands, press the rice down firmly, smearing it to the sides of the nori. Draw a thin line of wasabi along the centre of the rice and lay 1 or 2 strips of cucumber along the wasabi. Roll up firmly and carefully so that the rice encloses the filling, and seal the far edge of the nori with a little vinegar. Leave with the sealed edge downwards and prepare 3 more rolls in the same way.

Make 4 more rolls omitting the wasabi and sprinkling the cucumber with sesame seeds before rolling.

Wet a sharp knife and cut each roll into 3, trimming the ends neatly. Serve in groups of 6, 3 of each type, with soy sauce to dip.

Daikon Radish

Daikon literally means 'big root', and wherever you go in Japan you can see the big white daikon roots, growing halfway out of the soil, pushing up in little vegetable patches and huge commercial fields alike. Even in the suburbs of Gifu, right behind my flat, were daikon fields, and I used to stand on my balcony and watch the women in their indigo work bonnets digging them up. My landlord, Mr Nomura, had a vegetable patch where he grew daikon, tending them as lovingly as the carp in his ornamental pond.

The daikon is as common a vegetable in Japan as the potato in England. In theory it is a winter vegetable, and the mid-winter daikon is still the sweetest; but with modern agricultural methods it is available in the shops all year round, in many different varieties, shapes and sizes, sometimes up to 18 in (45 cm) long and 4 in (10 cm) across. Legend has it that daikon can grow up to 5 ft (150 cm) and weigh 20–30 lbs (10–15 kg), but I was never lucky enough to see such a mammoth specimen. In any case, it is nothing like the small red vegetable that we call radish.

The Japanese attribute all kinds of virtues to the daikon. My friends always assured me that it has no calories, so I could eat it to my heart's content. It is also said to be extremely good for the digestion. Grated raw it is always served as a condiment to counteract the oiliness of deep-fried dishes such as tempura, and a salad of finely cut daikon makes a refreshing accompaniment to many rich dishes. When cooked, it becomes sweet and juicy, and is often served on its own in big rounds to be eased apart with chopsticks. It is frequently used in miso soup and oden (Japanese winter stew). Yellow, pungent daikon pickle, known as Takuan after the Zen monk who invented it, is the most common and popular of all the many Japanese pickles, and a staple of the Zen monks' diet.

Daikon is now widely available in English vegetable shops and markets, as well as in Chinese and Indian shops; it is sold as mooli, daikon or white radish. Those available in England tend to be smaller than in Japan. Choose firm, fresh, unwrinkled daikon. The greens as well as the root itself can be used in cooking.

Daikon is first peeled and then cut in a variety of different ways depending on how it is to be used. For cooking, it is cut into large succulent chunks neatly bevelled at the edges. For use as a salad vegetable it is cut into very fine julienne strips, or into threads using the following method: take a 3–4 in (8–10 cm) length of daikon and hold it in your left hand; pare the daikon with a very sharp knife into one long continuous even sheet, using the thumb of your right hand to control the knife. Roll the sheet of daikon tightly and cut it across into very fine strips. This technique takes a little practice; but having mastered it, you will find that it has many uses. To make an attractive garnish, spread the sheet on a chopping board and cut into thin strips; place the strips in cold water to form 'curls'.

GRATED DAIKON

To use as a condiment, peel 1–2 in (2½–5 cm) of daikon and grate very finely; a Japanese grater with a tray to collect the juices is convenient, but any fine-toothed grater will do. Squeeze out excess water with your fingers or, following the Japanese method, put the grated daikon into a piece of muslin and squeeze gently.

RED MAPLE RADISH

Dried chillies grated with daikon give a tang and a red colour poetically associated with autumn maple leaves. Peel a piece of daikon about 2 in (5 cm) long and pierce 3 or 4 times with a chopstick. Remove the seeds from 3 or 4 dried chillies and push one pepper into each hole. Grate the daikon and chillies together, then gather the grated mixture in a piece of muslin and squeeze out as much liquid as possible. Shape into small mounds and put one on the side of each dish.

CLEAR SOUP WITH DAIKON AND DEEP-FRIED TOFU

Daikon makes a deliciously sweet addition to soup, and sliced finely cooks very quickly. This clear soup is served in winter; the grated daikon is said to resemble snow.

2 oz (60 g) daikon radish
1 sheet thin deep-fried tofu (usuage)
1½ pts (900 ml) dashi (page 143)
1 tsp each light soy sauce, sugar or honey and salt
8 slivers lemon rind

Cut the daikon across into 2 halves. Slice one half lengthwise, and slice very finely to make half moons. Grate the remaining half using a Japanese or very fine-toothed grater; gather the grated daikon into a piece of muslin and squeeze gently to remove excess water.

Rinse the deep-fried tofu with boiling water; drain and slice into fine julienne strips.

Bring the dashi to the boil. Add the daikon slices and deep-fried tofu and simmer for 1 minute until the daikon is tender. Season with soy sauce, sugar or honey and salt, tasting as you go.

Warm 4 soup bowls and put a mound of grated daikon in each bowl. Ladle the soup over the grated daikon, float a sliver of lemon peel on each bowl, and serve immediately.

SIMMERED WINTER VEGETABLES

This is a popular winter dish combining root vegetables with deep-fried tofu. The vegetables vary according to the cook, but there is always a large proportion of daikon radish.

4 oz (115 g) daikon radish
1 medium carrot
1 medium onion
½ sheet deep-fried tofu
sesame oil
2 fl oz (60 ml) dashi (page 143)
2 tsps light soy sauce
1 tsp sugar or honey
1 tbsp sake (optional)
seven-spice pepper

Wash and trim the vegetables; peel the daikon and onion and scrape the carrot. Cut the daikon and carrot into fine julienne strips of roughly the same size and slice the onion finely. Rinse the deep-fried tofu with boiling water, drain, pat dry, and cut into fine julienne strips.

Brush a small saucepan with sesame oil and sauté the onion slices; add the daikon, carrot and deep-fried tofu and sauté to coat the vegetables lightly with oil. Add the dashi and soy sauce, sugar or honey and sake if used, cover, preferably with a drop lid, and simmer for 15–20 minutes, shaking the pan occasionally, until the vegetables are tender and well flavoured and the pan is nearly dry.

Arrange in neat mounds in the centre of small deep bowls and spoon over any remaining cooking liquid. Pass seven-spice pepper separately.

DAIKON ROUNDS WITH HOT SESAME SAUCE

Mrs Misono, who taught me flower arrangement, often prepared traditional dishes using vegetables from her own garden. In this dish the daikon rounds are prepared very simply and given piquancy with a rich contrasting sauce. The rounds are usually cut from big fat daikons, 2½in (7 cm) across, the edges slightly bevelled, and served one per person, each round completely filling the little bowl. If using more slender daikon, serve 2–3 rounds per person. The length of time required to cook the daikon depends on its size and age (turnips can be used instead). Daikon rounds are also delicious simply served with a dab of freshly made English mustard.

½ large daikon radish or 2 small daikon radishes
salt

hot sesame sauce
4 tbsps white sesame seeds
2 tbsps white miso
2 tsps honey or mirin
½ tsp dry English mustard
1 tbsp dashi (page 143)

Peel the daikon and cut into 1 in (2½ cm) slices. Lightly bevel both the top and bottom edges. Put into lightly salted water to cover, bring to the boil and simmer for 20–40 minutes, depending on the size of the daikon, until very soft. Drain, reserving the cooking water to use as stock, and put into 4 small bowls.

While the daikon is cooking, prepare the sesame sauce: lightly toast the sesame seeds and set some aside to use as a garnish. Grind in a suribachi until oily, and blend in the miso, honey or mirin and mustard. Heat the dashi and dilute the mixture with it to give a thick creamy consistency.

Top each daikon slice with a spoonful of hot sesame sauce and sprinkle over the remaining sesame seeds to garnish. Serve hot or at room temperature.

RED AND WHITE SALAD

New Year is a time for donning kimonos and engaging in traditional activities, such as passing out gifts of money (carefully wrapped in small envelopes tied with red and white string) to all one's nephews and nieces. The New Year's meal of course includes a red and white salad, consisting of daikon radish and carrot. This salad is usually made one or two days in

advance, and seems to taste better after being refrigerated.
Japanese cooks usually make quite a large quantity as the salad
keeps in the refrigerator for at least a week.

6 oz (170 g) daikon radish
4 oz (115 g) carrot
½ tsp salt

dressing
2 tbsps rice vinegar
2½ tbsps dashi (page 143)
2 tsps honey or mirin
1 tsp light soy sauce

1 small piece kombu seaweed
shredded orange or lemon rind

Cut the vegetables into long chunks, then trim each chunk to
form a rectangle. Shave each rectangle into paper-thin slices
like tiny playing cards. Put the vegetables into a large mixing
bowl, sprinkle with salt, and leave for 10 minutes to soften.
Knead thoroughly until the daikon radish becomes soft and
translucent, and squeeze out as much water as possible. Pat dry
with absorbent paper.

Combine the dressing ingredients in a small saucepan and
bring just to the boil; remove from heat and chill.

Put the vegetables into a clean bowl; pour over the dressing
and mix well. Lay the kombu on top of the vegetables to give
flavour, cover the bowl and refrigerate. The salad may be
served after 30 minutes, but will have a better flavour if it is left
overnight. Refrigerated in a tightly sealed container, red and
white salad will keep for up to 2 weeks.

Serve very small portions, chilled or at room temperature,
and garnish with a little orange or lemon rind. Remove the
kombu before serving.

DAIKON SALAD WITH KOMBU AND ORANGE

Daikon combined with kombu and orange makes a tangy and colourful salad. Be careful to grate only the rind of the orange and not the zest, which is bitter.

4 oz (115 g) daikon radish
1¼ tsps salt
10 in (25 cm) kombu seaweed (about ¼ oz, 7 g)
1 tsp grated orange peel
4 fl oz (120 ml) rice vinegar
slivers of orange peel

Peel the daikon and slice very finely. Halve the slices to make half moons. Sprinkle with ¼ tsp salt and set aside for 10 minutes to soften. Knead thoroughly and squeeze out as much water as possible; pat with absorbent paper to dry.

Soak the kombu in warm water to cover for 20 minutes. Drain, reserving the water to use as stock, and cut the kombu with a sharp knife or scissors into small squares.

Combine the daikon, kombu and orange peel in a bowl. Mix the rice vinegar with the remaining 1 tsp salt and pour over the daikon mixture. Leave to marinade for 30 minutes.

Drain and serve in very small portions, garnished with a little orange peel.

Leeks and Spring Onions

You will find leeks all year round in Japan, sold in great bunches in markets and supermarkets; every Japanese kitchen has a stock, for they are one of the most essential of Japanese vegetables. There are many different varieties in Japan, from the 'long leeks' of the Tokyo area to the smaller 'green leeks' of the west. The sweetest leeks are said to come from Namba, now a business district and enormous railway junction right in the centre of the Osaka metropolis, but once full of leek fields.

Leeks in Japan, no matter what the type, are smaller, thinner and more delicately flavoured than English ones; use small young leeks or spring onions in Japanese recipes. Trim the root, remove the outer leaves and wash with care before or after cutting, removing all the mud from between the leaves.

Leeks are very versatile; different cooking techniques produce totally different tastes and textures. In Japan leeks are usually cooked for the shortest possible time, until barely

tender and still sweet, crisp and green. Cut into long chunks or sliced on the diagonal to make an interesting shape they may be grilled or deep-fried, and make a delicious tempura. They are often rinsed in cold water before cooking to remove bitterness. They are practically essential in winter one-pot dishes, and are a basic ingredient in many much-loved daily dishes such as miso soup.

Leeks or spring onions are one of the most important garnishes in Japanese cookery. To use as a garnish, leeks need to be shredded and rinsed: shred or chop extremely finely, rinse in cold water and squeeze, or wrap in muslin, rinse and wring out the water.

LEEK SALAD WITH HOT MISO DRESSING

Leeks lightly cooked to retain their crispness and sweetness are combined with a rich miso and mustard dressing to make this classic salad. Use fresh, very young leeks, preferably straight from the garden, for this salad. To make a more complex salad, add a few strands of wakame seaweed, softened in water and cut into thin strips, or half a sheet of deep-fried tofu, rinsed in boiling water and finely sliced.

4 young leeks
salt

dressing
4 tbsps flavoured white miso (page 152) or plain white miso
¼ tsp dry English mustard
1 tbsp rice vinegar
3–4 tbsps dashi (page 143)

1 tbsp sesame seeds, toasted

Wash and trim the leeks and cut into ¾in (2 cm) lengths. Parboil in lightly salted boiling water for 1–2 minutes or until just tender. Drain immediately and rinse in cold water to stop further cooking. Pat lightly to dry.

Blend the dressing ingredients in a suribachi or with a fork, adding enough dashi to make a dressing of mayonnaise consistency. Fold the leeks into the dressing, and arrange in small heaps in the centre of 4 deep bowls. Garnish with sesame seeds.

Mushrooms

Throughout the year, but particularly in the autumn, shops and markets in Japan have an abundance of mushrooms. In fact, the range and variety is so great that the word 'mushroom' as such is seldom used; each variety is referred to by its individual name. There are as many, probably more, kinds of wild and cultivated mushroom as in France, ranging from the clumps of tiny golden, grey or brown mushrooms which float in clear soups or appear in one-pot dishes, to the succulent brown shiitake mushrooms which are the most common, and culminating in the famous matsutake mushroom. Single matsutake mushrooms are often sold beautifully arranged on pine leaves in gift boxes; and the matsutake is so expensive that the highly prized aroma is sometimes eked out by using just one mushroom to flavour enough soup for four people. Some of my acquaintances were wealthy enough to own their own matsutake mountains, always heavily guarded in the autumn. Less fortunate amateur gardeners often find space, even in the smallest of gardens, for a branch or two inoculated with shiitake spores, so that they can grow their own.

Our flat and button mushrooms have recently begun to appear in Japanese shops, but their uses are more limited than Japanese mushrooms, and their flavour and texture are rather different. Dried Japanese mushrooms have a rich flavour and texture, and in Japan are prized above many varieties of fresh mushroom. In England they can be found in many health-food shops and all Japanese and Chinese shops; they are rather expensive but well worth it.

Choose both fresh and dry mushrooms which are large and fleshy and which have a good smell. Soften dried mushrooms by soaking for 30 minutes in warm water; cut off the hard stem before using according to the recipe. Mushroom soaking liquid is always reserved, and makes a delicious stock. To make a more strongly flavoured stock, put the dried mushrooms into boiling water and simmer for 5–10 minutes, then strain. The mushrooms can then be simmered in seasoned stock or used in any mushroom recipe. Their delicate flavour is best appreciated if they are served whole and alone.

Fresh mushrooms should be wiped, trimmed, and peeled if they are dark. They may be cooked whole, with or without the stems, thinly sliced or finely chopped to use as a filling ingredient. Fresh shiitake mushrooms can occasionally be found in Chinese or Japanese shops; the best shiitake have firm fleshy caps, slightly curled under at the edges. The shiitake stem is usually discarded and a cross is cut in the cap before cooking whole. Fresh shiitake are full of flavour, succulent and well worth seeking out.

Mushrooms are most versatile and may be prepared in a wide variety of ways. They can be grilled, make delicious tempura, and are very often used in soups and one-pot dishes or mixed with rice. They are perhaps most delicious very simply simmered and served whole.

SIMMERED WHOLE SHIITAKE MUSHROOMS

The time-honoured way of serving dried mushrooms in Japan is just by themselves, cooked as simply as possible to accentuate their succulence and flavour. Any large, unbroken, dried mushrooms may be cooked in this way, but Japanese dried shiitake mushrooms are particularly delicious. The best shiitake mushrooms are said to come from Kyushu, the warm southern island of Japan. Sake is often added to this dish to give a richer flavour.

12 large fleshy whole dried mushrooms
8 fl oz (240 ml) water
1 tbsp soy sauce
1 tsp sugar or honey
1 tbsp sake (optional)

Put the mushrooms in the water to soak for 30 minutes. Drain, reserving the water. Trim away the stems and lightly score the mushroom caps in a crisscross pattern. Lay the caps in a small saucepan and pour over enough of the reserved soaking water to cover. Stir in the soy sauce, sugar or honey and sake, if used, and bring to the boil. Stir to ensure that the sugar or honey is dissolved, cover, preferably with a drop lid, and simmer over very low heat for 45 minutes until the mushrooms are tender and well flavoured and most of the cooking liquid is absorbed. Leave the mushrooms to cool in the cooking liquid. Remove with chopsticks or a slotted spoon and arrange neatly in small shallow bowls. Any remaining cooking liquid should be reserved and used as stock for thick soups.

WHOLE SHIITAKE MUSHROOMS SAUTÉED AND SIMMERED

Dried shiitake mushrooms are sautéed in sesame oil and simmered in a sake–soy-sauce mixture to make a richly flavoured dish.

12 large fleshy whole dried mushrooms
1 tbsp sesame oil
2 fl oz dashi (page 143) or reserved mushroom soaking water
1 tbsp sake
1 tbsp soy sauce
1 tsp poppy seeds, lightly toasted

Soak the mushrooms in enough water to cover them for 30 minutes. Drain, reserving the soaking water. Trim away the mushroom stems and lightly score the caps in a crisscross pattern. Heat the sesame oil in a saucepan and sauté the caps for a few minutes over medium heat. Add the dashi (or mushroom

soaking liquid), sake and soy sauce and simmer, shaking the
pan occasionally, for 15 minutes, until the mushrooms are
glossy and the pan is nearly dry. Allow to cool to room
temperature. Arrange the mushrooms neatly in small shallow
bowls and sprinkle over a few poppy seeds.

DOBIN MUSHI: STEAMED SOUP WITH DRIED MUSHROOMS

The matsutake is a thick-stemmed, reddish-brown mushroom
which grows under red pine trees on mountain slopes. It is so
prohibitively expensive that it is usually used in tiny quantities;
one mushroom may be used to lend its delicate flavour to soup
or rice for a family of four. It is frequently simply wrapped in
foil with a couple of pine needles and grilled, or it is served in
dobin mushi.

The dobin is a little earthenware teapot which is stored away
all year and brought out in the matsutake season just to
make this delicate matsutake soup. Sadly, dobins are as rare
as matsutake mushrooms in England. However, this soup is
delicious using any wild mushroom or large, firm, cultivated
mushroom. Cook it in an earthenware container over a
steamer; or abandon such attempts at authenticity and use an
ordinary saucepan.

2 dried mushrooms
1½ pts (900 ml) dashi (page 143)
2 large, firm, fresh mushrooms
8 watercress leaves, or chrysanthemum leaves or small spinach leaves
1 tbsp soy sauce
¼ tsp salt
1 tbsp fresh lemon juice
8–12 slivers lemon peel

Soak the dried mushrooms in some of the dashi for 30 minutes.
Drain, reserving the dashi. Wipe and trim the fresh mushrooms. Remove the stems of the dried and fresh mushrooms
and slice the caps finely. Wash the watercress or other green
leaves and pat dry.

Put the dried and fresh mushrooms into a small earthenware

pot with a lid. Bring the reserved dashi to the boil and pour over them; cover with the lid. Place the pot in a preheated hot steamer, and steam over boiling water for 15 minutes. Remove the lid, add the watercress (or chrysanthemum or spinach leaves) and steam for just 30 seconds.

Remove from the heat and season carefully with soy sauce, salt and lemon juice, adding the seasonings little by little and tasting as you season. Ladle the soup into 4 warmed soup bowls, float a few slivers of lemon peel on the surface, and serve immediately.

This soup may also be prepared in 4 separate cups (see chawan mushi recipe, page 249), or cooked in a saucepan over very low heat.

MUSHROOMS WITH TOFU AND DEEP-FRIED WALNUTS

The rich cookery of Kyushu, the southern island, seems to owe as much to China, which is almost a neighbour, as to the austere traditions of Japan. In a small temple near Nagasaki I was served a rich dish of fresh and dried mushrooms combined with tofu and crisp walnuts, which I learnt were first deep-fried. If you use sesame oil it will give a Chinese tang to the dish. Cornflour may be used as a substitute for kuzu.

8 dried mushrooms
3 oz (85 g) walnut halves
5 oz (140 g) tofu, drained
1 young leek or spring onion
1 small carrot
4 oz (115 g) fresh mushrooms
vegetable oil for deep-frying
vegetable oil or sesame oil for sautéeing
1 tsp sake
1 tsp soy sauce
pinch salt
1 tsp kuzu

Soak the dried mushrooms in enough water to cover them for 30 minutes; drain, reserving the soaking water. Remove the stems and quarter the caps. Discard any discoloured walnuts and prepare 3 oz (85 g) walnut halves or large pieces. Cut the drained tofu into 1 in (2½ cm) cubes. Cut the leek or spring onion on the diagonal into fine slices. Cut the carrot into thin slices or flowers (page 64). Wipe and trim the fresh mushrooms and halve if large.

Fill a small saucepan with oil to a depth of 2 in (5 cm) and heat to 325°F (160°C). Deep-fry the walnut halves for 1 minute, turning, until lightly browned; they become bitter if even slightly burnt. Set aside on absorbent paper to drain. Heat a little vegetable or sesame oil in a frying pan and sauté the tofu cubes until all sides are golden and crisp. Drain on absorbent paper.

Heat a little vegetable or sesame oil in a large saucepan. Add the dried mushrooms, leek or spring onion and carrot and sauté to coat all surfaces with oil. Add 4 tbsps of the reserved mushroom soaking water, the sake, soy sauce and salt and bring to a simmer. Cover, preferably with a drop lid, and simmer for 5 minutes or until the vegetables are tender. Uncover and stir in the fresh mushrooms and tofu, and simmer for 2 more minutes. Dissolve the kuzu in 1 tbsp cold water. Over very low heat, stir the kuzu solution into the vegetables, stirring continually until the sauce thickens. Stir in the walnuts.

Arrange small portions in individual dishes or serve in one large dish and put in the centre of the table.

MUSHROOMS STUFFED WITH TOFU

Tofu is often combined with dried mushrooms – in this dish it is used as a stuffing for large flat mushroom caps. Japanese cooks usually steam each portion separately, artistically arranged on the plate in which it will be served. If this procedure seems too time-consuming, steam the mushrooms on a single large plate and arrange on individual plates once cooked.

12 large, flat, dried mushrooms
2 tbsps soy sauce
5 tsps sugar or honey
12 oz (340 g) tofu
salt

1 tbsp sesame seeds, toasted and lightly ground
1½ tsps kuzu
1 tbsp sake (optional)
flour
mustard and cress

Soak the mushrooms in enough water to cover them for 30 minutes. Drain, reserving the soaking water, and trim away the stems. Put the caps into a small saucepan and add enough of the reserved soaking water to cover. Add the soy sauce and 3 tsps sugar or honey, bring to the boil and simmer for 30 minutes. Leave to cool in the cooking liquid.

Bring plenty of salted water to a rolling boil, put in the tofu, and boil for 1 minute. Remove and allow to cool slightly. Mash with a fork, blending in 1 tsp salt, 2 tsps sugar or honey, the sesame seeds and the kuzu to make a stiff paste.

Drain the mushroom caps, pat dry, and dust the inner surface of each cap with flour. Stuff with the tofu mixture, shaping it into a smooth round. Arrange the mushroom caps on 4 small plates, sprinkle with sake if used, place in a preheated hot steamer, cover, and steam over boiling water for 5 minutes. Divide the mustard and cress into 4 small bunches and add to each group of 3 mushrooms just before the end of steaming. Steam uncovered for a few seconds, and serve immediately.

MUSHROOM RICE

Every season has its characteristic 'coloured rice', and mushroom rice, plain rice enriched with the mellow flavour of dried mushrooms, is a classic autumn dish.

10oz (285g) short-grain white or brown rice
5 dried mushrooms
1 4in (10cm) piece kombu seaweed (about ¼oz, 7g)
1 tbsp soy sauce
½ tsp salt
1½ tsps sake

Wash the rice several times, and put aside in a strainer. Soak the dried mushrooms and kombu in enough water to cover them

for 30 minutes. Drain, reserving the soaking water. Trim away
the mushroom stems and slice the caps very finely.

Lay the kombu in a heavy-bottomed saucepan and add the
rice. Measure out 15 fl oz (450 ml) mushroom soaking water,
adding more water if necessary, and season with the soy sauce,
salt and sake. Pour over the rice. Level the surface of the rice
and lay the mushroom slices on top. Cover and set aside to
soak for 1 hour.

Bring to the boil and simmer, covered, over very low heat
for 10–15 minutes for white rice and 40–50 minutes for
brown, until the rice is cooked, adding a little dashi if the rice
becomes dry. Let the rice stand, covered, for 10 minutes before
serving. Mix the mushrooms into the rice and serve as the rice
course of the meal.

FRESH MUSHROOM SALAD WITH WALNUT DRESSING

This delicate dressing is traditionally served with grilled shiitake mushrooms; it goes well with any fresh mushrooms, wild
or cultivated. The dressing is best made using a suribachi, a
Japanese ceramic mortar and pestle. If not available the walnuts
may be ground in an electric blender or crushed with a rolling
pin. Equal proportions of sesame seeds and walnuts are
sometimes substitutes for plain walnuts in this dressing.

4 oz (115 g) fresh mushrooms
vegetable oil

walnut dressing
1 oz (30 g) walnuts
2 tbsps dashi (page 143)
1 tsp soy sauce
¼ tsp sugar or honey

sprigs of watercress, parsley or coriander leaf

Wipe and trim the mushrooms and remove the stems. Thread
the caps on to bamboo or metal skewers (page 153) and brush
lightly with oil. Grill under a preheated hot grill, turning once,
for about 4 minutes, until lightly browned. Do not overgrill or
they will become dry. Remove from skewers and slice finely.

Put the walnuts into a suribachi and grind coarsely. Stir in the remaining dressing ingredients to make a moderately thick dressing. Fold the mushroom slices into the dressing.

Arrange the mushrooms in small mounds in the centre of small deep bowls, and garnish with a sprig of watercress, parsley or coriander leaf.

AUTUMN SALAD

In the autumn every private garden in Gifu seems to have its own persimmon tree, laden with orange fruit. My friends used to give me sacksful, which I ate for every meal, and even made into pies (most unorthodox). There are many different varieties. I spent a quiet afternoon threading small oval ones used for making dried persimmons on to a long piece of string which I hung along my balcony: I was rewarded after a few weeks by the deliciously sweet dried fruit. The following recipe is one of the ways in which the ladies of Gifu deal with the annual glut. Dried persimmons, if available in England, must be very expensive, so I have substituted dried apricots.

8 dried mushrooms
8 fl oz (240 ml) dashi (page 143)
1 tbsp soy sauce
1 tbsp sugar or honey
1 tbsp sake or mirin
¼ cucumber
salt
8 dried apricots

dressing
2 tbsps sesame seeds
8 oz (225 g) tofu, drained
1 tbsp rice vinegar
1 tbsp sugar or honey
1 tsp salt

slivers of lemon peel to garnish

Soak the mushrooms in enough water to cover them for 30 minutes. Drain, remove the stems and slice the caps thinly. Put the slices into a small saucepan and add dashi to cover. Season with soy sauce, sugar or honey and sake or mirin and bring to the boil. Simmer for 30 minutes, uncovered, stirring occasionally, until most of the cooking liquid has been absorbed. Leave to cool in the cooking liquid, then drain and set aside.

Wash the cucumber, halve and scrape out the seeds. Cut into paper-thin slices; sprinkle with salt, knead lightly and set in a colander to drain. Slice the dried apricots into julienne strips.

Lightly toast the sesame seeds; tip into a suribachi and grind until oily, or crush very thoroughly with a rolling pin. Boil the tofu in rapidly boiling water for 1 minute; remove, drain and mash, combining it with the sesame seeds in the suribachi. Blend in the remaining dressing ingredients. Taste and add more sugar or honey, salt or vinegar if required.

Rinse the cucumber and pat dry. Mix into the dressing in the suribachi together with the mushrooms and apricots. Arrange in small mounds in individual dishes. Garnish with a little lemon peel and serve at room temperature.

Onions

The Japanese name for the onion is tamanegi, 'round leek', because it is seen as a member of the leek family. It is a relative newcomer to Japan, but has rapidly come to be used in many traditional dishes. Japanese onions come in all sizes. Small ones, like our pickling onions, may be simmered whole, rather than fried, to bring out the sweetness. Large onions, sliced across, the rings carefully held together with wooden cocktail sticks, are grilled or used for a particularly delicious tempura.

Choose firm, golden-skinned onions with no sprout; top and tail and remove the peel.

Spring onions are the closest Western equivalent to the small, mild Japanese leek. The green leaves as well as the bulb are used. Wash, remove wilting leaves and slice finely.

SIMMERED ONIONS YOSHINO-STYLE

In this dish the sweet juices from boiled onions are thickened with kuzu to make a light and translucent sauce. Kuzu is legendary for its health-giving properties, and the best kuzu is said to come from Yoshino. After adding kuzu, the sauce needs to be continually stirred to prevent lumpiness. Arrowroot or cornflour can be used instead of kuzu.

4 small onions
12 fl oz (360 ml) water
1½ tbsps soy sauce
1 level tbsp kuzu

Trim the base of the onions and peel, leaving the onions whole. Put into a small saucepan with the water and soy sauce and bring to the boil. Cover, preferably with a drop lid, and simmer until the onions are soft; this takes 10–20 minutes, depending on their size. Remove with a slotted spoon. Dissolve the kuzu in a little cold water and pour gradually into the simmering stock, stirring continuously. Continue to simmer over a very low heat until the sauce thickens.

Stand each onion in a small deep bowl and spoon over the sauce. Serve immediately.

ONION SALAD WITH LEMON SOY DRESSING

Onions, parboiled to remove the sharpness, are often served as a salad, with a delicately tangy soy-based dressing.

2 medium onions (about 7oz, 200g total)
salt

dressing
2 tbsps light soy sauce
1 tbsp freshly squeezed lemon juice
1 tsp mirin or sake

seven-spice pepper

Peel the onions, halve lengthwise, and slice very finely. Immerse the slices in a bowl of lightly salted water, and wash. Drain and rinse, then plunge into rapidly boiling water and boil hard for 1 minute. Drain, and pat dry with absorbent paper.

Combine the dressing ingredients and pour over the onion, turning so that the slices are well coated with dressing.

Serve small portions, and sprinkle over a little seven-spice pepper.

Peppers

The Japanese word for pepper is piman, from the French 'piment', which shows that the pepper is not a native of Japan. But nowadays it is an essential ingredient in Japanese cookery. You cannot buy just one pepper, as we do in the West – they are sold by the basketful on market stalls, or in bags of five or ten (the Japanese equivalent of our half dozen or dozen) in supermarkets. Japanese peppers are much smaller, thinner skinned and sweeter than ours; they are often served as part of a dish of tempura, or grilled over charcoal to accompany sake in a Japanese bar.

Choose firm, bright, unblemished peppers. The smallest, thinnest-skinned peppers are the most suitable for Japanese recipes. Cut off the stalk and carefully remove the seeds; then wash well to remove any that remain. Peppers, finely chopped, are often added to mixed vegetable dishes; add them last so that they cook for only 2–3 minutes and remain crisp and sweet. They make a delicious salad on their own or with other vegetables, either raw and finely chopped, or first grilled until the skin blackens and blisters and then skinned. The smoky taste and soft texture of grilled pepper gives a subtle flavour to salads or cooked dishes.

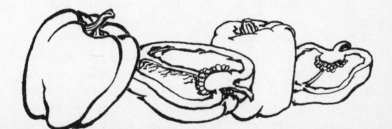

STUFFED GREEN AND RED PEPPER BOATS

Japanese stuffed vegetables are usually deep-fried rather than baked, and served with grated daikon radish and ginger to counteract any oiliness. If you can find seitan, a wheat gluten product, it gives a distinctive flavour and chewy texture to the filling; dried yuba shreds or even walnuts taste quite different, but are also delicious additions to the filling in their own right.

1 red and 1 green pepper

filling
1 young leek or spring onion
1 oz (30 g) fresh mushrooms
2 oz (60 g) tofu, well drained
1 tbsp seitan, finely chopped, or dried yuba shreds, or walnuts, coarsely chopped
½ tsp each soy sauce and sugar or honey
1 oz (30 g) plain flour
1–1½ tbsps dashi (page 143)

dipping sauce
8 fl oz (240 ml) dashi
2 fl oz (60 ml) soy sauce
1 tbsp sugar or honey

4 tbsps grated daikon radish
2 tsps freshly grated root ginger

batter
2 oz (60 g) plain flour
4 fl oz (120 ml) water

flour for dusting
vegetable oil

Halve each pepper across and then again lengthwise to form 4 shallow boat-shaped pieces; carefully remove the seeds without damaging the skin. Wash, pat dry and set aside.

Prepare the filling. Wash and shred the leek or spring onion. Wipe the mushrooms and dice finely. Cut the drained tofu into small cubes, and prepare the seitan, yuba or walnuts. Combine the soy sauce, sugar or honey and flour and stir in the leeks, mushrooms, tofu and seitan (or yuba or walnuts), mixing well to coat with the flour mixture. Add just enough dashi to bind.

Combine the dipping sauce ingredients in a small saucepan and bring just to the boil; keep warm. Prepare and drain the grated daikon and ginger.

Blend the flour and water to make a thin batter. Dust the inside of each pepper 'boat' with flour, and divide the filling between the 8 'boats', pressing in well. Keeping the 'boats' upright, dip into the batter, spooning batter over the top so that the 'boats' and filling are completely covered.

Half-fill a small saucepan with oil and heat slowly to 340°F (170°C). Lower the 'boats' a few at a time into the hot oil, and deep-fry for 1 minute until the batter is golden. Remove with chopsticks or a slotted spoon and drain on absorbent paper.

Arrange 1 red and 1 green pepper 'boat' each on 4 small dishes and put a mound of grated daikon topped with a little grated ginger on each dish. Serve with the dipping sauce. Each person mixes the daikon and ginger into the dipping sauce and dips the 'boats' into it before eating.

FLOWER PEPPERS

This colourful dish combines red and green peppers with a miso dressing; a little sugar or honey makes the dressing sweeter.

dressing
2 tbsps white miso
2 tbsps sake
1 tsp sugar or honey (optional)

1 red and 1 green pepper
1–2 tbsps vegetable oil
seven-spice pepper

Stir together the miso, sake and sugar or honey if used to make a smooth dressing and set aside. Wash, halve and deseed the peppers and cut into long julienne strips, ¼in (½cm) wide. Heat the oil in a frying pan, add the peppers, and sauté over medium to high heat for 2 minutes, until the strips are becoming tender but still crisp. Remove from heat and stir in the dressing, and a dash of seven-spice pepper, turning to coat well. Serve hot or at room temperature.

Potatoes

The potato is not a staple part of the diet in Japan as it is in England, but is quite a minor member of a large family of different tubers, which include the small hairy taro and the sweet potato, as well as more exotic tubers such as the 'sweet yam', the 'long yam' and the 'Satsuma yam' from southern Japan. The potato only arrived in Japan quite recently via Indonesia, and is known as jaga-imo, 'Jakarta yam'.

Japanese potatoes tend to be small. Whole ones, neatly trimmed into a round or hexagon, are often included in simmered dishes such as oden (Japanese winter stew, page 167), while thick, cooked slices may be served with a miso or sesame dressing. Potatoes are even used to make a filling for sweet cakes, or cut into a decorative shape and used as a garnish. Japanese cooks usually parboil potatoes before using them. Whole potatoes are put into cold water to be parboiled, while slices are put straight into boiling water. Potatoes come in many different varieties, from floury to firm. Select small, fresh ones for Japanese dishes. The cooking time varies according to the variety, size and age of the potato.

POTATOES SIMMERED WITH WAKAME

Starchy potatoes act as a natural thickener. In this country dish potatoes are simmered in seasoned stock, which thickens to become a rich sauce. Wakame adds a delicate flavour and texture.

4 small potatoes (about 12oz, 340g)
handful (⅛oz, 3g) wakame seaweed
8 floz (240ml) dashi (page 143)

2 tbsps soy sauce
1 tbsp sugar or honey

Scrub the potatoes and cut into small (½in, 1 cm) cubes. With a knife or scissors, cut the wakame seaweed into 1 in (2½ cm) lengths.

Combine the dashi, soy sauce and sugar or honey in a small saucepan; add the potatoes, cover and bring to the boil. Simmer for 5 minutes, stirring occasionally to ensure that the potatoes cook evenly. Stir in the wakame seaweed, which will absorb the stock and swell considerably. Cover and simmer for another 1–2 minutes or until the potatoes are soft. Remove from heat and leave to cool in the cooking liquid.

This dish can either be reheated or served at room temperature. To serve, arrange small portions in mounds in deep bowls and spoon over a little of the stock.

GRILLED POTATOES WITH PEANUT SAUCE

Grilled potatoes brushed with a thick peanut sauce make an unusual dish. Firm vegetables such as carrots, turnips and aubergine are also delicious prepared in this way.

4 small potatoes (about 12oz, 340g)

peanut sauce
½oz (14g) skinned peanuts or 1 tbsp (15ml) crunchy peanut butter
2 tsps sugar or honey
1 egg yolk
¼ tsp salt
½–1 tbsp dashi (page 143)

vegetable oil

Scrub the potatoes and cut into 1 in (2½ cm) cubes. Set aside in cold water to soak.

Roast the peanuts in the oven or in a covered frying pan until brown and nutty. Tip into a suribachi and grind to a paste; or use ready-made peanut butter. Stir in the peanut sauce ingredients in the above order, adding enough dashi to make a thick paste.

Drain the potato cubes, pat dry, and thread on to bamboo or, if not available, metal skewers. Brush with oil and grill under a very hot grill, turning, for a few minutes until the outside is crisp and brown and the inside is soft. Remove from heat and spread a little peanut sauce on one side of each piece. Return to the grill and grill lightly until the sauce begins to brown and bubble. Coat the opposite side of each piece with sauce and repeat.

Slide the potato pieces off the skewers on to small plates and serve immediately.

DEEP-FRIED POTATOES

Potatoes lend themselves to decorative cutting, often into seasonal shapes such as maple or gingko leaves. They are deep-fried without batter so that the outline remains clear, to make a crisp and delicious garnish. In Japan vegetable cutters in a variety of shapes are used.

4 small potatoes (about 4 oz, 115 g, each)
vegetable oil
parsley

Scrub the potatoes and cut into ¼ in (½ cm) slices. Either use the slices as they are or cut them into gingko leaves or some other decorative shape. To make gingko leaves: cut each slice into a roughly triangular shape with 2 concave and 1 convex sides, and cut a notch on one side of the convex top of the 'leaf'. Rinse the slices well in cold water to remove as much of

the cloudy starch as possible, changing the water several times.

Half-fill a small saucepan with oil and heat to 320°F (160°C). Deep-fry the slices a few at a time, quite slowly, for 3–4 minutes, until crisp and golden. Remove and drain on absorbent paper.

Scatter a few 'gingko leaves' on a small dish to serve, and garnish with parsley. Or use them to garnish a mixed vegetable dish.

DEEP-FRIED STUFFED POTATOES

Cooked mashed potatoes are stuffed with a vegetable filling and deep-fried, making a crisp shell. A variety of different vegetables can be used in the filling; the following recipe uses ones easily available in England.

12oz (340g) potatoes
2oz (60g) plain white or wholemeal flour
½ tsp salt
1 tbsp vegetable oil
boiling water (see recipe)

filling
1 young leek
½ medium carrot
¼ green pepper
4 dried mushrooms, softened in water
1oz (30g) freshly cooked corn kernels or peas
½ tsp freshly grated root ginger
1oz (30g) walnuts
1 tbsp vegetable oil
dash sesame oil
1 tsp kuzu or cornflour
2 floz (60ml) dashi (page 143)
salt

vegetable oil
tiny sprigs of watercress, parsley or coriander leaf
lemon wedges

Scrub the potatoes and cut into large chunks. Boil in lightly salted water until soft; drain and mash. Blend the flour and salt with the oil and add just enough boiling water to make a stiff dough. Mash the flour mixture with the potatoes; turn out on to a floured surface and knead lightly. The potato dough should be quite soft, but stiff enough to keep its shape. Set aside.

Wash and trim the vegetables. Chop the leek, carrot and green pepper very finely. Drain the mushrooms, remove the stems and slice the caps finely. Prepare the corn or peas and ginger and chop the walnuts coarsely. Heat the oils in a saucepan, add the leek, carrot, green pepper and mushroom and sauté; cover the pan, lower the heat, and continue to cook, shaking the pan occasionally, for a few minutes, until the vegetables are tender. Stir in the corn or peas and ginger. Blend the kuzu or cornflour with the dashi and stir into the vegetable mixture over very low heat. Continue to stir over low heat until the sauce thickens. Stir in the walnuts and season with a little salt to taste.

Divide the potato dough into 6 portions. With floured hands knead each portion lightly and flatten into a round about 3 in (8 cm) across. Divide the filling between the rounds and close the potato dough over the filling to make a neat oval.

Fill a small saucepan with oil to a depth of 3 in (8 cm) and heat to 340°F (170°C). Deep-fry the potato balls 2 at a time, turning, for 1–2 minutes, until the balls swell and become crisp and golden. Drain on absorbent paper.

Slice each potato ball into 1 in (2½ cm) slices, and divide the slices between 4 small plates. Garnish with watercress, parsley or coriander leaf and lemon wedges.

POTATO CHESTNUTS

Potatoes are often used to make simple sweetmeats at home, particularly at New Year. Small balls of sweetened mashed potato are deftly shaped into 'chestnuts' using a small square of cotton cloth, traditionally the cloth used to wipe the cup in the tea ceremony. For festive occasions, tiny pieces of real chestnut are added. Peel the potatoes to make a very smooth purée, or leave them unpeeled for more texture.

4 small potatoes (about 10 oz, 285 g total)
2 tsps sugar or honey
2 egg yolks

¼ tsp salt
a few chestnuts, peeled and boiled (optional)

Quarter the potatoes and boil in lightly salted water to cover for 5–6 minutes until soft. Drain well, reserving the cooking water. Allow to cool a little and mash, adding the sugar or honey, egg yolks and salt. Mash together thoroughly, adding just enough of the reserved cooking water to make a firm paste. The remaining water can be used for stock. Put the potato mixture into the top of a double boiler and heat over gently simmering water, stirring carefully so that it does not stick, until the mixture becomes fluffy and holds its shape. Remove from the heat and cool to room temperature. Divide into 12 portions and form each into a ball.

Dampen a square of cotton such as a handkerchief, and put a ball of potato into the centre of the cloth; put a few small pieces of chestnut into the centre if using. Gather the cloth around the potato and gently squeeze, twisting the top to form a chestnut shape; unmould the 'chestnut' on to a plate. Rinse the cloth and repeat with each of the potato balls. Arrange 3 chestnuts on each small plate, and serve with a small fork. Potato chestnuts look particularly attractive on delicate porcelain plates.

The tips of the 'chestnuts' may be coloured to make a particularly festive dish. The traditional colouring is bright green tea-ceremony tea. Take 1½ tsps of the potato mixture and mix with ⅓ tsp powdered green tea; form the remaining potato mixture into 12 balls. Put a tiny ball of the green mixture at the top of each ball, just off the centre, and shape as above, to make a 'chestnut' with a green tip. A little aduki bean paste (page 183) may be used in the same way to make a red tip.

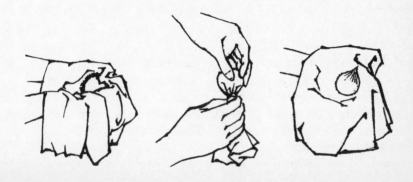

Pumpkin

In the summer the shops are full of small round pumpkins, with knobbly orange, dark-green or even beige skins, and you can see pumpkins scattered across the fields, half hidden by their big leaves. Japanese pumpkins are much smaller than those commonly available in England, and very sweet, with firm, bright orange flesh; the rind is edible too. Pumpkin is often served very simply, simmered or as tempura, to make the most of the contrast between the orange flesh and dark-green skin.

Small Japanese pumpkins can sometimes be found in markets, Chinese or West Indian shops, and some health-food shops; they are often sold as Hokkaido pumpkins. Chop them in half, remove the seeds, and cut according to the recipe. The most common shape is a thin crescent of orange flesh edged with the edible rind, about ¼in (1 cm) thick and 2in (5 cm) long. Any pumpkin, if it is as young and small as possible, makes a good substitute. Cut away the peel, scrape out the seeds and tough fibre, and cut the flesh into small chunks.

Pumpkin rapidly turns into purée. To retain its shape it must be cooked just enough to make it tender and sweet and removed from the heat before it begins to disintegrate. It can be cooked simply in its own juices, covered, over very low heat.

SWEET SIMMERED PUMPKIN

The Japanese like to sweeten vegetables; omit the sugar or honey from the cooking stock if you prefer a less sweet dish.

1 lb (450 g) pumpkin
4 fl oz (120 ml) dashi (page 143)

1 tsp light soy sauce
1 tbsp sake or mirin
¼ tsp salt
1 tsp sugar or honey
sprigs of parsley

Scrape out the pumpkin seeds and tough fibre, and peel (leave the peel of Japanese pumpkin intact). Cut Japanese pumpkin into ¼in (½cm) slices about 1 × 2in (2½ × 5cm). Other types of pumpkin can be cut into thin slices or 1in (2½cm) cubes.

Combine the dashi, soy sauce, sake or mirin, salt and sugar or honey in a saucepan. Add the pumpkin and bring to the boil. Cover, preferably with a drop lid, and simmer for 3–5 minutes until the pumpkin is tender but not disintegrating.

Drain, reserving the cooking liquid, and arrange a few slices of pumpkin attractively in 4 small bowls. Spoon over a little of the reserved cooking liquid and garnish with sprigs of parsley. Serve hot or at room temperature.

PUMPKIN SIMMERED WITH MISO

Onions and miso give the pumpkin a rich savoury taste.

1 lb (450g) pumpkin
1 medium onion
¼in (½cm) fresh root ginger
1 tbsp vegetable oil
2 tbsps white miso
2 tsps sugar or honey
4 fl oz (120ml) dashi (page 143)
1 tbsp sake or mirin

Prepare the pumpkin as in the previous recipe and cut into slices or cubes. Peel the onion and slice thinly. Peel and slice the ginger.

Heat the oil in a small saucepan and sauté the onion till translucent and beginning to soften. Add the pumpkin and ginger and sauté briefly. Cream the miso and sugar or honey in a little of the dashi, then blend in the remaining dashi, add the sake or mirin and pour over the pumpkin. Cover, preferably with a drop lid, bring to the boil, and simmer for 3–4 minutes until the pumpkin is tender but retains its shape.

Drain, reserving the cooking liquid. Arrange small portions of the pumpkin–onion mixture in 4 small deep bowls and spoon over a little of the cooking liquid. Serve hot or at room temperature.

PUMPKIN TEMPURA

Pumpkin makes a particularly sweet and delicious tempura, and is sometimes served with fresh ginger and parsley tempura to provide a contrast.

8oz (225g) pumpkin
2oz (60g) fresh ginger root
8 sprigs parsley
vegetable oil

batter
1oz (30g) plain white or wholemeal flour
2 floz (60ml) cold water
¼ tsp salt

plain white or wholemeal flour to dust
salt

Scrape out the pumpkin seeds and tough fibre, and peel; if you are using a Japanese pumpkin leave the peel intact. Cut the pumpkin into thin slices about 1 × 2in (2½ × 5cm). Peel the ginger and cut along the grain into fine julienne strips. Wash the parsley. Pat them all dry with absorbent paper.

Half-fill a small saucepan with vegetable oil and heat to 340°F (170°C). While the oil is heating, lightly mix together the batter ingredients to make a somewhat lumpy batter.

Dust the pumpkin slices with flour and dip into the batter so that each slice is completely coated. Gently place the slices in the hot oil and deep-fry for 1–2 minutes until the batter is golden and the pumpkin is tender. Drain on absorbent paper.

Hold each sprig of parsley by its stalk and dip the leaves into the batter. Deep-fry for 1 minute until the batter is pale golden; set aside to drain.

Mix the ginger strips into the remaining batter so that they are well coated. With chopsticks or a small spoon, slide small portions of the ginger into the hot oil and deep-fry for 1 minute; drain on absorbent paper.

Neatly fold 4 napkins and place on 4 plates. Arrange a few slices of pumpkin, 2 sprigs of parsley and some ginger on each plate and serve immediately. Pass salt separately.

Pumpkin tempura may also be served with tempura dipping sauce (page 156).

Spinach

Japanese markets and supermarkets seem to have an abundance of green leafy vegetables all year round, always quite perfect and dripping with cold water, which is splashed over them to keep them gleamingly fresh and crisp; vegetables which are beginning to droop are immediately marked down or discarded. Sadly, most of these leafy vegetables are not available in England. However, spinach is one of the most popular and frequently used.

Japanese spinach is a little smaller and more delicate in taste and texture than English spinach, akin to Swiss chard or leaf beet. It is always sold tied in bundles, complete with its pink root, with the leaves all neatly laid together and the roots at one end. The bundles are often cooked as they are, and the spinach is rolled and cut into small neat cylinders. The root itself and the pink base of the stems is often served separately from the leaves, and is quite a delicacy. It has a delicate sweet flavour, reminiscent of asparagus.

Spinach complete with its pink root can often be found in English shops and street markets. Any fresh unblemished

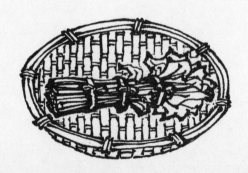

spinach may be used; tender young leaves in spring are the most delicious, served simply in the Japanese way.

Spinach needs the minimum cooking time, and can be steamed in its own juices and the water remaining on the leaves after washing. Japanese cooks usually cook it in rapidly boiling water for only 1 minute and immediately put it into cold water to stop further cooking and retain the bright green colour. The pink roots and stems need to be carefully washed and take a little longer to cook than the leaves.

SPINACH WITH SESAME DRESSING

The sesame dressing has a rich nutty flavour which complements the sweetness of the spinach in this classic of Japanese home cookery. The Japanese usually make the dressing in a suribachi; you may use an ordinary mortar and pestle, an electric grinder or even a rolling pin to crush the sesame seeds. Other green vegetables such as parboiled broccoli are delicious served with this dressing.

8 oz (225 g) spinach

sesame dressing
2 tbsps white sesame seeds
1 tsp sugar or honey
2 tsps soy sauce
1–1½ tbsps dashi (page 143)

toasted white sesame seeds

Wash and trim the spinach and parboil in a little rapidly boiling water for 1 minute until the stems are just tender. Rinse immediately in cold water. Drain and chop roughly. Squeeze lightly to expel some of the moisture, then set aside in a strainer or colander to drain a little more while you prepare the dressing.

Toast the sesame seeds until golden. Tip into a suribachi and grind until pasty. Add the sugar or honey and soy sauce and enough dashi to make a paste. Add the spinach to the suribachi and toss lightly in the dressing.

Heap the spinach in the centre of small deep bowls and sprinkle over a few sesame seeds to garnish.

SPINACH ROLLS

In this dish 3 or 4 rolls of spinach are topped with sesame seeds or peanuts and arranged upright like stooks of corn. Spinach rolls are often included in packed or picnic lunches.

8 oz (225 g) spinach
salt
1 oz (30 g) sesame seeds or raw peanuts
soy sauce

Wash the spinach. Parboil in lightly salted, rapidly boiling water for 2 minutes, until the stems are tender and the leaves have wilted. Rinse immediately in cold water to stop further cooking. Arrange half the spinach near the front of a bamboo rolling mat, putting the leaves on top of each other so that stems and leaves are at alternating ends. Fold the front of the mat over and press firmly to squeeze out excess moisture.

Finish rolling up in the mat and leave to rest for a few minutes. Unroll the mat and gently remove the spinach roll. Repeat with remaining spinach.

With a sharp knife, cut each roll neatly into 1 in (2½ cm) pieces. Toast the sesame seeds. If using peanuts, toast in a medium oven or over medium heat until golden and crunchy, and chop coarsely. Put the sesame seeds or peanuts in a bowl and press one end of each spinach roll lightly into the sesame seeds so that they adhere in an even layer.

Set 3 or 4 rolls upright in small deep bowls of a contrasting colour. Serve with a little soy sauce.

To make a simpler version of this dish, chop the spinach

leaves coarsely and parboil; drain well and serve in small mounds scattered with sesame seeds or peanuts.

SPINACH SALAD WITH RICH TOFU DRESSING

Lightly cooked spinach is very often served topped with a creamy tofu dressing, making an attractive combination of green and white.

8 oz (225 g) young spinach leaves
salt

dressing
1 oz (30 g) white sesame seeds
6 oz (170 g) tofu, lightly drained
1 tbsp sugar or honey
1 tsp mirin or sake
½ tsp salt

⅛ sweet red pepper to garnish

Wash and trim the spinach and parboil in a little lightly salted water for 1 minute, until the stems are just tender. Rinse immediately in cold water. Drain, chop roughly and pat with absorbent paper to dry.

Lightly toast the sesame seeds; tip into a suribachi and grind until pasty. Blend in the tofu, sugar or honey and mirin or sake, and season with salt to taste.

Blanch the pepper in lightly salted boiling water, drain and chop very finely.

Mound the spinach in the centre of small deep bowls. Spoon a little dressing over each portion, and scatter over a few tiny pieces of sweet red pepper to garnish.

STEAMED SPINACH BUNS

During the Second World War many children were evacuated to the countryside and were brought up by a second set of 'parents'. My friend Mieko took me to visit her parents, now quite elderly, living in a thatched farmhouse with acres of vegetable garden, over which her father still painfully toils. We helped her mother to prepare freshly cooked greens wrapped in dough to make round buns, which she steamed in a big, multi-tiered wooden steamer. These glossy buns with their moist green filling can be made in a Chinese bamboo steamer or any flat-bottomed steamer.

dough
½ tsp sugar or honey
4 fl oz (120 ml) hand-hot water
½ tsp dried yeast
5 oz (140 g) wholemeal or plain white flour
¼ tsp salt
2 tsps vegetable oil

spinach filling
8 oz (225 g) spinach
½ tsp salt
1 tsp sugar or honey

Make the dough. Stir the sugar or honey into 2 fl oz (60 ml) of the hand-hot water; sprinkle over the yeast and set aside in a warm place for 10–15 minutes until frothy. Combine the flour and salt in a large mixing bowl; make a well in the centre and pour in the yeast mixture, the oil and the remaining hand-hot water. With a knife gradually draw the liquid ingredients into the dry and mix together thoroughly. Turn on to a lightly floured surface and knead well, adding extra flour if necessary to make a manageable but not dry dough. Put the dough into an oiled bowl, cover with a damp cloth, and set aside in a warm place to rise for about 1 hour until double in bulk.

While the dough is rising, prepare the spinach filling. Wash the spinach and chop finely. Put into a saucepan, cover, and cook over very low heat for 5–10 minutes. The spinach will cook in its own juices; add a little dashi if the spinach becomes dry. It will quickly wilt and become dark green and much reduced. Drain the cooked spinach very well and season with a little salt and sugar or honey.

Punch down the dough and divide into 8 balls. Knead each ball lightly and roll out on a lightly floured surface to a thin round about 5 in (13 cm) across. Divide the filling between the rounds, and gather the dough gently around the filling, twisting it at the top to seal.

Prepare 8 squares of rice paper or greaseproof paper about 3 in (8 cm) square, and put each bun on a square of paper. Arrange the buns carefully on 2 flat steaming racks or flat Chinese bamboo steaming trays. Cover and leave in a warm place for 15 minutes to rise.

Put the buns on their steaming racks into a preheated steamer and steam, covered, over boiling water for 15 minutes, until the dough is no longer sticky. Remove from the steamer and serve immediately.

CLEAR SOUP WITH SPINACH AND EGG

This tasty clear soup with its floating strands of egg can be prepared in a matter of minutes and frequently appears on Japanese tables. Small cubes of tofu are sometimes added to the soup just before the egg.

2 leaves spinach
1½ pts (900 ml) dashi (page 143)
2 tsps light soy sauce
1 tsp sugar or honey
½ tsp salt
2 eggs
½ tsp freshly grated root ginger

Wash the spinach and cut into strips about 1 in (2½ cm) wide. Bring the dashi to the boil, add the spinach and simmer for 1

minute. Season to taste with soy sauce, sugar or honey and salt.
Beat the eggs lightly; they should not become frothy. Pour on
to the slowly simmering dashi in a thin stream, to float on the
surface of the soup. The eggs will set almost immediately.

Remove the soup from the heat and ladle into 4 warmed
soup bowls, distributing the spinach and egg evenly. Float a
little grated ginger on the surface and serve immediately.

SPINACH ROOTS

To enjoy spinach roots, look for bunches of spinach joined at
the base, with the pink root still attached. Serve a few roots at a
time so that the delicate flavour can be fully appreciated.

12–16 spinach roots
salt

Cut off the bottom 1–1½in (3–4cm) of stem and the pink
fleshy root of the spinach and trim away any brown or
tough-looking parts. Wash very well, carefully dislodging any
dirt that is caught up in the root. Steam or parboil in a very
little lightly salted water for 4–5 minutes until tender. Drain.
Serve the roots whole; large roots may be sliced lengthwise.

Spinach roots are delicious served plain, hot or at room
temperature, or with a scattering of sesame seeds and a dash of
soy sauce or a simple sesame dressing (page 121). For a richer,
more festive dish, serve with walnut dressing.

WALNUT DRESSING

2oz (60g) walnuts
2 tsps soy sauce
½ tsp sugar or honey
4–6 tsps dashi (page 143)

Walnut dressing is best made in a suribachi; it can also be made
in an electric grinder, which gives a less chunky texture.
Whichever way you choose, grind the walnuts, not too finely,
and mix in all the other ingredients, adding enough dashi to
give the consistency of peanut butter.

Serve the roots hot, topped with a little walnut dressing.

Sweetcorn

Festival time is the time for corn on the cob in Japan. You buy it from a street vendor, who takes it straight from the charcoal brazier where it has been roasting. Passing the hot cob from hand to hand you walk down the street munching, enjoying the sweetness and the smoky roasted taste.

Sweetcorn is grown in Hokkaido, the cold northern island of Japan. It is often simply eaten on the cob; or the kernels are stripped from the freshly cooked cob and used in soups and mixed vegetable dishes.

Always use the freshest possible corn; straight from the field is ideal. Look for plump, well-formed, pale gold cobs. Remove the leaves and silky threads; wash the cobs and boil hard in lightly salted boiling water for 12–20 minutes, until the kernels are just tender and can be just pierced with a fork. Older cobs will take longer to cook; be careful not to overcook or the corn will become tough. Either eat straight away with salt or, Western style, with butter; or strip the kernels from the cob with a sharp knife and use in any recipe calling for corn.

ROASTED CORN ON THE COB

4 cobs fresh corn
salt

Cook the cobs for 12–20 minutes, until the kernels are just tender. Drain; the cooking water may be reserved and used as stock. Grill the cobs under a hot grill, over a gas flame, or best of all over charcoal, turning, until the kernels are beginning to brown. Serve immediately, with a little salt if required.

SWEETCORN SOUP

Puréed sweetcorn is used to thicken this rich sweet soup, with the contrasting chewiness of rice cakes and dried mushrooms.

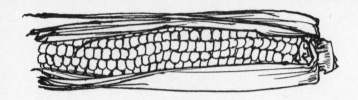

4 dried mushrooms
2 cobs fresh corn or 8 oz (225 g) frozen corn
salt
2 rice cakes
dashi (see recipe and page 143)
2 tbsps white miso
¼ tsp English mustard, mixed to a paste with a little water

Soak the dried mushrooms in water to cover for 30 minutes. Drain, reserving the water, cut off the stems and dice the caps. Return to the water, bring to the boil, and simmer for 10 minutes. Drain, reserving the water.

If you are using fresh corn, cook in lightly salted boiling water for 12–20 minutes (see page 127), until the kernels are just tender; drain and allow to cool. With a sharp knife, scrape the kernels into a large bowl. Cook frozen corn kernels in lightly salted boiling water for 3 minutes, and drain.

Chop half the fresh or frozen kernels coarsely, and grind to a paste in a suribachi or food processor. Press through a sieve to make a smoother purée if you wish.

Soften the rice cakes under a preheated hot grill for 2 minutes on each side until soft but not brown. Cut each rice cake into 4 pieces.

Add dashi to bring the reserved mushroom soaking water up to 1½ pts (900 ml). Put into a saucepan and bring to the boil. Stir in the puréed sweetcorn, corn kernels, mushrooms and rice cakes, and bring back to the boil. Dissolve the miso in a little of the hot stock, return to the soup and heat until nearly boiling. Stir in the mustard. Ladle into 4 bowls, distributing the corn kernels, mushrooms and rice cakes evenly.

Sweet Potatoes

Amidst the skyscrapers and traffic of modern Tokyo, you may suddenly come across the sweet-potato man, a reminder of old Japan, wheeling his cart full of sweet potatoes baking in a bed of glowing charcoal. Secretaries, mothers with babies on their backs and schoolgirls with their satchels quickly start to queue up, summoned by his distinctive yodelling cry; sweet potatoes are, after all, traditionally for the ladies. One by one they vanish, gingerly holding the hot potatoes in a gloved hand.

Sweet potatoes are available in a wide variety of types, shapes and sizes in Japan. The sweet-potato man sells small purple yams, which are eaten with a little salt as a sweet snack. At home sweet potatoes are cut into thick slices and simmered in seasoned stock, or deep-fried to make a particularly sweet tempura. They are often slivered and used in mixed vegetable dishes. Sweet potato is the basis for some of the sweet cakes that precede the bitter tea in the tea ceremony, nowadays largely a feminine activity. Mashed with chestnuts they make kuri kinton, a sweet New Year's dish.

They are available in many English markets nowadays as well as in Indian and West Indian shops. Choose smooth, firm, unscratched and unblemished sweet potatoes, and wash carefully; the skin is quite delicate. Japanese cooks usually cut them into rounds and soak them in cold water to reduce bitterness.

BAKED SWEET POTATOES

The simplest and perhaps the most delicious way to cook any of the many kinds of sweet potato is to bake them. Japan's sweet-potato men bake them in charcoal; less romantically, they may be cooked in the oven. Scrub the sweet potato gently, taking care not to break the skin, and pierce a few times with a fork. Bake at 400°F (205°C) for about 45 minutes, until soft, and serve plain or with a little salt, or, Western-style, with butter.

GRILLED SWEET POTATOES

Another simple and delicious way of cooking sweet potatoes is to grill them, and serve them plain or topped with flavoured miso.

4 medium sweet potatoes
salt
vegetable oil
flavoured misos (page 152)
toasted sesame seeds

Scrub the sweet potatoes gently, taking care not to break the skin. Put into a saucepan with water to cover. Add a little salt and bring to the boil; parboil for 10 minutes until semi-soft. Drain; the cooking water may be reserved for stock. Halve the sweet potatoes lengthwise, and score the cut face in a crisscross pattern. Brush with oil and arrange under a hot grill, cut face down. Grill for a few minutes. Turn. Either brush the cut face with oil or spread with flavoured miso, and return to the hot grill. Grill for 2–3 more minutes, until the sweet potato is brown and crisp and cooked through, and the flavoured miso, if used, is bubbling. Sprinkle over a few sesame seeds to garnish.

Arrange 2 sweet potato halves on each small plate, and serve very hot. Plain sweet potato halves may be served with soy sauce or salt.

SWEET POTATO STUFFED WITH MISO

The sweet potato is often used to make sweet dishes and seems to go particularly well with the rich flavour of miso. Like many sweet dishes, these sweet potato cakes are served and eaten as part of the main course of a meal.

2lbs (900 g) sweet potatoes
salt
1 tbsp lemon juice

filling one
3 tbsps white miso
2 tsps sugar or honey
2 tsps ginger juice
1–2 tbsps dashi (page 143)

filling two
2 oz (60 g) walnuts
1 tbsp dashi
pinch salt

vegetable oil

Slice the sweet potatoes and boil briskly in lightly salted water
for 10–15 minutes until soft. Drain, reserving the water, and
mash well, adding the lemon juice and a pinch of salt, and
about 4 fl oz (120 ml) of the reserved cooking water to bind; the
mashed potato should be creamy but still firm.

Prepare the 2 fillings. Blend the miso with the sugar or
honey and ginger juice, adding just enough dashi to make a
stiff paste. Grind the walnuts in a suribachi or electric grinder
and stir in the dashi and salt.

Divide the sweet potato into 8 portions. Knead each portion
and form it into a cup shape. Fill 4 cups with Filling One and 4
cups with Filling Two. Close the potato around the filling to
enclose it completely, and flatten the balls to make flat cakes
½–1 in (1½–2½ cm) thick.

Brush a frying pan with vegetable oil and heat over medium
heat. Fry the sweet potato cakes for a few minutes, turning
once, until both sides are browned.

To serve, cut each cake into 2 half moons, and arrange 2
halves of each type of cake on each plate, turned so that the
filling is visible.

SWEET POTATOES SIMMERED WITH HIJIKI

Hijiki is a particularly delicious sea vegetable, and its distinctive flavour brings out the sweetness of the sweet potatoes. It is easy to use and softens very quickly.

1 lb (450 g) sweet potato
handful hijiki seaweed (½ oz, 15 g)
2 tbsps vegetable oil
2 tsps light soy sauce
2 tsps sugar or honey
2 tsps sake or mirin
2 tbsps sesame seeds, toasted

Scrub the sweet potato and cut into matchsticks. Soak for a few minutes in cold water. Break the hijiki into short lengths and soak in water to cover. Drain the sweet potato and pat with absorbent paper to dry.

Heat the oil in a medium-sized saucepan, add the sweet potato and sauté for a few minutes. Drain the hijiki, reserving the soaking water; squeeze out excess water. Add to the sweet potato and toss lightly so that all surfaces are coated with oil.

Blend 8 fl oz (240 ml) of the reserved hijiki soaking water with the soy sauce, sugar or honey and sake or mirin and pour over the sweet potato and hijiki mixture. Cover, preferably with a drop lid, lower the heat and simmer for 7–8 minutes until the sweet potato is cooked. Uncover and cook for 2 minutes over medium-high heat to reduce the liquid. Stir well, then drain the vegetables and stir in the sesame seeds.

Serve hot or at room temperature, in small mounds in the centre of small deep bowls.

Turnips

The climax of the Japanese New Year is the festive meal, artistically arranged in lacquer boxes. Most of the dishes are chosen for their auspicious name, shape or colour as well as for their festive taste. The auspicious colours are red and white, and there are always several dishes which feature combinations of these two – sometimes small white hexagonal vegetables scattered with red stars, or neat red and white rolls secured with toothpicks, or, a spectacular centrepiece, a huge white 'chrysanthemum' with a red centre, nestled on two or three real chrysanthemum leaves. These dishes are all made from turnip, one of the most popular autumn and winter vegetables in Japan, whose firm crisp texture makes it an ideal base for decorative cutting techniques. Apart from 'chrysanthemum cutting', a part of every Japanese cook's repertoire, turnips are cooked in thick or thin slices, julienne strips or small rectangles ('playing cards'), or grated; small turnips are cooked whole or pared into hexagons.

Turnips are usually served either raw, probably marinaded in a vinegar dressing, or simmered in a seasoned stock. The turnip lends itself to long simmering, and is a standard ingredient in winter one-pot dishes such as Oden (Japanese winter stew).

Choose small, firm, fresh-looking turnips, avoiding ones which are soft or withered. After cutting, they are often soaked in lightly salted water and may be parboiled before simmering.

TURNIPS SIMMERED IN DASHI

This well-loved dish is served throughout autumn and winter. Large chunks of turnip are most suitable for this type of cooking. Small turnips may be simply washed and cooked whole, unpeeled, or cut across into halves, or carved into hexagons: cut a slice from the top and base of each turnip to make it level and pare the sides to form small hexagonal blocks. Large turnips are usually cut into thick slices or large cubes.

4 small turnips or 2 medium turnips, washed and trimmed
1 pt (600 ml) dashi (page 143)
2 tsps light soy sauce
2 tsps sugar or honey
¼ tsp salt
2 tsps sake or mirin (optional)

Cut the turnips into large pieces, using any of the cutting methods described above. Bring the dashi to the boil, put in the turnips and cook for 10 minutes. Add the soy sauce, sugar or honey, salt and sake or mirin, cover, reduce the heat, and simmer for 20 minutes, until tender. Leave the turnips in the cooking liquid to cool, so that they can absorb more of the flavour.

Serve at room temperature or reheat in the stock before serving. To serve, remove the turnips from the cooking liquid with a slotted spoon or chopsticks, arrange in the centre of small deep bowls and spoon over a little of the liquid.

TURNIP CHAWAN MUSHI (STEAMED TURNIP CUSTARD)

Gifu boasts the largest lacquer Buddha in the country, and quite possibly in the world. Behind the temple housing the imposing Buddha is a small restaurant, serving vegetarian food to the many visitors. One day in late autumn, having duly admired the maple leaves of the temple courtyard, we retired to this restaurant to be served a light meal, which included a delicately flavoured version of chawan mushi, savoury vegetable custard. None of us could identify the main ingredient, and were amazed to learn that it was turnip.

3 small (2–3oz, 60–75g) turnips, peeled
1 medium carrot
1 young leek
2 chestnuts, shelled and boiled
4 small pieces dried yuba or ¼ sheet deep-fried tofu, finely sliced
4 small fresh mushrooms, wiped and trimmed
4 heaped tbsps well-cooked white or brown rice
10 floz (300ml) dashi (page 143)
1 tsp light soy sauce
1½ tbsps kuzu or arrowroot
4 small sprigs coriander leaf or parsley

Grate the turnip very finely with a Japanese grater or food processor, and set aside in a strainer to drain. Cut the carrot into thin flowers (page 64); cut the leek diagonally into thin slices. Parboil the carrot and leek slices in lightly salted water. Halve the chestnuts and mushrooms. Arrange the vegetables and yuba or deep-fried tofu in 4 lidded chawan mushi cups, ramekins or mugs.

Mash the rice in a suribachi or with a fork; measure out 8 heaped tbsps of the grated turnip and mix it into the rice. Spoon the mixture over the vegetables, pressing it in firmly. Cover the cups with a clean cloth and steam in a preheated steamer for 10 minutes.

While the mixture is steaming, prepare the sauce. Combine the dashi, soy sauce and kuzu or arrowroot in a small saucepan and bring to a simmer over a very low flame, stirring continuously, to make a thick sauce. Carefully remove the cups from the steamer and ladle the sauce over the turnip mixture; top each cup with a sprig of coriander or parsley. Return the cups to the steamer, cover, and steam for 5 more minutes.

Cover each cup with a lid and serve immediately. This dish may be eaten with chopsticks or a spoon.

DEEP-FRIED TURNIP PUFFS

The first sign of spring in Japan is the pink plum blossoms, which appear even when branches are still covered in snow. After a day of plum-blossom viewing, the family may return to a dish such as these delicate turnip puffs with their crisp coating, served with bright vegetables.

12 oz (350 g) turnip (4 small turnips)
1 medium carrot
salt
8 mangetout peas, trimmed
2 tbsps plain white or wholemeal flour
1 egg white
vegetable oil for deep-frying

Trim the turnips and grate finely with a Japanese grater or very fine-toothed grater. Set aside in a strainer to drain.

Cut the carrot into thin flowers (see page 64). Bring a little lightly salted water to a rolling boil, add the carrot 'blossoms' and parboil for 1–2 minutes until just tender. Drain and immediately plunge into cold water. Parboil the mangetout peas in the same way in fresh water; drain and refresh.

Squeeze the turnip in your hands to expel as much water as possible. Combine thoroughly with the flour in a bowl. Beat the egg white until it forms peaks. Measure out 2 tbsps stiffly beaten egg white and fold lightly into the turnip mixture.

Pour oil to a depth of 2½ in (6 cm) into a small saucepan and heat to 340°F (170°C). Slide the turnip mixture by spoonsful into the hot oil and deep-fry, a few at a time, for 2–3 minutes until crisp and golden. Drain on absorbent paper. Continue until all the batter is used.

Arrange a few turnip puffs on small individual plates, and garnish each plate with 2 mangetout peas and 2 or 3 carrot plum blossoms.

CHRYSANTHEMUM TURNIPS

The coming of autumn is marked by the flowering of the much-loved chrysanthemum, the national flower of Japan. Even the tiniest flat has a windowbox where long-stalked chrysanthemums, the enormous heads supported on wire frames, are lovingly tended. Shrines and temples throughout the land celebrate autumn with chrysanthemum festivals, giving prizes to the growers of the biggest blooms. They even appear on the table, in the shape of chrysanthemum turnips.

4 small turnips (2–3 oz, 60–75 g each)
1 tsp salt
1 2 in (5 cm) piece kombu seaweed
2 tbsps rice vinegar

dressing
4 tbsps rice vinegar
4 tbsps dashi (page 143)
2 tbsps honey or mirin

1 dried red chilli pepper, seeded
few slivers lemon peel
fresh chrysanthemum leaves to garnish

Wash, peel and trim the turnips. Cut a slice from the top of each to make a flat base, and place each turnip on this base between 2 disposable chopsticks. With a sharp knife, make parallel cuts through the turnip about ¼ in (½ cm) apart, to within ¼ in (½ cm) of the base, so that the turnip remains joined at the base. Turn 90° and slice finely across, turning the turnip into a multi-petalled 'chrysanthemum'. Repeat with the remaining turnips.

Put the salt and the kombu with 3 cups water in a deep bowl, and soak the turnips for 20 minutes. Remove and gently squeeze out the excess water. Sprinkle with 2 tbsps rice vinegar and squeeze again.

Combine the dressing ingredients in a small saucepan and

heat gently. Chop half the chilli pepper finely and add to the dressing.

Put the turnips in a deep bowl, pour over the dressing, and leave to marinate for at least 30 minutes, preferably overnight.

Before serving, drain well, gently easing the 'petals' apart. Slice the remaining chilli pepper. Mound red pepper slices in the centre of 2 'chrysanthemums', and put a few slivers of lemon peel in the centre of the remaining 2.

Serve the 'chrysanthemums' in small individual dishes, decorated with 2 or 3 fresh chrysanthemum leaves.

MARINATED TURNIP AND APRICOT ROLLS

These crisp turnip rolls with a sweet apricot centre, making a festive combination of red and white, appear in the fourth of the New Year's boxes, with the vinegared foods. In Japan these rolls are made with dried persimmons.

2 small turnips (2–3oz, 60–75g each)
½ tsp salt
4 dried apricots, cut into julienne strips
1 tbsp sake

dressing
2 tbsps rice vinegar
1 tbsp sugar or honey
1 tbsp dashi (page 143)

1 tbsp rice vinegar

Peel and trim the turnips and slice across into very thin slices. Sprinkle with salt, turning the slices so that all surfaces are salted. Leave for 15 minutes to soften.

Sprinkle the apricot strips with sake and set aside.

Combine the dressing ingredients in a small saucepan and heat to dissolve the sugar or honey.

Gently squeeze the turnip slices, sprinkle with 1 tbsp rice vinegar, knead and squeeze lightly. Drain and gently squeeze the apricot strips.

Lay 1 or 2 apricot strips at the end of one turnip slice and roll firmly; insert a toothpick to secure the roll and trim the apricot ends neatly, reserving the trimmings. Continue in the same way with the remaining apricot strips and turnip slices.

Arrange the rolls in a small bowl and pour over the dressing. Leave to marinate for at least 15 minutes, or preferably overnight.

To serve, drain well and serve on small individual dishes, garnished with the finely chopped apricot trimmings.

TURNIP AND MUSHROOM SALAD

This salad combines turnips with grilled mushrooms in a light lemon and vinegar dressing.

2 small turnips (2–3 oz, 60–75 g) each, washed and trimmed
17 fl oz (500 ml) dashi (page 143)
12 small fresh mushrooms, wiped and trimmed
vegetable oil

dressing
3 tbsps dashi
2 tbsps rice vinegar
1 tbsp each freshly squeezed lemon juice, soy sauce and sugar or honey

1 sheet nori seaweed, lightly toasted

Quarter the turnips and slice very finely. Bring the dashi to the boil, add the turnips and parboil for 1–2 minutes until just tender; drain well, pat dry with absorbent paper and set aside. Trim the mushroom stems and thread a bamboo or metal skewer through both sides of each mushroom cap, taking care not to pierce the top of the cap. Brush the mushroom caps with oil and cook under a preheated hot grill for 2–3 minutes on each side, turning once. Set aside to cool; then combine in a small bowl with the turnips.

Combine the dressing ingredients in a small saucepan and heat just enough to dissolve the sugar or honey. Pour the warm dressing over the turnips and mushrooms and leave to cool to room temperature.

To serve, drain well and arrange small portions in deep individual dishes. With scissors cut the nori into thin strips and garnish each portion.

Seaweeds

Since time immemorial the Japanese have harvested the fruits
of the sea as much as the land. With great ingenuity they have
extended the variety of tastes and textures in their diet by
cultivating and processing many different types of seaweeds.
To them there is nothing remarkable or strange about using the
harvest of the sea. The word 'seaweed' as such is seldom used,
for seaweeds vary as much as land vegetables. In any Japanese
kitchen you will find crisp, dark-green sheets of nori stored in
long, oblong boxes, fronds of kombu and wakame, packages
of black, stringy hijiki and feather-light sticks of agar. All these
seaweeds have different tastes, textures and uses, and are quite
essential in Japanese cuisine – some of its most distinctive and
delicious tastes are based on them. Every meal contains
seaweed in some form, from kombu-based dashi which is used
in so many Japanese dishes, to plain sheets of nori used to wrap
rice at breakfast. The Japanese swear by the health-giving
properties of seaweeds, which apart from being nutritious are
said to give a pure unblemished complexion and glossy hair.
Seaweeds contain all the goodness of the sea, iodine, minerals
and vitamins, including vitamin B12, which is important for
vegetarians. They are normally used in dried form, although
fresh seaweed, particularly fresh wakame, is considered to be a
delicacy; most dried Japanese seaweeds are available in Japanese

shops and health-food shops in England. In theory they need to be softened in warm water for 20 minutes before use; in practice I have found that many soften immediately, and can be added to soups or simmered dishes without prior soaking time.

HIJIKI

Hijiki does not taste or look like our conception of a seaweed. It is black and stringy, with a distinctive sweet flavour and substantial rather chewy texture, which seems to appeal immediately to non-Japanese palates. All around the coast of Japan hijiki can be seen spread across the rocks. It is harvested between January and May, and young hijiki, harvested in January or February, is particularly sweet and tender. Hijiki softens almost immediately, and does not need to be soaked in water before use. It is often simmered in seasoned dashi, either alone or in mixed vegetable dishes. Sautéeing hijiki before simmering gives it added richness. It is also often added to miso soup.

RICH SIMMERED HIJIKI WITH TOFU

In this dish hijiki is combined with tofu and vegetables and first sautéed, then simmered in a piquant mixture of sake and soy sauce, giving it a very rich flavour. I tbsp honey may be substituted for the sake, to make a sweeter, milder flavour.

½oz (15g) hijiki
2 medium carrots
1 small leek
12oz (340g) tofu, drained
vegetable oil
2 tbsps light soy sauce
2 tbsps sake

Soak the hijiki in enough water to cover it for 5–10 minutes. Drain, reserving the soaking water to use as stock, and cut into 2in (5cm) lengths. Peel and trim the vegetables. Sliver the carrots into matchsticks; slice the leek finely and wash carefully. Cut the tofu into small cubes.
    Heat a little oil in a saucepan and sauté the carrots and leeks

over medium heat for 2–3 minutes. Add hijiki and tofu and continue to sauté, stirring carefully so as not to break up tofu.

Add soy sauce and sake, bring to a simmer, and continue to simmer uncovered over low heat for 7 minutes, until nearly dry.

Heap neatly in the centre of 4 small deep bowls and serve hot or at room temperature.

HIJIKI WITH SESAME SEEDS

Hijiki and sesame seeds make a classic and delicious combination. This is a dish for true lovers of hijiki.

½oz (15g) hijiki
2 tbsps sesame oil
1 tbsp soy sauce
1½ tsps sugar or honey
2 tbsps sesame seeds

Soak the hijiki in enough water to cover it for 10–15 minutes. Drain, reserving the soaking water. Heat the oil in a small saucepan and sauté the drained hijiki over medium heat for 2–3 minutes. Add the soaking water, soy sauce and sugar or honey, bring to the boil, and simmer for 10 minutes over medium heat until nearly dry.

Toast the sesame seeds and crush lightly in a suribachi or with a rolling pin. Mix with the hijiki.

Serve in small portions in individual bowls, hot or at room temperature.

KOMBU

Kombu, dried kelp, is an essential ingredient of Japanese cookery. It is harvested from small boats with hooked poles, and if you visit the northern island of Hokkaido you can see the long black strands strung up along the beach to dry. Kombu is the basis for classic dashi, the stock which gives the characteristically Japanese flavour to so many dishes. It is also a delicious sea vegetable in its own right, with a rich smooth texture and delicate flavour, and is often served simmered in seasoned stock or shredded and added to mixed vegetable dishes or stuffings. It is sold in Japanese and health-food shops in long dried strands, of which a very little is sufficient to make well-flavoured dashi. It should be lightly wiped but not washed before using, as the flavour is mainly on the surface; it is often scored or slashed to release more flavour. It should be simmered rather than boiled hard to avoid bitterness. Store opened packets of kombu in an airtight tin.

DASHI

Dashi is stock. The stock which is used in Japanese cookery tends to be light, giving a subtle underlying flavour to soups, simmered dishes and sauces. Classic dashi is made from kombu, and in Japan, where kombu is relatively cheap and easily available, this is the dashi which is most frequently used. Kombu seaweed may be simply wiped and soaked in water overnight, to give a light dashi. To make a delicate dashi suitable for clear soups, kombu is put into cold water and brought slowly to the boil; the kombu is removed just before the water reaches the boil.

Japanese cooks use a variety of other dashis to provide different background flavours. The water in which dried mushrooms are soaked is always kept, and makes a particularly delicious dashi; the soaking water from any seaweed too is used as dashi. Japanese cookery is extremely economical, and every part of most vegetables is used; any part which cannot be eaten can be used to make dashi. In the Zen temple in Kamakura where I stayed, nothing was ever wasted. A particularly tasty dashi was made from the skins peeled from daikon radish, and the water in which vegetables had been parboiled or simmered made a rich stock base for miso soup. The liquid in which beans or noodles are cooked is always saved, as is the whey which is a by-product of tofu making.

Classic kombu dashi, for which the recipe follows, will yield the most authentically Japanese flavour. However, in the time-honoured Japanese tradition of making use of what is locally available, any light vegetable stock or even water may be used instead.

2 pts (1200 ml) water
¼ oz (7 g) kombu seaweed

Put the water and kombu in a saucepan and heat slowly until

nearly boiling. Reduce the heat and simmer uncovered for about 20 minutes until the water is well flavoured and slightly reduced. Remove the kombu and reserve to use in other dishes.

KOMBU ROLLS

In Japan kombu is symbolic of happiness, prosperity and longevity, and, rather as we use holly, ivy and mistletoe, is used as a New Year decoration. It invariably appears in the New Year meal, usually in the form of kombu rolls, small, dark-green rolls stuffed with carrots and tied with gourd ribbon looking a little like cigars. In Japan, kombu rolls are often made with burdock root, which has an earthy taste which complements the smoothness of the kombu; if you can find fresh burdock root, use it instead of some or all of the carrot.

12 wide strips kombu seaweed, about 3 × 6 in (8 × 15 cm)
3 medium carrots (6–8 oz, 170–225 g)
12 6 in (15 cm) strips gourd ribbon (kampyo) or kombu
4 tbsps light soy sauce
2 tbsps sugar or honey
2 tbsps sake
dashi (see recipe)

Wipe the kombu with a damp cloth and soak in water to cover for 10–30 minutes, until pliable. Wash and trim the carrots and cut lengthwise into long julienne strips about ¼ in (½ cm) across. Soak the gourd ribbon or kombu strips in warm water for 10–15 minutes until pliable.

Drain the kombu, reserving the soaking water. Spread 1 sheet of kombu on a working surface and lay 3 carrot strips on it about 1 in (2 cm) from the shorter edge; lay 2 more carrot strips on top of the first 3. Roll the kombu tightly around the carrot strips and tie securely with a strip of gourd ribbon or kombu, finishing off with a neat knot. Trim the ends. Make 11 more kombu rolls in the same way.

Lay the rolls in a saucepan. Mix the soy sauce, sugar or honey and sake with enough of the reserved soaking water to cover the rolls, and pour over them (add dashi if you don't have enough water). Cover, preferably with a drop lid, and bring to the boil. Simmer over very low heat for 1–1½ hours, until the rolls are very soft and richly flavoured, topping up the cooking liquid if necessary with more soaking water or dashi and sake, soy sauce and honey or sugar.

Leave the rolls to cool in the cooking liquid. To serve, arrange them in 4 small deep bowls, and spoon over a little of the cooking liquid.

Kombu rolls will keep for up to a week in the refrigerator. Japanese housewives make enough for the whole New Year holiday and serve a few every day.

NORI

Crisp nori with its sweet seaweedy taste appears on most Japanese tables at breakfast time, for it is the seaweed which is rolled around rice, both at home and in sushi bars. We know nori as laver or porphyra, and it is one of our own native seaweeds, which is used as a food in Wales. In Japan nori is perhaps the most frequently used seaweed, and is farmed in vast quantities, mostly around the coast of the southern island of Kyushu. Nori grows best during the winter, and the first harvest is before the end of January. The nori is washed many times and stretched out on bamboo frames in the shallows to dry, like handmade paper. The best and most expensive nori is said to be Asakusa nori, first produced 300 years ago when much of Asakusa, now part of Tokyo, was under water, and still produced today, in spite of pollution, in Tokyo Bay.

Nori is normally sold in large 7 × 8in (18 × 20 cm) sheets which need to be toasted before use. Whole sheets are used to wrap nori rolls and rice balls; they can also be cut with scissors into small 1 × 2in (3 × 5 cm) sheets for wrapping rice at breakfast or into thin strips for garnishing, or simply crumbled on to rice. In Japan many different sizes, thicknesses and qualities of nori are available, including red, green, purple and black. In England nori can be found in all Japanese shops and some health-food shops. Store opened packets in an airtight tin.

To toast nori: toast the shiny side of the sheet over a hot flame for a few seconds, moving it gently to prevent burning, until it changes colour and becomes fragrant.

SALAD NORI ROLLS

Crisp salad vegetables wrapped in nori and flavoured with rich sesame miso make a colourful and refreshing summer side dish or *hors d'œuvre*. Choose sweet young vegetables for salad nori rolls; fresh perilla leaves, if available, have a particularly delicious flavour. A bamboo rolling mat is helpful but not essential for making neat, firm rolls.

2 sheets nori seaweed
4 oz (115 g) young carrots
¼ green or red pepper
1 oz (30 g) sesame seeds or 2 tbsps sesame paste
1 tbsp red or white miso
1 tsp sugar or honey
1 tsp ginger juice or fresh lemon juice
6–8 fresh perilla leaves or small lettuce leaves
4 sprigs watercress

Toast the nori lightly to bring out the flavour; do not overtoast as it will crack when you try to roll it.

Wash and trim the vegetables. Cut the carrots and pepper into long julienne strips. Pat all the vegetables dry with absorbent paper. Toast the sesame seeds, and grind in a suribachi until pasty; or use ready-made sesame paste. Blend the sesame with the miso, sugar or honey and ginger or lemon juice; adjust the quantities of the ingredients to taste.

Lay 1 sheet of nori on a bamboo rolling mat or on a working surface and spread half the sesame–miso mixture in a 2 in (5 cm) strip along the nori 1 in (2½ cm) from the edge. Lay 3 or 4 lettuce or perilla leaves along the sesame–miso mixture to cover it. Lay half the carrot and pepper strips to make a thick core along the centre of the lettuce leaves. Holding the ingredients in place with your fingers, roll the nori firmly around them, using your thumbs to roll. Dab a little water along the loose edge and press the roll firmly down on the moistened edge to seal; leave with the sealed edge downwards for a few minutes. Make a second roll with the remaining ingredients.

Moisten a sharp knife and cut each roll into 1–1½ in (3–4 cm) slices. Arrange a few slices on 4 small plates and garnish with watercress.

WAKAME

Wakame is a dark-green seaweed with long lobed fronds and a silky texture. The most tender and delicious wakame is gathered from the whirlpools at Naruto, off the coast of Shikoku, and in early spring, the season for fresh wakame, it is much in demand as a gift from returning travellers. Wakame literally means 'young leaf', and fronds, symbolising youth, are often included in the offerings at shrines and temples.

Wakame is frequently used in soups and salads. It is also delicious simmered with vegetables and beans, and is sometimes dried and served as a snack with beer or sake. It softens so quickly that it can be used as an instant ingredient in soups, to be added just before serving. Combined with a vinegar dressing it makes a delicious salad. The time-honoured way of preparing wakame as a salad ingredient is to scald it in boiling water so that it turns bright green, and immediately dip it into cold water to retain the colour; it can also be simply soaked for 10–15 minutes. It sometimes has a tough spine which should be trimmed away after soaking.

Dried wakame is available from Japanese and some health-food shops. It is very light, and expands greatly when added to water; one packet will provide enough for several meals.

It is difficult to measure: simply break off a few strands.

WAKAME AND CUCUMBER SALAD

Wakame and cucumber is a refreshing combination which appears on most Japanese tables nearly every day during the long hot summer.

½ cucumber or 1 small Japanese cucumber
½ tsp salt
½oz dried wakame seaweed

dressing
3 tbsps rice vinegar
3 tbsps dashi (page 143)
1 tbsp soy sauce
1 tsp sugar or honey
1 tsp mirin or sake (optional)

If using an ordinary cucumber, halve lengthwise and scrape out

the seeds; Japanese cucumbers do not need to be deseeded. Cut
the cucumber into paper-thin slices. Put them in a bowl with
water to cover, add the salt, and set aside to soak for 20
minutes.

Soak the wakame in lukewarm water for 10 minutes; it will
swell and become a rich glossy green. Drain and plunge briefly
into boiling water, then rinse in cold water to give a more
intense colour. Drain well and pat dry with absorbent paper.
With a sharp knife trim away the tough stem and chop the
wakame coarsely. Drain the cucumber and pat dry.

Combine the dressing ingredients in a small saucepan and
heat to dissolve the sugar or honey; remove from heat immediately and chill. Combine the cucumber and wakame and
pour over the chilled dressing just before serving. Toss gently.
Arrange neat mounds of salad in individual bowls.

CLEAR SOUP WITH WAKAME AND MANGETOUT PEAS

This recipe is the strictly orthodox method of preparing clear
soup with wakame: the wakame and mangetout peas are
precooked and carefully arranged in the bowl and hot dashi
poured over them. French beans may be used instead of the
mangetouts.

¼oz (7g) dried wakame seaweed
12 mangetout peas (about 1oz, 30g)
½oz (7g) kombu
½ tsp salt
2–3 tsps light soy sauce
½ tsp freshly grated ginger

Holding the wakame with chopsticks, dip it into boiling water
and swirl it around for a few seconds. Immediately put it into
cold water and leave to soften; depending on the variety of
wakame, this may take up to 20 minutes. Drain, pat dry, trim
away the tough stem, and chop the wakame coarsely.

Wash and trim the mangetout peas, and cut each pea on the
diagonal into 1in (2½cm) slices. Drop into fresh rapidly
boiling water and parboil for 1 minute until bright green.

Immediately rinse with cold water, then drain and pat dry.

Put the kombu into a saucepan with 1½ pts (900 ml) water and heat slowly. Remove the kombu just before the water boils; the kombu may be used again in any kombu recipe. Season with a little of the salt and soy sauce; taste and add more if required.

Warm 4 soup bowls with hot water; dry the bowls and arrange a mound of wakame and some peas in each bowl. Ladle in the hot dashi, filling the bowls no more than three-quarters full. Float a little grated ginger on each bowl and serve immediately.

Mixed Vegetable Dishes

Traditionally a Japanese meal consists of tiny portions of various different dishes. But at home with the family, particularly in the winter, many cooks like to provide a more robust meal, such as a large warming dish of mixed vegetables to be cooked at the table and shared by all, or plates of assorted tempura or grilled vegetables. Mixed vegetable dishes generally come not from the traditions of the refined temple cuisine, but originate in the countryside or come to Japan from abroad; tempura, apparently one of the most Japanese of dishes, was in fact introduced to Japan by the Portuguese fathers only a few centuries ago. In their cooking methods, however, mixed vegetable dishes remain very Japanese. Cooking is usually light and quick, and although a variety of vegetables are cooked by the same method, the individual flavours and textures remain distinct; they do not merge to become a vegetable mixture. Mixed vegetable dishes are popular family fare in Japan; they demand less time and effort on the part of the cook, and ensure a relaxed and convivial atmosphere.

Most mixed vegetable dishes make a complete meal, accompanied by a cooked salad, rice, pickles and miso soup.

VEGETABLES SAUTÉED AND SIMMERED IN KUZU SAUCE

Japan presents enormous contrasts from north to south in climate, people and culture. The warm southern island of Kyushu is but a ferry ride away from Korea and the Chinese mainland, and has for centuries played host to colonies of Chinese and Korean settlers. Its cooking methods reflect this cosmopolitan spirit. In this dish the vegetables are stir-fried before being simmered, a technique similar to that of neighbouring China.

1 young leek, washed and trimmed
1 medium onion, peeled
4 oz (115 g) carrots, scraped
½ green pepper
4 oz (115 g) white cabbage
4 oz (115 g) fresh or tinned bamboo shoot (optional)
1–2 tbsps vegetable oil
15 fl oz (450 ml) dashi (page 143)
1 tbsp soy sauce
2 tbsps kuzu or arrowroot

Cut the leek diagonally into ½ in (1½ cm) slices. Halve the onion and cut into thin half moon slices. Slice the carrots or cut into thick flowers (see page 64). Quarter the green pepper and cut into chunks. Cut the cabbage into chunks. Cube the bamboo shoot.

For the best flavour, the vegetables should be parboiled separately in lightly salted water, rinsed, drained and patted dry with absorbent paper.

Heat the oil in a large, heavy-bottomed pan (cast-iron is best) over medium to high heat. Add the vegetables in the order given, sautéeing a little between each addition, until the vegetables are lightly cooked and evenly coated with oil.

Add the dashi and soy sauce, bring to the boil, cover and simmer for 5 minutes. Drain the vegetables and keep warm; reserve the cooking liquid. Dissolve the kuzu in a little cold water and stir into the stock. Bring to a simmer over very low heat, stirring continuously with a wooden spoon or chopsticks until thick.

Serve the vegetables in small individual portions, hot or at room temperature, with the sauce ladled over them.

VEGETABLE DENGAKU: GRILLED VEGETABLES TOPPED WITH MISO

There is a tiny restaurant in Kamakura which must have been there since the days of the samurai. Eight or ten customers squeeze in to sit around the heaped charcoal fire, over which hangs a steaming cast-iron kettle on the traditional large wooden hook carved like a fish. The mama-san, the proprietress, continually replenishes pots of tea and flasks of sake, while grilling vegetables and tofu on bamboo skewers propped around the fire. Finally she applies a liberal layer of flavoured miso from one of the earthenware jars lined up along the hearth. Although the smoky atmosphere and taste will be lacking, this dish is equally delicious prepared using an ordinary grill. The flavoured misos can be made in relatively large quantities and stored in the refrigerator for several months.

flavoured miso one
3 tbsps red miso
3 tbsps dashi (page 143)
1 tbsp sake or mirin
2 tbsps sugar or honey

two
3 tbsps white miso
2 tbsps dashi
1 tbsp sake or mirin
1 tbsp sugar or honey
1 tbsp freshly squeezed lemon juice
½ tsp grated lemon rind

three
3 tbsps sesame seeds, lightly toasted
3 tbsps white miso
2 tbsps dashi
1 tbsp sake or mirin
2 tsps sugar or honey

1 aubergine (about 8oz, 225g)
4 small leeks
8 large flat mushrooms
1 green pepper
½ cake konnyaku (optional)
vegetable oil

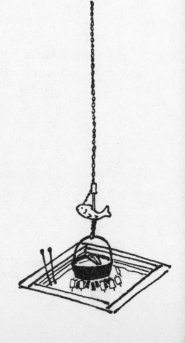

garnishes
lightly toasted white sesame seeds
poppy seeds
sprigs of fresh coriander or parsley

Combine the ingredients for misos number one and two in 2 small saucepans. To prepare miso number three, grind the sesame seeds in a suribachi until pasty and blend with the remaining ingredients in a third small saucepan. Add more dashi if necessary to each mixture to give a thick, creamy consistency. Heat the misos, stirring frequently, over very low heat until they begin to bubble. Remove from the heat immediately and set aside. They may be used at once or refrigerated indefinitely.

Wash and trim the vegetables. Cut the aubergine into ½ in (1 cm) slices. Slice the leeks diagonally into ½ in (1 cm) slices. Remove the mushroom stems and cut 2 notches in each cap to make a cross. Cut the green pepper lengthwise into 1 in (2½ cm) strips. Slice the konnyaku ½ in (1 cm) thick and sauté in a dry frying pan for a few minutes.

Soak long bamboo skewers in water. Thread each type of vegetable separately on to 2 of them or on to barbecue skewers, skewering carefully so that the vegetable will be secure while cooking and will keep its shape. Lay the aubergine slices on the table and slide 2 skewers sideways through the skin; the skewers should not pierce the cut face. The 2 skewers should not be parallel but should fan apart slightly. Skewer the mushroom caps flat in the same way. Thread 2 or 3 slices of leek on to 2 parallel skewers. Run 2 skewers through the top and bottom of each pepper strip, and lengthwise through each slice of konnyaku.

Brush the vegetables lightly with oil, and grill under medium heat, turning occasionally, until lightly browned. Remove from the grill and spread 1 side with one of the flavoured misos. Return to the grill and grill for 1–2 minutes until the miso begins to bubble. Quickly slide the vegetables off the skewers on to small plates, garnish, and serve immediately.

VEGETABLE BARBECUE

On cold winter evenings, and on warm summer nights too, people crowd into the 'robata-yaki' restaurants, where cheerful young chefs, white cotton scarves wound in workmanlike fashion around their heads, grill vegetables strung on bamboo skewers over a charcoal fire that stretches all the way along the counter, brushing them with a rich sweet sauce before passing them piping hot to the expectant customer. Although charcoal is ideal, an ordinary grill is perfectly adequate. Any firm vegetable, cut into small chunks, can be grilled. Prepare plenty of sauce and chop all the vegetables before the meal. When you are ready to eat, grill the vegetables, brush with sauce and serve straight away. The remaining sauce keeps well in the refrigerator and can be used again. You can also use it to baste whole vegetables baked in the oven, or to accompany sautéed vegetables.

sauce
4 fl oz (115 ml) dark soy sauce
4 fl oz (115 ml) sake
2 fl oz (60 ml) mirin and 1 tbsp sugar or honey, or 2 tbsps sugar or honey

2 medium carrots
2 small potatoes
2 onions
4 small leeks
1 green pepper
4 oz (115 g) small mushrooms
vegetable oil
seven-spice pepper

Bring the sauce ingredients to the boil in a small saucepan and set aside. Wash and trim the vegetables. Cut the carrots into ½ in (1 cm) slices, and cut the potatoes into small chunks. Peel the onions, halve and slice into half moons. Slice the leeks into 1½ in (4 cm) lengths. Cut the pepper into 1 in (2½ cm) squares. Wipe and trim the mushrooms and remove the stems; cut a cross in each mushroom cap. Soak long bamboo skewers in water. Thread each type of vegetable separately on to them or on to barbecue skewers. Simply skewer the carrots, potatoes, leeks and green pepper chunks. Lay the onion slices on the table and carefully slide through a skewer to hold the slices together in neat half moons. Slide a skewer horizontally through the mushroom caps. Pat the vegetables with absorbent paper to ensure that they are perfectly dry, and brush with oil.

Preheat the grill to very hot and grill the vegetables for 1 or 2 minutes, turning occasionally. Brush them thickly with sauce and return to the grill. Continue to grill, brushing 2 or 3 times with sauce, until they are tender. Be careful not to overcook the vegetables so that they become dry.

Slide the vegetables off the skewers on to small plates and serve immediately. Sprinkle with a little seven-spice pepper before eating.

If available, the following foods are delicious cooked in this way, and very popular in Japan: deep-fried tofu, in cubes; gingko nuts, shelled, boiled and skinned; quails' eggs, hard-boiled; lotus root, in thin slices.

TEMPURA

Tempura is magical food, retaining the crunchy sweetness of the vegetable within a crisp coating, light as air. In a tempura restaurant the white-coated chef behind the scrubbed pine bar prepares tempura in seconds, serving it up morsel by morsel as it is cooked, and arranging it elegantly on a neatly folded napkin in a little wicker basket. Tempura is best eaten freshly cooked at home too; in winter it is even sometimes cooked at the table. Before eating, tempura is usually dipped in a delicately flavoured sauce, into which a little grated daikon radish and fresh ginger have been mixed, to add a touch of

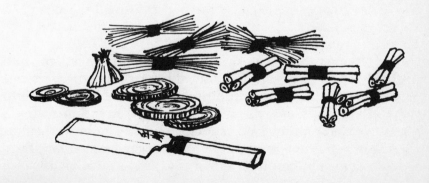

piquancy to the flavour and to help digestion. Crisp, light tempura needs the most delicate of batters, and, as in all Japanese cooking, the secret lies in lightness of touch. Made with chilled ingredients, the batter is barely mixed and still quite lumpy, and should be made just before it is used. Tokyo dwellers make a golden batter using only egg yolks; in the west of Japan, the whole egg is used to make a white batter.

1 large or 2 small aubergines (8 oz, 225 g)
1 medium carrot
1 green or red pepper, deseeded
2 small onions
8 mushrooms (about 4 oz, 115 g), wiped and trimmed, stems removed
2 young leeks
4 oz (115 g) sweet potatoes, scrubbed
24 French beans, topped and tailed (about 4 oz, 125 g)
1 oz (30 g) harusame noodles
½ sheet nori seaweed

dipping sauce
10 fl oz (300 ml) dashi (page 143)
3 tbsps soy sauce
2 tsps honey or mirin

4 tbsps grated daikon radish
2 tsps grated root ginger

batter
1 egg yolk
5 fl oz (150 ml) iced water
2 oz (60 g) unbleached white flour or fine wholemeal flour
pinch salt

extra flour for dusting
vegetable oil for deep-frying
a few drops sesame oil

Cut the aubergine into slices ¼ in (½ cm) thick, or into decorative fans (see page 45). Cut the carrot into flowers (see page 64). Slice the pepper into thin rounds, halve and cut into strips. Peel and halve the onions and cut across into slices, using wooden toothpicks or cocktail sticks to hold the rounds together. Cut a neat cross in the top of each mushroom. Trim the leeks and cut diagonally into 1 in (2½ cm) slices. Wash well and dry. Cut the sweet potato into ¼ in (½ cm) slices. Divide the French beans into groups of 3 of equal length. Cut the noodles in half with scissors and divide into 4 groups. Wrap a strip of nori firmly around each noodle and bean group, and wet the end of the nori to seal.

Combine the dipping sauce ingredients in a small saucepan and bring to a simmer; keep warm. Drain the grated daikon radish and ginger. Squeeze the daikon firmly into 4 small cones, and top each with a little ginger. Arrange neatly on 4 small plates with folded white paper napkins.

Half-fill a small saucepan with oil to a depth of 3 in (8 cm) and add a few drops of sesame oil. Heat slowly to 340°F (170°C) (to test this, see pages 40–1).

While the oil is heating prepare the batter. Stir together the egg yolk and iced water very lightly with chopsticks; do not beat. Add the flour and mix in very lightly; the batter will still be very lumpy with lumps of unmixed flour.

Make sure that all the ingredients are dry, and lay them out on a tray together with a bowl of flour for dusting and the bowl of batter beside the cooker. You will also need long cooking chopsticks or a skimmer, and some absorbent paper or a rack for draining the cooked tempura.

Dust a few vegetables with a light coating of flour, shaking off the excess. With chopsticks, dip the vegetables into the batter and slide gently into the oil, making sure that the vegetables do not touch and that the pan is not crowded. Deep-fry the vegetables, turning occasionally, for 2–3 minutes, until both sides are crisp and pale gold. Deep-fry the harusame noodles without dipping into batter. Drain briefly on absorbent paper or a wire rack before arranging neatly on individual plates. Pour the dipping sauce into 4 small bowls and serve with tempura immediately. Continue to deep-fry the remaining vegetables in the same way, a few at a time, until they are all cooked, and replenish the plates with fresh tempura as it is cooked. (It is easier on the cook to cheat and cook all the tempura first before serving it!)

The vegetables given above are the most popular, but in fact practically any vegetable makes delicious tempura. Use any of the following: sprigs of broccoli or cauliflower; mangetout peas; lotus root, thinly sliced and stuffed with miso; potatoes in

¼in (½cm) slices; burdock root in 1in (2½cm) lengths.

Tempura is usually served as a meal in itself, followed by plain boiled rice, Japanese pickles and miso soup; or serve with rice and a simple salad.

VEGETABLE FRITTERS

At the end of a tempura meal, the cook mixes small quantities of finely chopped vegetables into the remaining tempura batter and deep-fries them to make delicate fritters.

2 medium carrots, scrubbed
2oz (60g) white cabbage
1 young leek, washed
2oz (60g) French beans
batter as for tempura (page 156)
dipping sauce and condiments as for tempura (page 156)
vegetable oil for deep-frying

Shred all the vegetables and pat with absorbent paper so that they are quite dry. Lightly mix with enough batter to coat all the ingredients. Heat the oil to 340°F (170°C). Slide the vegetable mixture by spoonsful into the hot oil and deep-fry for about 1 minute on each side, until golden. Remove and drain on absorbent paper.

Serve with warm dipping sauce and condiments.

MRS MISONO'S SPECIAL TEMPURA

Mrs Misono teaches flower arrangement in Gifu, encouraging her students to respond to the line of the branch rather than impose a design on it. Her cookery is as sensitive and delicate as her arrangements. This tempura dish is one of her recipes. Choose small fine plates to serve it on. If you can find fresh perilla leaves, by all means use them.

12oz (340g) tofu
1 sheet (7 × 7in, 18 × 18cm) nori seaweed
vegetable oil for deep-frying
few drops sesame oil

batter
1 egg white
4 oz (115 g) flour
¼ tsp salt
5–10 fl oz (150–300 ml) iced water (see recipe)

8 chestnuts, peeled and boiled
8 gingko nuts, shelled, boiled and peeled
extra flour for dusting
8 fresh perilla leaves, washed and patted dry (optional)
8 sprigs parsley, washed and patted dry
salt and soy sauce

Cut the tofu into 8 rectangles and drain for 30 minutes. With scissors, cut the nori seaweed into small 1 × 2in (3 × 5cm) rectangles.

Half-fill a small saucepan with oil to a depth of 3in (8cm) and add a few drops of sesame oil. Heat slowly to 340°F (170°C).

While the oil is heating, prepare the batter. Lightly break up the egg white (do not whisk), and gently fold in the flour and salt. Stir in enough water to make a medium-thick batter.

Make sure that the ingredients to be deep-fried are all perfectly dry. With chopsticks, dip the tofu, chestnuts and gingko nuts first into flour, and then into batter to coat completely and deep-fry until golden. Dip only one side of the nori and perilla leaves into batter; holding the stem of the parsley, dip just the head into batter. Deep-fry the nori, perilla and parsley for only 30 seconds, to set and crisp the coating without burning the vegetable. Drain the tempura briefly, then serve on 4 small plates on top of folded white paper napkins. Serve salt and soy sauce separately.

WINTER ONE-POT COOKERY

Japanese winters are every bit as severe as English ones, and the cold tends to penetrate right inside the unheated houses. But far from being grim, life in the winter can be very cosy. Everyone gravitates to the kotatsu, the unique Japanese heated table, under which legs intertwine in friendly fashion, covered with a warm quilt. And the happy custom of tabletop cookery ensures warmth of spirit as well as of body.

A large earthenware casserole full of rich stock simmers on a portable gas burner in the centre of the table. Around it, artistically arranged on large platters, is an appetising array of vegetables in bite-sized pieces: chunks of Chinese cabbage, green spinach, orange carrots cut into flowers, little clumps of grey and yellow field mushrooms and soft white cubes of tofu.

Everyone shares in the cooking, filling the pot with the raw vegetables and helping themselves to food straight from the pot when it is cooked just to their taste. The piping hot vegetables are then dipped into a small bowl of seasoned sauce. At the end of a long and convivial evening, the stock, much enriched from the flavour of all the vegetables, is ladled into the bowls and drunk like soup.

A few pieces of equipment are practically essential for one-pot cookery. You will need a small gas or electric burner which can be used on the table, and a large and attractive flameproof casserole with a lid; the Japanese use earthenware or cast-iron casseroles. You will also need chopsticks for putting food into and taking it out of the casserole, and a ladle for dishing out the stock. If necessary the dish can be cooked in the kitchen and brought to the table piping hot; but although the taste will be the same, the atmosphere will be lacking.

Practically any seasonal vegetable can be used in one-pot dishes; but choose ingredients that will harmonise in flavour. They should all be cut into small pieces that will cook quickly; hard vegetables are usually parboiled beforehand. Make sure there is plenty to eat; cold winter nights produce big appetites. Serve rice and pickles after the one-pot dish to make a complete meal.

CASSEROLE OF TOFU AND VEGETABLES

This is the simplest and most popular one-pot dish. Perfectly fresh vegetables and tofu are lightly cooked in a delicate stock and dipped into a tangy lemon or rich sesame sauce. Finally, at the end of the meal, a couple of eggs are broken into the remaining stock, now full of flavour from the vegetables.

2 leaves Chinese cabbage
2oz (60g) spinach
4oz (115g) bean sprouts
4oz (115g) mangetout peas or French beans
4 young leeks
12 large flat mushrooms, wiped and trimmed
4 medium carrots
4oz (115g) bamboo shoots
12oz (340g) tofu
½ pkt (3½oz, 100g) shirataki noodles
6–8 sprigs parsley or watercress

lemon soy dipping sauce
4 floz (115ml) light soy sauce
2 floz (60ml) freshly squeezed lemon juice
2 floz (60ml) rice vinegar
1 tbsp mirin or sake

sesame sauce
1oz (30g) white sesame seeds
1 tsp sugar or honey
1 tbsp light soy sauce
1 tsp sake or mirin
4–5 tbsps dashi (page 143)

condiments
red maple radish (page 88)
fresh root ginger, finely grated
2 spring onions or young leeks

1 6in (15cm) piece kombu seaweed (about ¼oz, 7g)
2 eggs (optional)

Wash and trim the vegetables. Parboil the Chinese cabbage and spinach and form into a roll (see page 60); cut into 1in (2½cm) lengths. Top and tail the bean sprouts and peas or beans. Cut the leeks on the diagonal into 1½in (4cm) lengths. Remove the stems of the mushrooms and neatly notch a cross in the top of each mushroom cap. Cut the carrots into flowers (see page 64). Halve the bamboo shoots lengthwise and slice into half moons. Cut the tofu into 1 in (2½ cm) squares. Parboil the shira-taki for 1–2 minutes and drain. Arrange the vegetables and other ingredients on 1 or 2 large platters, grouping each type of ingredient together. Garnish with parsley or water-cress.

Stir together the lemon soy dipping sauce ingredients and pour into 4 small bowls. To make the sesame sauce, lightly toast the sesame seeds, then tip into a suribachi and grind until pasty. Gradually blend in the remaining ingredients, adding enough dashi to make a thin sauce, and pour into 4 small bowls. Prepare the condiments. Shred and rinse the spring onions or young leeks (see page 94). Arrange the condiments in small bowls on the table, and put a bowl of each dipping sauce at each place. Set a gas or electric burner on the table.

Wipe the kombu and score a few times to help release the flavour. Place in a large flameproof casserole and fill the casserole two-thirds full of water. Bring to the boil and remove the kombu. Bring the casserole to the table and set on the burner. Bring the water back to the boil and turn down to a simmer. Put a selection of vegetables into the pot to start the meal, beginning with hard vegetables which need longer cooking.

The diners add a little stock to their dipping sauces and season them with the condiments to taste. They then dip the vegetables into the sauce before eating, refilling the pot until all the ingredients are used. Leave a little stock in the pot after all the vegetables are cooked; add the eggs, stir well, and serve to anyone who still has an appetite, or simply serve the remaining stock as soup.

SNOW COUNTRY WINTER CASSEROLE

One February I was invited to visit Mr and Mrs Doi in Toyama, in the legendary Snow Country on the Japan Sea coast. I boarded a train in Gifu, which was enjoying a particularly mild winter that year, and set off. Within an hour the train was pushing its way between walls of snow a good 6 ft

(2 m) high. The rigours of the climate produce strong people and warming dishes. Mr Doi, at the age of eighty, had just returned from his first visit abroad; he had been mountain climbing in the Himalayas. While he told us his adventures, we feasted on this hearty vegetable casserole.

½ head Chinese cabbage (about 12 oz, 340 g)
4 young leeks
4 oz (115 g) chrysanthemum leaves or spinach
2 medium carrots
4 small potatoes
4 dried mushrooms, softened in water
12 gingko nuts (optional)
1 cake konnyaku
1 rolled omelette using 2 eggs (see page 243)
2 oz (50 g) harusame noodles

simmering stock
2 pts (1.2 l) dashi (page 143)
4 tbsps soy sauce
2 tbsps mirin, sake, sugar or honey
1 tsp salt

seven-spice pepper
4 oz (115 g) cooked rice (optional)
1 egg (optional)

Wash and trim the vegetables. Slice the Chinese cabbage into 1 in (2½ cm) rounds. Cut the leeks on the diagonal into long thin slices. Cut the chrysanthemum leaves or spinach into 2 in (5 cm) lengths. Cut the carrots into flowers (see page 64). Cut the potatoes into hexagons (see page 134). Remove the mushroom stems and cut a decorative cross in the top of each mushroom cap. Shell and peel the gingko nuts (see page 23) and thread 2 or 3 on to long pine needles or wooden cocktail sticks. Cut the konnyaku into ¼ in (½ cm) slices, make a slit down the centre of each slice, and thread one end through the slit to make a decorative knot. Cut the egg roll into 1 in (2½ cm) slices. Soak the harusame in hot water for 2 minutes, then dip in cold water and drain. Arrange the vegetables and other ingredients attractively on 1 or 2 large ceramic or wooden platters, grouping each type of ingredient together. Set a small bowl at each place and provide

seven-spice pepper for seasoning.

Pour the dashi into a large flameproof casserole and bring to the boil; season with the soy sauce, mirin, sake, sugar or honey and salt. Set on a burner in the centre of the table, and add some of the Chinese cabbage, leeks, carrots, potatoes, mushrooms and konnyaku. Simmer for a few minutes, then add some of all the remaining ingredients.

The diners ladle a little of the stock into their bowls to use both as dipping sauce and as soup, and help themselves to vegetables when they are cooked, putting more vegetables into the pot until all the ingredients are used. Serve the remaining stock as soup. Alternatively, stir cooked rice and an egg into the stock to make a thick soup.

ONE-POT DISH WITH NOODLES

The people of Osaka are said to be fond of money and good living, and this lavish one-pot dish is typical of their cooking. A colourful array of vegetables and other foods is laid out over a bed of cooked soba on a large platter, to be simmered at table in a rich stock. The soba is eaten last and takes the place of rice.

14oz (400g) buckwheat noodles (soba)
2 leaves Chinese cabbage
2oz (60g) spinach
4oz (115g) daikon radish

8 large flat fresh mushrooms, wiped and trimmed
4 oz (115 g) chrysanthemum leaves, spinach or watercress
4 young leeks
2 medium carrots
4 pieces dried gluten or dried yuba (optional)
2 cakes or 4 balls deep-fried tofu
4 rice cakes

condiments
fresh root ginger, finely grated
seven-spice pepper
lemon wedges
2 spring onions or young leeks

simmering stock
2 pts (1 l) dashi (page 143)
4 tbsps soy sauce
2 tbsps mirin, sake, sugar or honey
1 tsp salt

Cook the noodles as described on page 283. Drain well and arrange on 1 or 2 large platters. Set aside. Wash and trim the vegetables. Parboil the Chinese cabbage and spinach and form into a roll (see page 60). Cut the daikon into ½ in (1 cm) slices and parboil for 10 minutes. Remove the mushroom stems and cut a decorative cross in the top of each mushroom cap. Cut the chrysanthemum leaves, spinach or watercress into 2 in (5 cm) lengths. Slice the leeks thinly on the diagonal. Cut the carrots into flowers (see page 64). Break the yuba into bite-sized pieces if large. Halve the deep-fried tofu cakes. Rinse them or the deep-fried tofu balls in boiling water to remove oil and pat dry. Grill the rice cakes under a hot grill for 2–3 minutes on each side, or use raw. Arrange all the ingredients over the noodles, garnishing with the carrot flowers.

Prepare the condiments. Shred and rinse the spring onions or young leeks (see page 94). Arrange the condiments in small bowls on the table and set a small empty bowl at each place.

Put the dashi into a large flameproof casserole and bring to the boil; season with the soy sauce, mirin, sake, sugar or honey and salt. Set on a burner in the centre of the table, and put in some of each vegetable, the dried gluten or yuba, the deep-fried tofu and the rice cakes.

The diners ladle a little stock into their bowls and season to taste with the condiments, then dip the hot foods into the stock before eating. Replenish the pot until all the vegetables are used, adding more dashi if necessary. Finally put the noodles into the stock to heat through and serve with the remaining stock.

MISO RIVER-BANK CASSEROLE

In this colourfully named one-pot dish the whole casserole is coated with a thick layer of miso, which is scraped little by little into the simmering stock, flavouring it richly. Before eating, the hot foods are dipped into a little raw egg, which makes a delicate coating.

4 young leeks
8 oz (225 g) chrysanthemum leaves, spinach or watercress
12 dried mushrooms, softened in water
2 medium carrots
2 oz (60 g) daikon radish
2 cakes grilled tofu (yakidofu) or 12 oz (340 g) tofu, drained
8 rice cakes
4 eggs

miso 'riverbank'
4 tbsps white miso
4 tbsps red miso
1 tbsp mirin, sake, sugar or honey
a little cool dashi (see recipe)

1 6 in (15 cm) piece kombu seaweed (about ¼ oz, 7 g)
2 pts (1 l) dashi (page 143)

Wash and trim the vegetables. Cut the leeks on the diagonal into 1½ in (4 cm) slices. Cut the chrysanthemum leaves, spinach or watercress into 2 in (5 cm) lengths. Remove the mushroom stems and cut a decorative cross in the top of each mushroom cap. Cut the carrots into flowers (see page 64). Halve the daikon radish lengthwise and slice into thin half moons. Cut the grilled tofu or drained tofu into 1½ in (4 cm) cubes. Grill the rice cakes under a hot grill for 2–3 minutes on each side; or simply use raw. Arrange all the ingredients attractively on 1 or 2 large platters, grouping each type of ingredient together, and garnish with the carrot flowers. Set a bowl with a fresh egg in it by each place.

Mix together the 2 misos and the mirin, sake, sugar or honey, adding enough cool dashi to make a thick but spreadable paste. Spread the paste evenly around the inner walls of a flameproof ceramic or cast-iron casserole, to make a bank about ¼in (½cm) thick. Put the casserole over a low flame to cook the miso a little.

Wipe the kombu and score a few times to help release the flavour, and lay in the casserole. Add the dashi and bring to the boil. Put in some of each of the vegetables and simmer for a few minutes; add some cubes of tofu. The diners break the egg into the bowl and lightly beat it with chopsticks; they then help themselves to cooked food directly from the casserole, dipping it into the egg. Replenish the casserole with vegetables and tofu, gradually scraping the miso into the stock. Add the rice cakes when the stock has become rich and flavoursome. At the end of the meal, ladle the remaining stock into bowls to be drunk as soup.

ODEN: JAPANESE WINTER STEW

On winter evenings the lanes that surrounded my flat in the Gifu suburbs seemed to be full of hawkers pushing or pulling wooden carts of steaming food, calling out or blowing whistles to make their presence known. I soon learnt to distinguish the oden man's bell, and would join the neighbours around his cart, to enjoy a bowlful of vegetables, tofu and konnyaku in rich stock. Oden is one of the great winter foods all over Japan. At the foot of Tokyo's towering skyscrapers, businessmen queue at the little corner oden stalls, laughing and joking with the red-faced oden sellers in their fingerless gloves who seem to belong to a completely different world. The big rectangular saucepans simmering over charcoal are divided into compartments, each for one particular type of food, and each item of food is skewered on a flat wooden stick. Oden is often prepared at home, simmered for hours in a big ceramic casserole, which is brought steaming hot to table. If you have time, oden is best prepared the previous day and left overnight in the stock, then reheated before serving. Any firm winter vegetable may be included in oden; vary the ingredients depending on what is in season.

2 medium carrots
4 small potatoes
2 small turnips
8 6in (15cm) strips gourd ribbon
8in (20cm) daikon radish
4 Shinoda rolls (see page 58) or cabbage rolls (page 60)
4 eggs, hardboiled
1 cake konnyaku
4 tofu purses (page 207) or 1 cake deep-fried tofu
4 kombu rolls (page 144) or 4 2in (5cm) pieces kombu seaweed

simmering stock
2pts (1.2l) dashi (page 143)
4 tbsps soy sauce
4 tbsps mirin, sake, sugar or honey
½ tsp salt

1 6in (15cm) piece kombu seaweed (about ¼oz, 7g)
freshly made English mustard

Wash and trim the vegetables. Cut the carrots into thick slices and halve or quarter the potatoes and turnips. Soak the gourd ribbon in water to soften. Peel the daikon radish and cut into 8 1in (2½cm) slices. Tie a strip of gourd ribbon around the rim of each slice of daikon, tucking in the end securely. Prepare the Shinoda or cabbage rolls. Shell the hardboiled eggs and cut the konnyaku into 4 triangles. Prepare the tofu purses or cut the deep-fried tofu into 4 triangles. Prepare the kombu rolls, or tie each piece of kombu seaweed into a neat knot.

Wipe the 6in (15cm) piece of kombu and score a few times. Place in a large flameproof ceramic casserole. Arrange the ingredients over the kombu, with the foods that need longer cooking (daikon, kombu rolls) at the centre. Pour over the simmering stock ingredients and bring to the boil. Simmer uncovered over very low heat for at least 1½ hours, adding more dashi if necessary; the simmering liquid will reduce and thicken. Do not stir the oden; simply shake the pot a little occasionally.

Either serve immediately or cover the pot, leave overnight and reheat the following day. Bring the casserole piping hot to table so that everyone can serve themselves, and pass freshly made mustard.

MISO ODEN: WINTER STEW WITH MISO

Just outside Gifu, at the end of the tram line, where the paddy fields end and the mountains begin, is a famous old temple, which attracts thousands of pilgrims. On the way back to the station it is impossible to resist stopping for a bite of miso oden at one of the stalls which line the road. Over the charcoal brazier the rectangular pans bristle with bamboo skewers, each holding a chunk of vegetable, tofu or konnyaku. In the middle of the pan stands a bowl of sweet miso into which the hot vegetables are dipped. Serve this dish at table in a large flameproof casserole, with a cup in the casserole for the miso sauce; or serve small bowls of miso sauce for dipping.

6oz (170g) daikon radish
2 medium carrots
4 small potatoes
2 small turnips
12 quails' eggs or 4 small hens' eggs, hardboiled
1 cake konnyaku
12oz (340g) tofu, well drained
flavoured miso (see page 152)
1 6in (15cm) piece kombu seaweed
2pts (1.2l) dashi (page 143)

Wash and trim the vegetables. Peel the daikon and cut into half moons ½in (1cm) thick. Cut the carrots into thick slices and halve or quarter the potatoes and turnips. Parboil each vegetable separately till nearly cooked and skewer each piece with a bamboo skewer. Shell the eggs and thread 3 quail's eggs or 1 hen's egg on to each of 4 bamboo skewers. Cut the konnyaku into ½in (1cm) slices and sauté in a dry frying pan for 2 minutes, then skewer each piece. Cut the tofu into ½in (1cm) slices and carefully thread 2 bamboo skewers through each slice.

Set a large flameproof casserole on a gas or electric burner on the table. Fill a clean deep cup half-full with flavoured miso. Wipe the kombu, score a few times, and place in the casserole.

Set the cup of miso on the kombu. Arrange the various ingredients in the casserole with the skewers upright or resting on the edge so that they can easily be retrieved. In a separate saucepan bring the dashi to the boil, and pour into the casserole to cover the ingredients.

Return to the boil and simmer for 5 minutes until all the ingredients are heated through. The diners help themselves to the hot ingredients, dipping them into the flavoured miso.

Pickles

While in Japan I did a great deal of travelling, and, like a good Japanese traveller, always returned laden down with gifts. Every town in Japan, even the smallest village, has its specialities, always edible, to be taken home as souvenirs for expectant friends and relations. One of the most welcome presents is a fine local pickle from the cold mountain areas, like those of my own Gifu region.

In the autumn the farmers hang row upon row of freshly harvested vegetables beneath the eaves of their big thatched houses, and town dwellers string up the big daikon radishes and turnips from their allotments. Vegetables are pickled whole, usually in rice bran, traditionally in big wooden pickle barrels weighted with heavy stones. Modern Japanese housewives, making a small amount of pickles for the family, use plastic pickling tubs with a lid which screws down little by little to press the pickles. Nowadays you can buy local pickles from all over Japan in the department stores in the big cities. The food sections down in the basement are full of men up from the country in their indigo happi coats and white cotton scarves, bawling their wares, and selling whole Chinese cabbages or daikons straight from the pickle barrel, coated in sandy yellow rice bran.

Pickles are one of the most characteristic and essential Japanese foods. Plain rice is always accompanied by a dish of crunchy, powerfully flavoured pickles – dark purple aubergines, pale Chinese cabbage or deep yellow daikon pickles – to be savoured with relish. In themselves rice and pickles are considered to make a complete and adequate meal, sufficient for a packed lunch or for the Zen monk's frugal diet.

Almost any vegetable may be pickled; the most popular are

daikon radish, Chinese cabbage, turnips, cucumber and aubergines. They are pickled raw in a variety of different mediums,
usually rice bran, miso, salt or rice vinegar, sometimes flavoured with a little kombu seaweed, lemon peel or chilli.

A wide variety of Japanese pickles is available in Japanese
shops and some Chinese supermarkets in England; once
opened the packets should be refrigerated. Tasty pickles may
also be made quickly and simply at home. For small quantities
an earthenware or glass bowl is an adequate container; use a
plate very slightly smaller than the top of the bowl as a lid, and
top with a jar of water for a weight.

Serve very small quantities of a variety of pickles of contrasting colours and types, in bite-sized pieces, mounded in the
centre of small individual plates. They may be seasoned with a
drop of soy sauce before eating.

SALT PICKLED VEGETABLES

Salt pickling is the most basic form of pickling and often
precedes other more complicated techniques. Simple salt pickling consists of layering raw vegetables with salt to make a
crisp and pungent pickle. Any firm vegetable may be pickled in
this way; Chinese cabbage, daikon radish and cucumber are
particularly delicious. Each type of vegetable is usually pickled
separately so that the flavours remain distinct. Use pure sea salt
or rock salt for the best flavour.

1 Chinese cabbage, or 2 cucumbers, or 4 pickling cucumbers, or 2
   daikon radishes
1 oz (30 g) salt

Wash and trim the vegetables. Quarter the Chinese cabbage
lengthwise and cut across into 1 in (2½ cm) chunks. Halve the
cucumbers lengthwise and scrape out the seeds; cut into 1 in
(2½ cm) lengths. Cut the pickling cucumbers into ½ in (1 cm)
slices. Peel, quarter and cut the daikon radish into 1 in (2½ cm)
lengths. Pat the vegetables with absorbent paper to dry.

Rub the salt into the vegetables. Put them into a ceramic
bowl, and cover with a plate to fit neatly inside the bowl on top
of the pickles. Set a weight such as a jar of water on the plate.

Leave the bowl in a cool dark place for 3–4 days; the brine will quickly rise above the level of the vegetables.

To serve, remove a small amount of pickled vegetable; rinse and gently squeeze, then cut into bite-sized pieces. Serve in very small quantities with rice. The remaining pickles will keep in a cool place for 2–3 months in the brine.

MISO PICKLED VEGETABLES

Miso pickling is both a simple and a versatile technique, giving a variety of subtly flavoured mellow pickles. Kombu and tofu (see page 201), as well as firm vegetables such as daikon radish, aubergine, cucumber and carrots, all make delicious miso pickles. The food to be pickled must first be dried. In Japan vegetables are strung up outside to dry, in the shade in summer and in the sun in winter; they may also be parboiled or salted to reduce the moisture content. Then, to pickle them, they are simply buried in miso. Vegetables cut into small pieces may be eaten after 1 or 2 days, while whole vegetables will need several months. The longer the vegetable is left in the miso the stronger the flavour becomes. The miso is often flavoured with sake, mirin or honey to give added flavour. To serve, remove the required amount of vegetable from the miso, scrape or wash off the miso, and chop the vegetable into small pieces. Miso which has been used for pickling may be used to make miso soup or in any miso recipe.

The following examples are intended only to suggest some of the possibilities of miso pickling. It is rather difficult to specify quantities. As it will keep for some time, it is sensible to make a relatively large quantity of pickle. You will need enough miso to cover the vegetable completely.

SIMPLE MISO PICKLES

2 medium carrots, or 1 small aubergine, or 2 pickling cucumbers, or
  1 daikon radish
salt
8-12 oz (225–340g) red miso or red flavoured miso (page 152)

Wash the vegetables; use whole, or cut to fit the container if

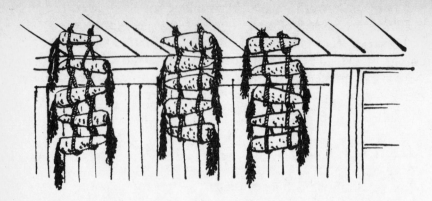

necessary. Carrots: parboil and allow to cool. Aubergine or cucumbers: sprinkle with salt and set in a bowl; cover with a lid and a light weight and set aside for 24 hours, then rinse and pat dry with absorbent paper. Daikon: whole daikons need to be salted and set under a weight for 3–4 days; halve the daikon and cut into 3 in (7 cm) chunks to speed up the process. Make sure the vegetables to be pickled are quite dry.

Prepare a lidded non-metal container which will comfortably hold the vegetable and the miso; spread a layer of miso over the bottom, and pack the vegetables neatly in. Cover the vegetables completely with miso, ensuring that all sides of each vegetable are covered. Fit on the lid and wrap the whole box in cling film. Put in the refrigerator. The vegetables should be left for at least 1 month.

QUICK AUBERGINE PICKLES

2 small or 1 medium aubergine
4 oz (115 g) white miso
2 tbsps sake

Wash the aubergine, remove the stem, and cut into thin slices. Sprinkle with salt and set in a colander under a light weight to drain for 30 minutes. Rinse, squeeze lightly, rinse again and pat dry with absorbent paper. Blend the miso with the sake, and spread over all surfaces of the aubergine slices. Put the slices into a bowl, cover with cling film, and leave for at least 2 hours. Wash off the miso before serving, and cut the slices into small pieces.

CELERY PICKLED IN MISO

2 stalks celery
2oz (60g) red miso
1 tbsp mirin, sake, sugar or honey

Wash the celery, strip away stringy parts, and cut into 1in
(3cm) pieces. Dry thoroughly with absorbent paper. Blend the
miso with the mirin, sake, sugar or honey. Mix the celery into
the miso so that all surfaces are coated. Put into a bowl, cover
with cling film, and leave for 2–3 days.

UMEBOSHI: PICKLED PLUMS

The best pickled plums are homemade. Every year in June, my
neighbour would summon me to her garden to pick the hard
green plums, which are apparently inedible raw even when
ripe. Apart from pickling, the plums are used to make plum
wine (umeshu); or 1 plum can be put into a jar of honey to
flavour it. I would salt my plums and wait a few days for the
juices to rise, then mix in red perilla leaves to make the plums
red. The most crucial step was to wait for the proverbial three
hottest days of summer, actually the three last days of July,
when the plums had to be laid in the sun on bamboo mats to
dry.

Pickled plums are usually served at breakfast, with the
pickles, rice and nori seaweed. The Japanese believe in a plum,
not an apple, a day to ensure good health; pickled plums are
said to be full of vitamin C and to do wonders for the digestion. I have met Japanese travellers very far from Japan who
always seem to have a supply of pickled plums.

Pickled plums are available in health-food stores and Japanese
shops. If you can find the ingredients, make your own, using the
following recipe; green apricots are a possible alternative for the
Japanese plum.

2lbs (900g) green Japanese plums
6–8oz (170–225g) sea salt
1lb (450g) fresh red perilla leaves

Wash the plums and soak overnight in water to cover. Dry

each plum very carefully with a tea towel. Mix the plums with 4–6 oz (115–170 g) salt and put into a large earthenware or glass jar. Set a weight on the plums and leave for 2–3 days until the juices rise above the level of the fruit.

Tear the perilla leaves from their stems and discard the stems. Wash and dry the leaves. Mix them with 2 oz (60 g) salt, and knead well; they will give off a large amount of dark bitter juice, and will reduce greatly in volume. Discard the bitter juices.

Put the perilla leaves into a large bowl, and drain the plum juices on to the leaves. Gently knead the leaves in the juice, which will become red. Pour the red juice back over the plums in the jar, and spread the leaves on top. Set a weight on the plums and store until the end of July, or until you can be sure of 3 days of continuous fine hot weather.

On the first hot day remove the plums and leaves from the juice and lay in the sunlight in a single layer to dry; in Japan the plums are laid on bamboo draining trays, but a piece of clean towelling would do. Turn the plums occasionally so that they dry thoroughly. At night return the plums and leaves to the juice. Repeat this procedure for a total of 3 days.

Store the plums in their juice in an earthenware or glass jar, and spread the leaves on top. Cover but do not weight them. The plums can be eaten immediately, but improve with time, and keep indefinitely.

Part Two

BEANS, SOYA BEAN PRODUCTS AND EGGS

Beans

Because of their high protein content, beans have always been an important part of the Japanese diet. Soya beans are the basis of some of the most original and essential foods of Japanese cuisine, foods as diverse as soy sauce, tofu, miso and natto, which, as well as providing protein in an easily digestible form, are highly versatile cooking ingredients. Soya beans also provide bean sprouts; a plateful of fresh green soya beans in their fuzzy pods, boiled and salted, invariably appears in summer with sake.

While soya bean products are important staples in Japan, the dried beans, together with black beans and aduki beans, tend to be reserved for celebrations and special occasions. Aduki beans are used to make red rice, obligatory at all important occasions, and are the basis for many Japanese sweets. Whole black or soya beans, simmered in sweetened dashi seasoned with soy sauce, and served in a little of the syrupy stock, make a rich and sweet dish which is always prepared for New Year. In November black beans cooked with rice are served to honour the god of wealth and good luck, Daikoku, and soya beans cooked with rice are the traditional meal on February 4th, when the evil spirits are driven out at the end of the lunar year.

SOYA BEAN RICE

At the beginning of February, the demons and evil spirits have to be cleaned out of houses, temples and shrines in preparation for spring. The father or the oldest son of the house goes into every room, throwing soya beans in the auspicious direction for that year and then in the opposite direction, and shouting,

'Good luck in: demons out'; and everyone rushes to collect up the lucky beans. The auspicious meal for the day is of course

soya beans cooked with rice. Black bean rice is prepared in exactly the same way.

2 oz (60 g) soya beans
8 oz (225 g) short-grain brown rice
15 fl oz (450 ml) water
1 tbsp light soy sauce
1 tbsp sake (optional)
2 tbsps black sesame seeds

Put the soya beans in a dry frying pan and sauté for a few minutes over medium heat, until they give off a nutty aroma and the skin cracks open. Leave to cool and rub off as many skins as possible.

Wash the rice thoroughly and combine with the soya beans, the measured water, soy sauce and sake in a heavy saucepan with a closely fitting lid. Leave to soak for 1 hour. Bring to the boil and simmer over very low heat for 40–50 minutes until the rice and soya beans are cooked. Turn off the heat and leave covered for 10 minutes, then fluff with a wooden rice paddle or spoon and serve in place of rice. Lightly toast the sesame seeds and scatter a few over each portion of rice.

Soya bean rice may also be cooked in a pressure cooker under high pressure; bring to pressure, then cook over very low heat for 20 minutes.

FIVE-COLOUR SOYA BEANS

This multi-coloured dish of soya beans and vegetables is often served at New Year. The exact ingredients vary according to the cook; here is one version.

8 oz (225 g) soya beans
3 dried mushrooms, softened in water
1 medium carrot
¼ cake konnyaku
1 8 in (20 cm) piece kombu seaweed
8 fl oz (240 ml) dashi (page 143)
1 tbsp light soy sauce
1 tbsp sugar or honey
1 tbsp sake or mirin
1 tbsp white sesame seeds, toasted

Soak the soya beans overnight. Put into a large saucepan and cover with water; bring to the boil and simmer, uncovered, for 10 minutes. Drain, discarding the water, and rinse. Return to the saucepan and add enough water to cover. Bring to the boil, cover and simmer for 1–1½ hours, until the beans are tender. Drain.

While the beans are cooking, prepare the vegetables. Cut off and discard the mushroom stems and slice the caps finely. Wash, trim and sliver the carrot into small matchsticks. Sauté the konnyaku in a dry frying pan for a few minutes until it becomes dry and shiny, then chop finely. Wash the kombu to soften it, squeeze gently, and sliver, using a large sharp knife.

Combine the soya beans with the vegetables in a saucepan, and pour over the dashi mixed with the soy sauce, sugar or honey and sake or mirin. Bring to the boil and cover, preferably with a drop lid. Simmer over very low heat for 30 minutes, until the vegetables and kombu are tender and well flavoured. Drain, reserving the cooking liquid, and set aside to cool. Boil the reserved cooking liquid over high heat, stirring, for 2–3 minutes, until reduced and thickened. Serve small portions at room temperature and spoon over a little of the reduced cooking liquid. Scatter over a few sesame seeds to garnish.

SWEET-SIMMERED SOYA BEANS

One dish which invariably appears in the third of the stacked lacquer boxes in which the New Year's meal is served, among the simmered foods, is sweet-simmered soya beans or sweet-simmered black beans, which are prepared in exactly the same way. A wooden drop lid is helpful in preparing this dish (see page 35).

8 oz (225 g) soya beans
2 tbsps sugar or honey
1 tbsp sake or mirin (optional)
½ tsp salt

Soak the soya beans overnight. Put into a large saucepan and cover with water; bring to the boil and simmer, uncovered, for 10 minutes. Drain, discarding the water, and rinse the soya beans. Return to the saucepan and add enough water to cover. Stir in the honey and sake or mirin if used. Bring to the boil and cover, preferably with a drop lid. Simmer over very low heat for 1–1½ hours, until the beans are tender and the simmering liquid is much reduced. Season with a little salt. Serve small portions, hot or at room temperature; spoon over a little of the simmering liquid.

RED RICE

Red is a very auspicious colour in Japan, and rice cooked with aduki beans to make it red is invariably served at weddings, birthdays and all the annual festivals. A lacquer box of red rice moulded into an auspicious shape is always among the gifts presented to each guest after a wedding. On festive days the ancestors too eat red rice, which is set before the family shrine. This rather unorthodox version of red rice is made with brown rice; the aduki beans give a pleasant flavour and chewiness and even a slight red colour.

4 oz (115 g) aduki beans
8 oz (225 g) brown rice
15 fl oz (450 ml) water

1½ tbsps soy sauce
2 tbsps black sesame seeds
salt

Soak the aduki beans overnight and drain. Wash the rice several
times, drain, and combine with the aduki beans in a heavy
saucepan with a closely fitting lid. Add the water and soy sauce
and leave to soak for 1 hour. Cover, bring to the boil, and
simmer over very low heat for 40–50 minutes until both the
rice and beans are soft. Turn off the heat and leave covered for
10 minutes, then fluff with a wooden rice paddle or spoon and
serve in place of rice. Lightly toast the sesame seeds, mix with a
little salt, and scatter over each portion of rice.

Red rice may be eaten hot, but is usually served at room
temperature.

ADUKI BEAN PASTE

In Japan a guest is always welcomed with a cup of unsweetened
green tea and a small cake to sweeten the palate before
drinking. Most families buy their cakes from the local cake
shop, whose exquisite confections change with the seasons;
spring is greeted with cakes shaped and coloured to resemble
pink cherry blossoms, wrapped in cherry leaves, or flavoured
with fresh spring herbs, while autumn cakes feature chestnuts
or are tinted like maple leaves. A few simple cakes and sweets
are made at home, particularly at festival time. Most Japanese
cakes, both shop and homemade, include aduki bean paste,
together with rice, agar and seasonal ingredients such as
chestnuts and sweet potatoes. In the past aduki bean paste was
used unsweetened, with simply a pinch of salt to bring out the
natural sweetness of the mild aduki beans. Nowadays aduki
bean paste is sweetened with sugar.

The following quantities will yield 8–10 oz (225–85 g) purée
or 12–13 oz (345–70 g) of thick aduki bean paste.

4 oz (115 g) aduki beans
1½–2 oz (45–60 g) sugar

Soak the aduki beans overnight in plenty of water. Drain and put in a large saucepan with fresh water to cover. Bring to the boil and boil hard for 10 minutes, then drain and discard the water. Bring back to the boil in fresh water and simmer, covered, for 20–30 minutes or until the beans are very soft. Drain, reserving the water.

To make thick aduki bean paste, simply mash the beans, adding just enough of the reserved cooking water to make a stiff paste.

To make a purée, rub the beans through a sieve to remove the bean skins; set the sieve in the reserved cooking water so that the pulp dissolves into the water. Strain the liquid through muslin, gently squeezing out the water.

Put the mashed or puréed beans in a saucepan with the sugar. Heat gently, stirring backwards and forwards (not round and round) with a wooden spoon or rice paddle until the sugar has dissolved and is well blended.

YOKAN: ADUKI BEAN JELLY

While Mrs Suzuki took care of all the practical household affairs, sometimes her aged and frail mother would slowly and painstakingly prepare dishes which young people today seldom take the trouble to make. She showed me how to make yokan, which is actually extremely simple to make at home. Two or three slabs of this cool, jelled sweetmeat are served on small plates to accompany tea. Most Japanese kitchens contain yokan moulds, small square containers with a detachable base; however, any small, straight-sided, rectangular container will serve as a mould.

½ stick agar (kanten)
10 fl oz (300 ml) water
¼ tsp salt
10 oz (285 g) aduki bean paste (page 183)

Tear up the stick of agar, hold under running water, and wring and squeeze a few times. Combine with the water and salt in a saucepan and bring slowly to the boil to dissolve the agar. Do not stir until the agar has dissolved; then skim off the foam and stir frequently.

Stir in the aduki bean paste and simmer for 5 minutes. Remove from heat and place the pan in cold water to cool the mixture rapidly. Moisten a mould. Stir the mixture; as soon as it begins to thicken, pour into the mould.

Leave the jelly to cool and set. To serve, cut neatly into oblongs 1 × 2in (2½ × 5cm). Arrange 2–3 pieces per person neatly and asymetrically on small plates. Each piece could be wrapped in a cherry, oak or perilla leaf before serving.

OHAGI: RICE AND ADUKI BEAN BALLS

Around the autumn equinox, the bush clover, hagi, appears in the woods, and in shops and homes appear great wooden trays full of ohagi. Ohagi is a typical Japanese sweetmeat, soft and chewy and subtly sweet, made of rice and aduki bean paste, often rolled in roasted soya flour, which with its sweetly nutty flavour is a favourite coating for sweet foods. The rice for ohagi needs to be cooked until it is very soft.

10oz (285g) well cooked short-grain white or brown rice,
   freshly cooked
salt
10oz (285g) aduki bean paste (page 183)
3 tbsps roasted soya flour (kinako)
1 tbsp poppy seeds, toasted

Mash the cooked rice in a suribachi or food processor, and knead, adding a very little water to make a stiff paste; season with a little salt. Arrange the roasted soya flour and poppy seeds in 2 small plates. Work quickly while the rice is still warm and soft.

Moisten your hands, take a small portion of aduki bean paste and form into an oval. Take about 3 tbsps rice, knead, and press into a flat round in the palm of your hand. Place the aduki bean oval in the centre and close the rice round it to cover it completely. Roll the ball in roasted soya flour. Continue in the same way until half the rice and aduki bean paste are used.

Form the remaining rice into small ovals and enclose each oval in aduki bean paste. Press a few poppy seeds into the top surface of each.

Arrange 1 rice-coated and 1 aduki-coated ohagi on each

plate, and serve with green tea. Provide a small fork or cocktail stick to eat the ohagi.

ZENZAI: ADUKI BEAN SOUP WITH RICE CAKES

Whenever I visited friends on cold wintry days I was offered a bowl of sweet red aduki bean soup containing a rice cake or two. This is one sweet dish that everyone seems to make at home. The rice cakes should be eaten with chopsticks, and the soup is drunk direct from the bowl.

4 oz (120 g) aduki beans, soaked overnight
1–2 tbsps sugar or honey
¼ tsp salt
4 rice cakes

Cook the aduki beans until soft (see pages 183–4). Season with sugar or honey and salt; taste and add more sugar or honey to make a sweeter soup. Add more water if necessary to make a thick soupy consistency, and simmer over medium heat for 15 minutes, stirring occasionally.

Grill the rice cakes under a hot grill or over a hot flame, for 2–3 minutes on each side, until both sides are crisp and brown.

Put each rice cake into a small deep bowl and ladle over the soup. Serve piping hot.

Tofu

Sengai, a celebrated Zen painter with a sense of humour, has a very simple ink painting depicting a block of tofu on a plate; the accompanying poem explains that this is a portrait of the ideal man, white, bland and rectangular, pure and unadulterated. If nothing else, it is a true portrait of most tofu-makers I have come across, simple honest kindly people who even look a little like a block of tofu.

Tofu, soya bean curd, is one of Japan's great foods and has recently become celebrated in the West for its high protein content and its versatility as a cooking ingredient. For me tofu is absolutely essential; the preparations for any meal always begin with a visit to the tofu shop. A tofu shop is a little like a cold version of a Japanese public bath; the white slabs of tofu are kept cool and fresh in huge troughs of water which continually overflow as fresh water is pumped in through hose pipes. I would pick my way gingerly across the wet floor to be greeted by Mr Ishikawa, a small, cheerful man in rubber boots, who would pass on the latest gossip as he plunged his hands into the water, separating off a block of tofu which he deftly inserted into a plastic container. He told me that he set to work at two every morning to prepare the day's batch of tofu; I used to make a special effort to arrive early, to enjoy freshly made tofu, still slightly warm, fresh deep-fried tofu and treasure balls. In the late afternoon Mr Ishikawa would set off to make deliveries on his bicycle, with tofu and deep-fried tofu stacked in wooden containers on the back, sounding his horn as he went along, and attracting queues of customers.

Tofu is made from soy milk, coagulated and pressed in a process very similar to the making of cottage cheese. Standard tofu, known as cotton tofu, has a subtle, slightly nutty flavour.

It is an extremely nutritious food, a versatile cooking ingredient, and the basis for a wide variety of other products, including grilled tofu, deep-fried tofu, treasure balls, and freeze-dried tofu (koya dofu). Tofu makers also produce a soft and delicate tofu, known as silken tofu, which, being a luxury food, is usually simply served so that its flavour and texture can be fully appreciated.

At home tofu is served simply, chilled in summer with a little soy sauce and simmered in winter. However, it is also the basis for a varied and sophisticated cuisine, the speciality of many restaurants and temple restaurants, where you can enjoy such dishes as tofu waterfall (tofu transformed through the chef's virtuoso cutting skills to resemble a waterfall) and dishes of complex flavour and texture, far removed from their humble origins.

When drained, tofu becomes stronger and easier to handle, and readily absorbs flavours. It can be drained a little so that it remains moist and tender, and fried or deep-fried; well drained, it can be mashed, seasoned and reshaped, or mixed with other

ingredients to give a chewy texture. The uses of tofu are practically endless, and it is particularly valuable to the vegetarian cook as a source of protein and of variety of taste and texture.

Buying Tofu

The best tofu is made fresh every day and is sold in large 1½lb (685 g) blocks in Chinese supermarkets and Japanese shops. Tofu is also available in health-food and wholefood shops. A variety of silken tofu is marketed by Morinaga in long-life packs. Deep-fried tofu is available frozen in Japanese shops. Good fresh tofu is white with no smell. When you buy tofu, immerse it completely in fresh water and put it in the refrigerator. Change the water every day. Stored in this way, tofu will keep 4–5 days.

Draining Tofu

One simple method will suffice: slice the tofu into ½in (1 cm) slices and lay the slices separately on several layers of clean towelling; put more towels on top. Leave for 30 minutes to drain lightly; the longer you leave it the drier it will become. To speed up the process, place a chopping board on top of the towels.

Making Tofu

In Japan tofu is so widely available and in such variety that most Japanese home cooks never make it. In England fresh, good quality tofu can now be found with relative ease in most cities. But everyone should try making their own at least once, if only to experience for themselves the miraculous transformation of yellow soya beans into white blocks of tofu. Homemade tofu, like homemade bread, may be less perfect than the commercial product, but is infinitely more delicious and interesting, and very simple to make, using everyday ingredients and utensils which can be found in any kitchen. Like bread it is as easy to make a large quantity as a little, and it is worth making in bulk to feed the family for a few days.

Tofu making yields two other products, both of which can also be used. Okara is the strained-off soya bean husks, which are used to make a variety of different dishes. The soya milk whey makes a rich stock for soups and vegetable dishes; brown rice is particularly delicious cooked in it. Tofu makers in Japan use it as a natural detergent-free cleanser for the tofu-making equipment.

Tofu may be made using a variety of different coagulants, which result in different textures and slightly different flavours. Most modern commercial tofu shops use calcium sulphate, which gives a rather bland white tofu. A few of the very best tofu shops in Kyoto and Tokyo still produce traditional tofu using nigari, a coagulant derived from sea water, giving a distinctively tasty and solid tofu, slightly beige rather than white in colour. Nigari is sold in some health-food and oriental shops in England. Inexpensive everyday ingredients such as lemon juice or rice vinegar also produce very satisfactory tofu. The juice of the salted plum (umeboshi) gives a delicately pink tofu.

To make tofu you will need two large saucepans, a blender, a strainer or colander and two large pieces of muslin, cheesecloth or coarsely woven cotton cloth. It is possible to buy special rectangular tofu-pressing boxes, full of holes for the whey to drain away, and with a lid for pressing that fits inside the box. A strainer topped with a plate is just as effective, but produces round rather than rectangular tofu.

1 lb (450 g) soya beans

coagulant
1 of the following:
2–3 tsps nigari dissolved in a little warm water
juice of 2–3 lemons
3 tbsps rice vinegar
3 tbsps umeboshi juice

Soak the soya beans overnight in plenty of water. Drain and rinse thoroughly. Put one-third of the beans in a blender with enough water to cover and grind thoroughly; the finer the purée, the greater the yield of tofu. Continue in the same way until all the beans are ground.

Meanwhile bring 4 pts (2·4 l) water to the boil in a large saucepan. Pour the soya bean purée into the boiling water and bring gradually back to the boil, stirring continuously with a wooden spoon. When the mixture froths and begins to rise, quickly sprinkle with cold water so that the temperature drops and the mixture sinks. Repeat this process a total of three times, to ensure that the soya beans are cooked; the soya beans will boil up very quickly and need to be watched carefully. Alternatively simply simmer the soya bean purée in the water for 5–7 minutes.

Line the strainer with muslin or cheesecloth and set in a second large saucepan. Pour the soya bean mixture through the muslin to separate the husks from the soya milk. Gather the muslin around the husks and squeeze thoroughly to press out as much soya milk as possible. Complete the squeezing by pressing with an empty jar. Set aside the husks; this is okara.

Heat the soya milk until it is nearly boiling. Remove from heat, stir well, and while the soya milk is still moving sprinkle the coagulant little by little on to the surface until the soya milk begins to curdle, stirring very gently if necessary. Cover the pan and leave for 5–10 minutes; the soya milk will have separated into soft white curds and clear whey. If the liquid is still cloudy, add a little more coagulant, cover and wait another 5–10 minutes.

Line the strainer with the second piece of muslin, and

moisten with a little whey. Without disturbing the tofu curds, gently ladle out as much of the whey as possible into a container. Gently pour the tofu curds into the strainer, breaking the curds as little as possible. Fold the cloth over the curds and cover with a small plate. Set a weight such as a jar of water on the plate and leave for 10–15 minutes, until whey no longer drips. The longer the tofu is pressed, the firmer it will be.

Set the tofu in its muslin in cold water. When the tofu is required, gently remove the muslin under water.

Fresh homemade tofu deserves to be served very simply so that its flavour can be fully appreciated. Serve as it is with just a dash of soy sauce, or follow the recipe for Summer Tofu (see below). Homemade tofu may be used in any recipe calling for tofu. Stored under water in the refrigerator, it will keep for up to 5 days.

VARIATION

Japanese tofu makers sometimes add small quantities of finely shredded vegetables to the soya milk before adding the coagulant. The following are traditional combinations: grated carrot, slivered dried mushroom (soaked) and peeled and boiled gingko nuts, soaked and shredded kombu seaweed, finely chopped spring onion and toasted sesame seeds.

SUMMER TOFU

One of the most refreshing dishes during Japan's long stifling summer is chilled tofu in a bed of ice cubes. This is the simplest way to serve tofu (connoisseurs maintain that it is the only way); it depends for its flavour on the quality of the tofu, which should be extremely fresh. Eating this dish with chopsticks requires a little skill; use pointed Japanese chopsticks and open them like scissors to ease the tofu apart into bite-sized pieces. Either standard or silken tofu can be used for this dish.

1½lbs (685g) tofu
2 spring onions
4 tsps finely grated root ginger

½ sheet nori seaweed
seven-spice pepper
soy sauce

Chill the tofu. Slice the spring onions very finely and rinse (see page 94). Form the grated ginger into 4 mounds. Lightly toast the nori seaweed and cut with scissors into thin strips. Divide the condiments between 4 small dishes and set 1 at each place. Provide small containers of soy sauce and seven-spice pepper.

Cut the tofu into 4 equal blocks and arrange in 4 deep bowls; the Japanese usually use glass bowls. The blocks may be left whole or cut into 4 squares and reassembled to form a block. Surround the tofu with ice cubes and serve immediately.

The diners select condiments to taste, sprinkle them on the tofu, and pour over a little soy sauce.

KAMINARI JIRU: THICK VEGETABLE SOUP WITH TOFU

Tofu is the basis of this thick and nourishing winter soup. Well-drained tofu is crumbled into hot oil and crackles like thunder, so this soup is known as Kaminari Jiru, thunder soup.

8 oz (225 g) tofu
1 medium carrot
2 small potatoes
1 small leek
6 fresh or dried and soaked mushrooms
½ cake konnyaku
vegetable oil
1½ pts (900 ml) dashi (page 143)
1½ tbsps soy sauce
1 tbsp kuzu dissolved in 2 tbsps dashi

Wrap the tofu in tea towels and set aside to drain. Wash and trim the vegetables. Slice the carrots into thin half moons and cut the potatoes into chunks. Cut the leek on the diagonal into long thin slices. Trim away the mushroom stems and slice the caps finely. Cut the konnyaku into small chunks.

Heat a little oil in a large heavy saucepan. Crumble the tofu and add. Sauté over medium to high heat for 2 minutes until the tofu is dry. Add a little more oil and stir in the carrot and potatoes; sauté for 2 minutes, then add the leek, mushrooms and konnyaku, and sauté until the vegetables are lightly browned and evenly coated with oil.

Pour the dashi into the pan and bring to the boil. Season to taste with soy sauce and simmer for a few minutes until the vegetables are soft. Over a very low flame pour in the kuzu solution and stir continuously until the soup thickens. Serve immediately.

YUDOFU: SIMMERING TOFU

Mrs Takenouchi is a motherly and merry lady with a most distinguished ancestry. She grew up in Ginkakuji, the Silver Temple, one of the most venerable temples in Kyoto. I went with her to visit the present abbot and admired the raked sand garden and ancient wooden pavilion where she used to play. In the evening we gathered around the kotatsu and enjoyed yudofu, a Kyoto speciality. Very fresh tofu is simply simmered in a light dashi, in a special casserole which holds the dipping sauce in a separate container in the hot dashi. This dish is a classic of both temple and home cooking; either standard or silken tofu can be used.

condiments
2 spring onions or young leeks
red maple radish (see page 88)
fresh root ginger, finely grated
½ sheet nori seaweed
seven-spice pepper

1½lbs (685 g) tofu

dipping sauce
8 fl oz (240 ml) soy sauce
2 tbsps mirin, sugar or honey

1 6in (15 cm) piece kombu seaweed (about ¼oz, 7 g)

First prepare the condiments. Shred and rinse the spring onions or leeks (see page 94). Lightly toast the nori seaweed and cut with scissors into thin strips. Arrange all the condiments in small bowls on the table.

Cut the tofu into 1–1½in (2–3 cm) cubes and arrange on a platter.

Combine the dipping sauce ingredients in a small saucepan and bring to the boil. Remove from heat and keep warm.

Set a gas or electric burner on the table.

Wipe the kombu and score a few times to help release the flavour. Place in a large flameproof casserole and fill it two-thirds full of water. Place on the burner and bring gradually to a simmer. Slide some of the tofu cubes into the simmering stock and cook over low heat for 2–3 minutes until they are heated through; be careful not to overcook.

While the tofu is heating, serve each diner with a small bowl of warm dipping sauce, into which they mix the condiments to taste. They help themselves to the heated tofu with a slotted spoon, and place it in the dipping sauce before eating. Continue to add fresh tofu to the stock until all the tofu is cooked.

MARINATED TOFU TATSUTA STYLE

The colours of the maple leaves in autumn at Tatsuta, near the ancient capital of Nara, are particularly splendid. In this dish well-drained tofu is marinated in a mixture of honey and soy sauce until it becomes a rich reddish brown like the maple leaves, then fried in a crisp coating. It is extremely simple to make; in fact it practically makes itself. Just ensure that the tofu has plenty of time to drain and to absorb the marinade.

1½lbs (685 g) tofu

marinade
8 tbsps dark soy sauce
8 tbsps honey
2 tsps fresh ginger juice
2 tbsps sake or mirin (optional)

1 oz (30 g) sesame seeds
2 oz (60 g) plain white or wholemeal flour
vegetable oil

Cut the tofu into ½in (1 cm) slices; spread on clean towels, cover with more towels, and set aside to drain for 1–2 hours.

The longer the tofu drains, the more marinade it will be able to absorb.

Blend the marinade ingredients and pour into a wide shallow platter. Lay the tofu slices in the marinade in a single layer and leave for 1 hour. Carefully turn the slices to marinate the other side for a further hour. The tofu will absorb most of the marinade and become quite brown and rather fragile.

Lightly toast the sesame seeds and grind in a suribachi. Combine with the flour. Heat a little oil in a frying pan. Carefully lift the tofu slices from the marinade, and dip in the flour mixture to coat both sides completely. Fry the slices a few at a time for 2–3 minutes on each side over medium heat until the coating is crisp and brown.

Transfer the remaining marinade to a small saucepan and cook over high heat for a few minutes, stirring, to reduce and thicken. Serve the tofu immediately topped with a little of the reduced marinade.

TOFU DENGAKU: GRILLED TOFU WITH SWEET MISO

Near my first home in Gifu is one of my favourite temples, tucked away among spectacular mountains. On Sundays it is crowded with pilgrims and sightseers, who sit gazing at the carp-filled lake with its little stone bridges, and eating steaming morsels of tofu coated in sweet miso. Matchbox-sized slabs of tofu on two-pronged bamboo skewers are grilled over charcoal and coated with flavoured misos of various colours, red, white, and even green. Tofu dengaku is made in homes and temples all over Japan; but Gifu's dengaku is particularly famous. Two bamboo skewers may be used to replace the pronged skewers used in Japan, and the tofu may be grilled under an ordinary grill, or alternatively fried or deep-fried. Leftover flavoured miso will keep indefinitely in the refrigerator.

1½lbs (685g) tofu

flavoured white miso
3 fl oz (90ml) white miso
3 fl oz (90ml) dashi (page 143)
2 tbsps sugar, honey, mirin or sake

2 egg yolks
2 tsps fresh lemon or ginger juice
pinch powdered green tea (optional)

flavoured red miso
3 fl oz (90 ml) red miso
3–4 fl oz (90–120 ml) dashi
2 tbsps sugar, honey or mirin
2 egg yolks
1 oz (30 g) sesame seeds

lightly toasted white sesame seeds
sprigs of fresh coriander or parsley
shreds of lemon peel

Carefully slice the tofu into 12 rectangular pieces, about 2½ × 1½ × ¾ in (6½ × 4 × 2 cm). Lay the tofu on tea towels, spread more towels on top, and set aside for at least 1 hour to drain. Soak 24 bamboo skewers in water.

While the tofu is draining prepare the misos. Combine the white miso, dashi, sugar (or honey, mirin or sake) and egg yolks in the top of a double boiler, and heat over simmering water, stirring continuously, until the mixture thickens; add more dashi if necessary to give a thick creamy consistency. Remove from heat and stir in the lemon or ginger juice. To make green miso, put half the flavoured miso into a bowl and stir in a little powdered green tea. Prepare the red miso in the same way as the white; lightly toast the sesame seeds, grind until pasty and add to the red miso.

Slide 2 bamboo skewers lengthwise through each piece of tofu. Grill the tofu slices under a preheated very hot grill, arranging them close to the flame, for 3 minutes on each side until the surface is speckled with brown. Spread each slice with white, green or red flavoured miso, and return to the grill with the miso side upwards; cook for 1 minute until the miso is heated through. Either garnish and serve immediately, or turn and spread the other side with miso of the same colour and grill again.

Garnish the red miso with sesame seeds, the white with lemon peel, and the green with tiny sprigs of coriander or parsley, and serve immediately.

TEMPLE TOFU

Hidden down a back street in the little town of Kamakura is a temple where one can sit quietly contemplating the garden and savouring delicate dishes of tofu and vegetables, all arranged on a lacquer tray decorated with a sprig of pine or a single autumn leaf. Lifting the lid of a porcelain bowl you will find a golden square of tofu in a thick sauce, subtly flavoured with lemon peel. The tofu is rolled in kuzu to give a light, crisp coating.

1½lbs (685g) tofu

sauce
8 floz (240ml) dashi (page 143)
1 tbsp kuzu
1 tbsp soy sauce
1 tsp each sugar or honey, lemon juice and lemon peel

1oz (30g) kuzu
vegetable oil for deep-frying
slivers of lemon peel

Cut the tofu into 4 large rectangles and wrap each piece in tea towels; set aside to drain for 30 minutes. Combine the sauce ingredients in a small saucepan and heat over a low flame, stirring continuously, until the sauce thickens; set aside and keep warm. Grind the 1oz (30g) kuzu finely in a suribachi or pestle and mortar; or simply crush to a fine powder with a rolling pin.

Fill a small saucepan with oil to a depth of 3in (7cm) and heat to 350°F (180°C). Dip the tofu in the kuzu, turning so that all sides are coated. Gently slide the tofu into the oil and deep-fry each piece separately for 3–4 minutes, turning until all sides are golden. Drain briefly on absorbent paper.

Warm 4 deep bowls, preferably with lids, and arrange 1 piece of tofu in each bowl. Stir the warm sauce and pour over the tofu, garnish with lemon peel and serve.

This dish can also be garnished with shredded and rinsed spring onion and grated daikon radish.

TOFU TREASURE BALLS

In my local tofu shop, while Mr Ishikawa prepared fresh tofu for the day, Mrs Ishikawa was busy making treasure balls from the previous day's unsold tofu. She would deftly shape the tofu into balls, mixing in multi-coloured slivers of carrot, mushroom and kombu seaweed, and pressing a whole gingko nut into the middle of each ball, and then deep-fry the balls, which would rapidly puff up and become crisp and golden. Tofu treasure balls can be simply made at home, and you can vary the ingredients which you put inside them.

2 lbs (900 g) tofu
¼ oz (7 g) kombu seaweed
2 dried mushrooms
1 medium carrot
1½ tsps sesame seeds
8 gingko nuts (optional)
1 tsp salt
vegetable oil

sauce
8 fl oz (240 ml) dashi (page 143)
2 tbsps soy sauce
1 tbsp honey, sake or mirin
2 tsps kuzu

Cut the tofu into ½ in (1 cm) slices and set aside wrapped in tea towels to drain. Soak the kombu and mushrooms in warm water for 30 minutes. Drain, reserving the soaking water; trim away the mushroom stems and shred the mushroom caps and kombu to make 2 tbsps of each. Pat lightly with absorbent paper to dry. Grate the carrot and measure out 2 tbsps. Lightly toast the sesame seeds. If gingko nuts are available, shell, boil and rub away the inner skin.

Mash the well-drained tofu to make 16 fl oz (480 ml) mashed tofu, and mix in the carrots, kombu, mushrooms, sesame seeds and salt. Knead for 2–3 minutes until the mixture holds together well. Fill a small saucepan with oil and heat to 340°F (170°C). Moisten your hands and form the tofu mixture into 8 balls or flat cakes; press a gingko nut, if using, into the centre of each. Deep-fry the balls a few at a time for 4–5 minutes, turning once, until they are golden brown and crisp. Remove with chopsticks or a slotted spoon; drain on absorbent paper.

Combine the sauce ingredients in a small saucepan and heat gradually, stirring continuously, until the sauce thickens.

Serve the treasure balls hot, topped with a little sauce.

MOCK EEL

Buddhist monks are forbidden to eat meat or fish, so tofu (along with yuba and gluten) is sometimes used in temple cookery to make dishes which theoretically resemble them. Eel prepared Japanese-style is tempting even to vegetarians, and is supposed to be an essential energy-giving food during the exhaustingly humid summer. This savoury dish of richly seasoned tofu on squares of nori, deep-fried and topped with sweetened soy sauce, looks and even tastes a little like slices of eel, and is an original and delicious dish in its own right.

12oz (340g) tofu
1 tbsp sesame seeds
1oz (30g) plain white or wholemeal flour
1 tbsp red miso
1 tsp sugar or honey
½ tsp freshly grated root ginger
2 sheets nori seaweed
vegetable oil

glaze
2 tbsps dark soy sauce
1 tbsp sugar or honey

Cut the tofu into ½in (1cm) slices and drain well wrapped in tea towels. Lightly toast the sesame seeds and grind in a suribachi until pasty. Stir in the tofu and add the flour to make a stiff paste. Blend in the miso, sugar or honey and ginger. With scissors cut each sheet of nori in half, then cut each half into 4 rectangles. Spread a thin layer of the tofu mixture on each rectangle of nori; score lightly with a fork.

Fill a small saucepan with oil to a depth of 2in (5cm) and heat to 340°F (170°C). Gently place the nori and tofu slices a few at a time in the hot oil, keeping the tofu side uppermost, and deep-fry for about 1 minute until puffed up and golden brown. Set aside on absorbent paper to drain.

Combine the soy sauce and sugar or honey in a small saucepan and heat to dissolve the sugar or honey. Arrange 4 slices on each plate and brush the slices with hot glaze.

TOFU PICKLED IN MISO

Pickled tofu is the nearest Japanese equivalent to a strong cheese. Slices of tofu, well drained to absorb as much flavour as possible, are layered with flavoured miso; after a few months the tofu is transformed into a deliciously salty, dark-brown substance with a texture rather like cheese, which is served either as it is or lightly grilled in small quantities to accompany rice, or used as a piquant addition to vegetable stuffings. The tofu can be used as soon as a day after it is pickled, in which case the flavour will be much milder; but it is usually left for about six months. Unused tofu pickle is kept covered with miso and the flavour gradually becomes stronger and stronger. Nor is the miso wasted; when it is no longer needed for the tofu pickle it can be used in any recipe calling for flavoured miso. To make pickled tofu you will need a small non-metal container with a tight fitting lid; in Japan wooden or earthenware containers are used, but glass or even plastic will do. The following quantities will give a small trial batch.

1½lbs (685 g) tofu
1lb (450 g) red miso
2 tbsps sugar or honey
1 tbsp ginger juice or fresh lemon juice
1 tbsp sake (optional)
pinch seven-spice pepper

Cut the tofu into ½in (1 cm) slices and drain well between tea towels. Mash the miso with the remaining ingredients. Prepare a lidded container which will comfortably hold the miso mixture and the tofu. Fill the container with layers of miso and tofu, beginning and ending with a layer of miso; ensure that all sides of each tofu slice are covered with miso. Fit on the lid and wrap the box in cling film. Put the box in the refrigerator.

When you want to use the pickle, open the box and gently scrape off the top layer of miso. Carefully remove a slice of tofu; replace the miso, cover the box and return to the refrigerator. The longer the tofu is left, the stronger the flavour will become.

SESAME TOFU

Every temple meal and every meal of tofu cuisine invariably includes a small cube of sesame tofu topped with a little bright green wasabi. For me this is the dish to be saved until last, and eaten very slowly, savouring the subtle flavour and silky texture. Sesame tofu is not in fact tofu, but pure sesame, set with kuzu, with a texture and appearance akin to tofu. Reputedly the monks of Mount Koya, the great Shingon Buddhist stronghold, first made sesame tofu, and theirs is said to be still the best. The flat mountain top of Mount Koya, south of Osaka, is covered in temples and temple complexes, with little shops and stalls selling mementoes; here you can buy prepacked sesame tofu to take home with you. I lodged in a temple where I was, of course, served with particularly fine sesame tofu. Sesame tofu is not traditionally made at home, although it is one of the simplest dishes to prepare. Ready-made sesame paste makes the preparation easier, but the finest flavour comes from freshly roasted and ground sesame seeds.

4 tbsps sesame seeds, or 2 tbsps sesame paste
2½ tbsps kuzu
½ tsp salt
16 fl oz (480 ml) water
1 tsp freshly made wasabi
soy sauce

Toast the sesame seeds until they are fragrant. Tip into a suribachi and grind until the seeds give off oil and form a smooth paste; this takes a long time and a lot of grinding.

Scrape the sesame paste into a small saucepan and mix in the kuzu, salt and water. Stir well to dissolve the kuzu. Heat very slowly over the lowest possible flame, stirring continuously with a wooden spoon or whisk. The mixture will suddenly thicken. Continue to cook and stir for another 12 minutes to give the sesame tofu a smooth, creamy texture.

Select a small, flat-bottomed, preferably square or rectangular mould, at least 1½in (4cm) deep, and rinse with water; do not dry. Pour in the sesame mixture, tapping the mould lightly to settle the mixture evenly. Set aside to cool to room temperature (do not refrigerate). Run a knife around the inside edge of the mould and gently invert it on to a plate so that the tofu slips out. Wet a sharp knife and cut the tofu into 8 rectangles. Place 1 or 2 rectangles in small deep bowls, top with a mound of wasabi, and serve with soy sauce.

Alternatively, rinse 4–6 small glass bowls with water and divide the sesame mixture evenly between the bowls. Allow to cool to room temperature and serve in the bowls, with wasabi and soy sauce or with a little flavoured miso (see pages 152, 196–7).

Peanut and walnut tofu can be made in the same way. Simply replace sesame seeds in the recipe above with the same quantity of walnuts or peanuts and proceed as above.

Deep-Fried Tofu

Although the little neighbourhood tofu shops survive these days, like the public baths they get fewer every year. My friend Akio Matsui in Akashi owns a big tofu concern, employing twenty girls who turn out huge amounts of tofu daily. Like every tofu maker, Akio makes several different kinds of deep-fried tofu – thin slices of well-drained tofu slowly fried in hot oil. In Akio's shop, they travel along a sort of conveyor belt in a trough of hot oil, beginning as tofu and gradually turning golden and becoming light and puffy, finally tumbling into a container to be shipped off to Osaka, Kyoto and western Japan.

Like tofu, deep-fried tofu is invaluable to the vegetarian cook. It is often simmered in lightly seasoned stock or slivered and mixed with vegetables. Cut in half, the thin tofu eases open to form little pouches, which can be stuffed with rice or a mixture of vegetables. These pouches, open and decorated with sesame seeds, or neatly tied with gourd ribbon, look most appealing and appetising.

In England, deep-fried tofu is available frozen from Japanese shops and some Chinese and health-food shops in packages of 3 sheets, each 6 × 3in (15 × 8cm). Before using, it should be rinsed in boiling water to remove excess oil. Deep-fried tofu tears quite easily and should be treated with care.

INARI SUSHI: STUFFED TOFU POUCHES

The equivalent of the sandwich bar in Japan is the local take-away sushi bar with its nori rolls and lovely inari sushi, golden tofu pouches stuffed with rice and other delicacies, and topped with sesame seeds, bright red vinegared ginger or dark-green dried herbs. Inari is the god of rice and the harvest, and the fox, his messenger, is famous for his love of deep-fried tofu. Inari sushi is an essential ingredient in the wooden lunch box, still frequently seen on train journeys, picnics or at the theatre.

4 sheets deep-fried tofu
16 fl oz (480 ml) dashi (page 143)
1 tbsp light soy sauce
2 tsps sugar or honey
1 tbsp mirin (optional)
sushi rice made from 15 oz (425 g) uncooked rice (pages 260, 262)
1 tsp sesame seeds, toasted

Cut the deep-fried tofu sheets in half and gently separate the two sides to make little pouches. Put into a bowl and pour boiling water over them. With chopsticks swirl the tofu about in the water to wash off excess oil, then remove and drain.

Combine the dashi, soy sauce, sugar or honey and mirin if used in a small saucepan; add the tofu sheets and bring to the boil. Simmer uncovered for 10 minutes until the simmering

stock is nearly all absorbed and the tofu is well flavoured. Leave in the simmering stock to cool, then drain well and squeeze lightly to remove excess liquid.

Fill each pouch to the brim with rice, pushing the rice in firmly; but take care not to tear the pouch. Sprinkle a few sesame seeds on top. Serve 2 pouches on each plate to replace rice; or fit snugly into a small box in a single layer for a packed lunch.

FIVE-COLOUR TOFU POUCHES

These colourful tofu pouches look delicious and very festive; the rice filling is speckled with red carrots, brown mushrooms, green parsley and black sesame seeds, and the pouches are garnished with yellow egg strands.

4 sheets deep-fried tofu
sushi rice prepared from 8 oz (225 g) uncooked rice (pages 260, 262)
2 dried mushrooms, softened in water
1 tbsp light soy sauce
1 tsp sugar or honey
1 tsp mirin or sake (optional)
½ small carrot
1 tbsp finely chopped parsley
1 tbsp black sesame seeds, toasted

egg strands
1 egg
1 egg yolk
1 tbsp dashi (page 143)
¼ tsp each light soy sauce and sugar or honey

vegetable oil

Prepare 8 tofu pouches from 4 deep-fried tofu sheets (see page 205). Prepare the rice following the instructions on page 259. While the rice is cooking, prepare the vegetables. Drain the mushrooms, reserving the soaking water, and remove the stems. Put the caps in a small saucepan with enough of the reserved soaking water to cover. Add the soy sauce, sugar or honey and mirin or sake if used. Bring to the boil, cover, preferably with a drop lid, and simmer for 20 minutes until the mushroom caps are well flavoured and soft. Leave to cool in the simmering stock, then drain well, reserving the stock, and dice finely. Parboil the carrot until just tender and shred. Chop the parsley, toast the sesame seeds and prepare the egg strands, following the recipe on page 247.

Lightly mix the mushrooms, carrots, parsley and sesame seeds into the cooled sushi rice, moistening with a little of the reserved mushroom cooking stock. Fill each pouch to the brim with rice, pushing the rice in firmly, being careful not to break the pouches, and garnish with egg strands. Serve as part of a meal or as a snack.

TOFU PURSES

Little sacks of deep-fried tofu can be filled with practically any stuffing (such as vegetable, tofu or rice mixtures) and neatly tied with gourd ribbon to make most attractive and intriguing purses. Leftovers can be transformed into a filling for tofu purses. Tofu purses are often included in oden (Japanese winter stew, page 167) or other one-pot dishes.

4 sheets deep-fried tofu
1 small carrot
1 young leek
¼ green pepper
1 oz (30 g) fresh peas
1 oz (30 g) fresh mushrooms
40 in (100 cm) dried gourd ribbon
8 fl oz (240 ml) dashi (page 143)
1 tbsp sake or mirin
1 tbsp soy sauce
1 tsp sugar or honey

Halve the deep-fried tofu sheets and gently separate the two sides to make little sacks. Rinse with boiling water and pat with absorbent paper to remove excess oil. Wash and trim the vegetables. Shred the carrot, leek and pepper, and dice the mushrooms. Mix the vegetables together and distribute evenly between the tofu sacks. Cut the gourd ribbon into 8 equal pieces. If it is fairly soft, simply use it as it is to tie the sacks neatly, finishing off with a bow; trim the ends. If the gourd ribbon is rather dry and hard, knead it with a little salt and rinse several times to soften, then use it to tie the sacks.

Fit the 8 purses snugly into a small saucepan, keeping them upright. Blend the dashi with the sake or mirin, soy sauce and sugar or honey and pour over the purses. Bring to the boil. Cover, preferably with a drop lid, and simmer gently for 10 minutes. Carefully lift out the purses with chopsticks or a slotted spoon. Boil the remaining cooking liquid for 3 minutes until thickened and reduced.

Put 2 tofu purses each on 4 small plates, and spoon over a little of the reduced cooking liquid. Serve hot or at room temperature.

GRILLED TOFU PURSES

Grilling deep-fried tofu gives it a richer flavour. Grill very briefly under medium heat, watching carefully; if the deep-fried tofu browns or becomes too crisp, it will be too delicate to stuff. Dip it in water to soften before stuffing. Tofu purses may be secured with gourd ribbon or wooden cocktail sticks instead of strips of kombu seaweed. If available, a few shreds of dried yuba make a delicious addition to the filling.

4 sheets deep-fried tofu
1 6in (15 cm) strip kombu seaweed
3 dried mushrooms
½ leek
¼ green pepper
2oz (60g) fresh mushrooms
4oz (115g) tofu, well drained
1 tsp sesame seeds, toasted
pinch salt
1 tbsp soy sauce
2 tsps sugar or honey
a little freshly made English mustard

Halve the deep-fried tofu sheets and gently separate the two sides to make little sacks. Grill the sacks under a medium-hot grill for 30 seconds on each side. Put the kombu and dried mushrooms in water or dashi to cover, and soak for

20 minutes. Remove the mushrooms from the water and cut off the stems; return the stems to the water to flavour it. Chop the mushroom caps finely.

Wash, trim and shred the leek and green pepper. Wipe the fresh mushrooms and dice finely. Mash the tofu and combine with the dried and fresh mushrooms, leek and green pepper. Crush the sesame seeds in a suribachi or with a rolling pin and stir into the tofu mixture.

Remove the kombu from the water and tear along the grain into thin strips. Dip the deep-fried tofu in fresh water to soften, and half-fill the purses with filling. Fold over the top front flap of each purse to enclose the filling; tuck in the sides and fold over the top back flap of the purse like an envelope. Tie a piece of kombu around the purse to secure it; or fasten with a wooden cocktail stick. Return any remaining kombu to the mushroom-soaking water.

Combine the water containing the mushroom stems and kombu with the soy sauce and sugar or honey in a small saucepan. Add the tofu purses, cover, preferably with a drop lid, and bring to the boil over moderate heat. Simmer covered for 5 minutes. Uncover and simmer for another 5 minutes, then turn off the heat and leave the purses to cool in the cooking water.

Drain well and serve at room temperature. Put 2 tofu purses each on 4 small plates, and spoon over a little of the cooking liquid. Pass a small dish of English mustard separately.

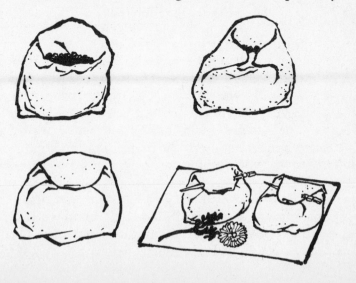

Yuba

Fresh yuba is the Japanese equivalent of caviare, a luxury food reserved for special occasions, hideously expensive but a rare delicacy. Like tofu, it is made from soy milk; but while every village has its local tofu shop, fresh yuba can only be found in a few shops specialising in Kyoto products. Fresh yuba features in temple cookery and the luxury cuisine that accompanies the tea ceremony, but as far as I know only one temple, set in paddy-fields a little to the west of Arashiyama in Kyoto, specialises in yuba cuisine. Most Japanese have never tasted fresh yuba, and the visitor to Japan is more likely to encounter it in its dried form, as delicate yellow ribbons floating in a bowl of clear soup.

Akio Matsui owns a big, modern tofu factory in Akashi, on the coast of the Inland Sea, not far from Kyoto, and it was he who introduced me to the delights of fresh yuba. While his twenty employees labour to produce vast quantities of tofu, Akio, like a master craftsman, concentrates on the fine art of yuba making, lifting the delicate white sheets without any fold from the pans of steaming soy milk and rolling them into perfect cylinders, which we savour slowly like fine wine, just as they are, without even soy sauce to mask the delicate taste.

Yuba is absurdly easy to make, but it is not so easy to make good yuba. The Japanese, who have a fine sense of propriety, prefer to leave yuba making to the master craftsman; but for us brash Westerners, yuba making can be a real discovery.

Yuba is the skin which forms naturally when soya milk is simmered, and in which all the goodness and richness of soya milk is concentrated. It needs simply to be lifted off and rolled to be served as fresh yuba. It is usually available only in its dried form, in brittle yellow sheets, small rolls or tied into bows, in Japanese shops and a few health-food shops. You can dry your own homemade yuba quite simply. Dried yuba needs to be softened in water. The freshest dried yuba softens immediately, and is simply dipped into water and removed at once; dried yuba which is less fresh may need to be soaked for 5–10 minutes to become pliable. Dried yuba is most often used in clear soups; it is put directly into the bowl and hot stock poured over it so that it softens immediately.

Both fresh and dried yuba are versatile cooking ingredients, which can be prepared in a variety of ways, and may be simmered, deep-fried or stuffed. Fresh yuba makes delicious tempura, while dried yuba, deep-fried, becomes a delicately flavoured crisp. Yuba readily absorbs flavours, and, simmered in seasoned stock, becomes rich and savoury with a texture almost reminiscent of meat. In Chinese vegetarian cuisine, a much thicker, chewier yuba, sold in Chinese shops as 'bean curd skin' or 'bean curd sheets', is actually used as a meat substitute, and vegetarian restaurants in Hong Kong and China abound with such dishes as 'Vegetarian Fish' and 'Vegetarian Chicken' which even look similar to the real thing. But fresh yuba, eaten just as it is, remains the most delicious.

Making Yuba

Yuba is very simple to make; in fact it makes itself, but the process does require plenty of time. You will need 2–3 hours to make enough yuba for 4, although your actual work will take only a few minutes; all you have to do is remove the sheets of yuba as they form. The quality of the yuba depends on the quality of the soya beans, the proportion of water to beans, the temperature of the fire and the precise moment when the yuba is removed. You can make yuba from commercial soya milk, but the best yuba is made from the best-quality soya beans, freshly ground. If you use commercial soy milk, make sure that it is unsweetened. To make yuba you will need a wide shallow pan, 1½–2in (4–5cm) deep; a large heavy frying pan will do, although to make perfectly shaped rolls you will need an oblong pan such as is used in Japan. In China yuba is made in a wok. Yuba needs to be made over the lowest possible heat. In Japan the oblong pans are set over simmering water; you can use an asbestos mat instead, or simply set the pan over a very low flame. You will also need several long chopsticks and a large saucepan on which to rest the chopsticks while the yuba drains. Yuba is extremely rich. The following quantities will produce 3–4 rolls, depending on the size of your pan, which will be more than enough for 4.

6 oz (170 g) soya beans
1 pt 12 fl oz (950 ml) water or 1½ pts (900 ml) commercial soya milk

If you are making your own soya milk, wash the soya beans and soak overnight in plenty of water. Drain and rinse thoroughly. Little by little grind the beans very finely in a blender, using some of the measured water. Stir in the remaining water and bring to the boil in a large saucepan. Strain through several layers of muslin, squeezing the muslin to extract as much milk as possible. Set aside the contents of the muslin: this is okara. Bring the milk back to the boil and simmer for 6–8 minutes. The soya milk is now ready.

Now pour either the homemade or commercial soy milk into a large frying pan, wok or oblong pan, to a depth of not more than 1½ in (4 cm). Heat over the lowest possible heat without stirring, so that it is steaming but not bubbling. When the soya milk is steaming, the yuba will begin to form. After 10–15 minutes there will be a firm even skin on the surface of the soya milk: this is yuba.

Gently slide a chopstick around the edge of the pan to loosen the yuba. With a finger slightly lift one edge, slide a long chopstick under the centre and lift the yuba off gently. It takes a little practice to slide it smoothly on to the chopstick without creating wrinkles. If using an oblong pan, you can also slide the chopstick under one end of the yuba and lift it off in a single large sheet.

Rest the chopstick on the saucepan, letting the yuba hang down inside to drain for 2–3 minutes. Then lay the yuba on a clean dish cloth, cut along the chopstick to free it and remove the chopstick. Lay 2 or 3 sheets of yuba on top of each other and roll up gently with your fingers into a neat cylinder.

Continue in the same way, removing the yuba every 8–10 minutes, when a firm film has formed, until most of the soya milk has disappeared. At the bottom of the pan will be a thick yellow layer of 'sweet yuba', rich and sweet. This is a true delicacy; scrape it off with a wooden spatula, and eat it yourself or arrange the scraps neatly in bowls.

Serve the yuba cut into 1½in (4cm) lengths. I think it is most delicious without any seasoning at all; however, in Japan it is usually served with a dash of soy sauce and a dab of freshly made wasabi.

Leftover yuba can be refrigerated and used the following day, either raw or cooked in some way. To make dried yuba, hang sheets of yuba, or arrange rolls in a single layer, in a warm dry place, in the sun or an airing cupboard, for 10–20 hours, until crisp and dry. Dry yuba is brittle and needs to be treated with care. Store in an airtight container until ready to use.

YUBA TEMPURA

In spite of the temptation to eat all your freshly made yuba just as it is, it is worth saving a little to make into yuba tempura, rich and creamy inside and crisp outside; or use leftover yuba to make yuba tempura the following day.

4 rolls fresh yuba

tempura batter
2oz (60g) plain white or wholemeal flour
1 egg yolk
5 floz (150ml) iced water
pinch salt

vegetable oil
soy sauce, salt or lemon juice, or tempura dipping sauce (page 156)

Use fat, tightly rolled yuba rolls for this dish; as you make the fresh yuba, lay several sheets on top of each other and roll tightly. Cut into 1½in (4cm) lengths.

In a small pan heat the oil to a temperature of 340°F (170°C). While the oil heats, prepare the batter, combining the ingredients very lightly and rapidly to make a rather lumpy batter.

With chopsticks dip the yuba rolls into batter and slide into the oil a few at a time. Deep-fry for just 30–45 seconds, turning, until the batter is crisp. Drain briefly on absorbent paper before serving attractively heaped on individual dishes, with a dash of soy sauce, salt or lemon juice, or with warm tempura dipping sauce.

DEEP-FRIED YUBA ROLLS

Fresh yuba, deep-fried, becomes crisp, sweet and nutty, and is often served topped with one of the sweet misos which are so popular in Japan. This dish is quick and simple to prepare, and is often served to pilgrims and visitors in the little restaurants beside the famous Kyoto temples.

4 rolls fresh yuba

red flavoured miso
3 tbsps red miso
3–4 tbsps dashi (page 143)
1 tbsp sake or mirin (optional)
2 tbsps sugar or honey

white flavoured miso
3 tbsps white miso
2–3 tbsps dashi
1 tbsp sake or mirin
1 tbsp sugar or honey
1 tsp fresh ginger juice

1 tbsp white sesame seeds
1 tbsp poppy seeds
vegetable oil

Use fat, tightly rolled yuba rolls for this dish; as you make the fresh yuba, lay several sheets on top of each other and roll tightly. Cut into 1½ in (4 cm) lengths.

Heat the ingredients for each flavoured miso in a small saucepan over very low heat, stirring; add more dashi if necessary to make a thick but spreadable paste, a little thicker than mayonnaise consistency. Remove from heat. Lightly toast the sesame seeds and poppy seeds.

In a small saucepan heat the oil to 325°F (163°C), a little lower than for tempura. Gently deep-fry the yuba rolls, a few at a time, over moderate heat, for about 1 minute, turning them – they will puff up and become golden.

Drain briefly on absorbent paper, and quickly spread with 2–3 tsps of the red or the white flavoured miso. Arrange 2 red-topped and 2 white-topped yuba rolls on each plate, and sprinkle a few sesame seeds on the red miso and poppy seeds on the white miso. Serve immediately.

DRIED YUBA, DEEP-FRIED AND SIMMERED

Dried yuba is sold in a variety of different shapes, and is often used for its attractive appearance as well as for its delicate taste. It is very brittle and can be easily broken into small pieces or cut with scissors. Simply deep-fried for 1 or 2 seconds, dried yuba swells dramatically and becomes crisp. These 'crisps', sometimes called Kyoto flowers, are often salted and served with sake, or may be added to soups or steamed dishes such as chawan mushi.

In this dish deep-fried yuba is simmered in seasoned dashi, and rapidly absorbs the flavours to become rich and savoury. Dried yuba may also be simply simmered in seasoned stock without being first deep-fried. Chinese 'beancurd skin' may be used, but will need to be simmered for at least 30 minutes.

4 large sheets or 12 small sheets dried yuba
vegetable oil
6 fl oz (180 ml) dashi (page 143)
1 tbsp soy sauce
1 tsp sugar or honey
1 tbsp sake

With scissors cut the dried yuba into pieces 2 in (5 cm) square. Heat the oil to 300°F (150°C), and deep-fry the yuba pieces, a few at a time, for 1–2 seconds. Remove immediately with a slotted spoon and drain on absorbent paper. Soak the deep-fried yuba in hot water for 5 minutes to soften; drain.

Combine the softened yuba with the remaining ingredients in a small saucepan and bring to the boil; simmer for 3–4 minutes. Remove the yuba with chopsticks or a slotted spoon and arrange in 4 small bowls. Spoon over a little of the simmering liquid and serve immediately.

SIMMERED DEEP-FRIED YUBA ROLLS

The biggest conurbation I have ever seen sprawls for two or three hundred miles south from Tokyo, through Yokohama and Nagoya down to Osaka. Within this urban sprawl are pockets of green, and, hard though it is to believe, it is possible to walk through mountains and paddy-fields all the way from Tokyo to Osaka on the Tokai trail. This path winds its way through the mountains surrounding Gifu, and I often walked the Gifu part of the footpath. A good afternoon's walk would take me to a lake nestling into the hillside, with a few swans and a small island on which stood a restaurant, where I would finally relax over dishes of wild foods and richly seasoned deep-fried yuba rolls.

4 rolls fresh yuba
vegetable oil
16 floz (480 ml) dashi (page 143)
2 tsps sugar or honey
1 tbsp light soy sauce
1 tbsp sake or mirin
8 mangetout peas
1 small carrot
salt

Cut the yuba rolls into 1½ in (4 cm) lengths and deep-fry in oil as deep-fried yuba rolls (page 214). Drain in absorbent paper.

Combine the dashi, sugar or honey, soy sauce and sake or mirin in a small saucepan and bring to the boil. Lower the heat and gently add the yuba rolls, and simmer uncovered for 10 minutes, occasionally turning the rolls and spooning over the sauce, until the rolls are a rich brown and the simmering liquid is thickened and much reduced.

While the rolls are cooking, wash the vegetables and top and tail the mangetout peas. Cut the carrot into thin flowers (see page 64). Parboil the vegetables separately in lightly salted boiling water for 1–2 minutes, until just tender, and drain.

Remove the rolls from the remaining simmering liquid with chopsticks or a slotted spoon and arrange on 4 small plates. Spoon over a little of the cooking liquid and garnish each plate with 2 mangetout peas and a few carrot flowers.

STUFFED YUBA

To the west of Kyoto is Arashiyama, a beauty spot famed for its wild rushing river and the brilliant colours of its autumn maple leaves. A little beyond Arashiyama, in a beautiful setting in the midst of paddy-fields, is a temple with a restaurant which specialises in yuba cuisine, serving a variety of different dishes all based on freshly made yuba, including a dish of dainty yuba rolls which I have tried to reproduce here.

Dried yuba may be used in this recipe in place of fresh. It will need to be soaked in water until soft and pliable, and after stuffing should be tied with a piece of gourd ribbon or secured with a wooden cocktail stick.

12 sheets fresh yuba

filling
3 dried mushrooms, softened in water
1 oz (30 g) French beans
1 small carrot
1 oz (30 g) bean sprouts
1 tsp red miso
½ tsp sugar or honey

vegetable oil
2 tbsps grated daikon radish
soy sauce

Prepare the yuba, lifting off 12 large single sheets (see page 212); do not stack the sheets but lay them out separately.

For the filling, trim away the mushroom stems and mince caps. Wash and trim the vegetables, and shred. Combine vegetables, binding the mixture with the miso and sugar or honey.

Place a little of the filling near the front of each sheet of yuba. Fold in the sides to cover the filling, then roll up tightly; the damp yuba will seal itself. Leave with sealed edge underneath until all the rolls are prepared.

Fill a small saucepan with oil and heat to 300°F (150°C); deep-fry stuffed yuba rolls, a few at a time, for 1 minute, turning them, until the yuba is crisp and golden. Arrange on 4 plates, and on each plate put a cone of grated daikon. Serve immediately with soy sauce. The diners mix the daikon with a little soy sauce and dip the stuffed rolls in the mixture before eating.

CHINESE-STYLE STUFFED YUBA TEMPURA

This rich and complex yuba dish is akin to the rich vegetarian cookery of China. Large sheets of yuba, stuffed with vegetables and tofu, are coated in batter and deep-fried, and suddenly undergo a dramatic transformation, puffing up to become golden and crisp. Use large single sheets of yuba (see page 212) or substitute large sheets of dried yuba, available from Chinese shops as 'beancurd sheets'. Chinese dried yuba is tougher and easier to use than Japanese, but still brittle, and it should be treated with care.

8 large single sheets fresh yuba or 4 large Chinese beancurd sheets

filling
4 dried mushrooms, softened in water
1 medium carrot
¼ green pepper
2oz (60g) bean sprouts
5oz (140g) tofu, drained
2oz (60g) fresh peas, shelled
2–3 tbsps vegetable oil
3 tsps plain white or wholemeal flour
2 floz (60ml) dashi (page 143)
1 tsp soy sauce
salt
4 8in (20cm) strips gourd ribbon (kampyo)

batter
2oz (60g) plain white or wholemeal flour
1 tsp baking powder
4 floz (120ml) water
1 tbsp vegetable oil

vegetable oil for deep-frying
2oz (60g) French beans or mangetout peas
1 medium carrot
sprigs of parsley

Prepare the yuba, lifting off 8 large single sheets (see page 212); stack the sheets in pairs to make 4 thick sheets of yuba. If using Chinese beancurd sheets, soak in warm water for 15 minutes or until soft and pliable.

 Make the filling. Remove the mushroom stems and dice

the caps. Wash and trim the vegetables and dice the carrot and green pepper. Chop the bean sprouts and dice the tofu. Heat the vegetable oil and sauté the mushrooms, carrot and peas for a few minutes over medium heat. Add the green pepper, bean sprouts and tofu and stir in carefully so as not to break up the tofu. Dissolve 1 tsp of the flour in 1 floz (30 ml) of the dashi and stir into the vegetable mixture over very low heat. Season with soy sauce and salt and continue to stir over low heat until the sauce thickens. Remove from heat and set aside.

Dissolve the remaining 2 tsps flour in just enough of the remaining 1 floz (30 ml) dashi to make a paste. Spread 1 thick sheet of fresh yuba or 1 softened beancurd sheet on a bamboo rolling mat and brush evenly with half the flour paste. Cover with a second sheet of yuba. Spoon half the filling in a long mound down the centre third of the yuba sheet. Fold in the 2 ends and, holding the filling in place with your fingers, firmly and evenly roll the yuba around the filling, using your thumbs to roll. If using dried beancurd skin, seal the edge with a little flour paste; fresh yuba will seal itself. Finally tie the roll securely at each end with gourd ribbon, trimming the ribbon ends neatly. (If the gourd ribbon is hard knead it with salt and soak briefly in just enough water to cover.) Make a second roll in the same way with the remaining ingredients.

If using beancurd sheets: steam the rolls over rapidly boiling water for 30 minutes, turning once, until the beancurd becomes paler and tender. This step is unnecessary if using fresh yuba.

Combine the batter ingredients, stirring well to make a thick batter, and set aside for 30 minutes.

In a large saucepan, heat oil to a depth of 3 in (8 cm) to 340°F (170°C). Coat the rolls evenly with batter and deep-fry, turning once, for 2 minutes each side. The rolls will puff up and become golden and crisp. Drain briefly on absorbent paper.

Wash and trim the vegetables and cut the carrot into flowers (see page 64). Parboil the beans or peas and carrots separately, drain and pat dry.

Slice the rolls into ½ in (1 cm) slices so that they are easier to eat with chopsticks, then neatly reassemble on a serving platter and garnish with beans or mangetout peas, carrot flowers and parsley.

CLEAR SOUP WITH YUBA

When yuba is used in home cookery it is usually in clear soup, elegant, simple and reminiscent of the refined cuisine of the temples and the tea ceremony. A clear soup is composed rather than cooked, and its preparation is simple and quick, emphasising aesthetics as much as flavour. Like a flower arrangement, a clear soup has a main ingredient or 'host', perhaps a slice of parboiled vegetable, a cube of tofu, or a roll, bow or ribbon of yellow yuba; the 'guest' may consist of a leafy vegetable, a slice of mushroom or a square of seaweed, complementing the 'host'. A shred of lemon peel or a tiny, sharply flavoured leaf floating on the surface provides colour and piquancy. The solid ingredients are precooked or, like yuba, need no cooking, and are carefully arranged in the bowl in tiny quantities; hot, subtly flavoured dashi is then ladled over. Yuba is available in Japan ready formed in bows, rolls or ribbons; alternatively cut large sheets of Chinese bean curd into small squares with scissors and soak them in warm water for 30 minutes.

8 sprigs watercress or 8 small leaves spinach
8–12 small pieces dried yuba or Chinese bean curd skin
1½ pts (900 ml) water
1 4 in square kombu seaweed
2 tsps light soy sauce
1 lemon

Wash and trim the watercress or spinach and parboil for just 30 seconds or until wilted; rinse immediately in cold water to retain the bright green colour. Arrange the yuba and watercress or spinach in the bottom of 4 soup bowls; in Japan small lacquered bowls with lids are used. Prepare 12 slivers of lemon rind or make lemon twists (see page 221).
Combine the cold water and kombu in a small saucepan and bring slowly to the boil. Remove the kombu just before the water boils, and season this very light dashi with soy sauce. The kombu may be used again to make standard dashi (page 143).
Pour the hot dashi over the watercress or spinach and yuba, float a few slivers of lemon rind or a lemon twist on the top of each bowl and serve immediately.

LEMON TWISTS

Cut 4 thin, neat rectangles of lemon rind about 1–1¼ins
(2½–3cm) by ½–¾in (1½–2cm). Make 2 cuts as illustrated
and twist to form a triangle, crossing the ends to secure.

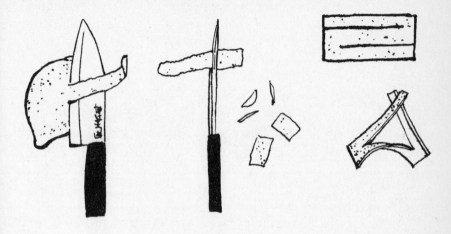

Okara

After making tofu, yuba or soy milk, you will be left with the soya bean husks, okara. Okara is white and fluffy and very bulky; it has little taste of its own but readily absorbs other flavours, and has plenty of texture. It has all the protein of the soya bean and, like bran, is full of fibre. Okara is nearly as versatile a cooking ingredient as tofu, and the Japanese make a variety of different and delicious dishes with it. The best-known okara dish is unohana, a delicate mixture of okara with slivered vegetables, which is often made at home or can be bought ready-made and somewhat more highly seasoned in delicatessens. Okara can be mixed into soups and is used to make a dressing for salads. Although outside the scope of this book, okara has many uses in Western-style cookery, and can be baked to make a type of granola or mixed into vegetable burgers. It keeps for only a very short time and should be used immediately.

UNOHANA: OKARA SIMMERED WITH VEGETABLES

Unohana is a wild spring flower with tiny white blossoms which okara is, rather romantically, supposed to resemble. Like many Japanese dishes unohana tastes best at room temperature and even better if the flavours are left to marry overnight before serving. Japanese main-course dishes tend to be sweet; the sugar or honey may be omitted or reduced in quantity if you wish. Deep-fried tofu and konnyaku, if available, are delicious additions.

2 dried mushrooms, softened in water
1 small leek
½ medium carrot
¼ sheet deep-fried tofu (optional)
¼ cake konnyaku (optional)
2 tsps vegetable oil
4 oz (115 g) okara
4–6 fl oz (120–180 ml) dashi (page 143)
1–2 tbsps light soy sauce
1–2 tbsps sugar or honey
1–2 tbsps sake or mirin
1 tbsp sesame seeds, toasted

Drain the mushrooms and remove the stems. Wash and trim the leek and carrot. Slice the mushroom caps very finely and shred the leek and carrot. Rinse the deep-fried tofu with boiling water and drain; pat dry and slice finely. Slice the konnyaku finely and sauté in a dry frying pan for a few minutes until quite dry.

Heat the oil and lightly sauté the vegetables, deep-fried tofu and konnyaku. Stir in the okara, and add 2 fl oz of the dashi, soy sauce, sugar or honey and sake or mirin to taste. Bring to the boil and simmer uncovered for about 10 minutes, stirring occasionally, until the mixture is well flavoured and coloured and nearly dry. Add more dashi and seasonings as required if the mixture becomes too dry.

Cool to room temperature, or preferably leave overnight. Serve in mounds in small deep bowls of a contrasting colour, and sprinkle over sesame seeds to garnish.

Miso

Miso is a rich and savoury bean paste: to most Japanese the word evokes warm memories of childhood, of appetising aromas wafting from cast-iron saucepans full of miso soup simmering over a charcoal fire on a frosty morning. Miso is one of the basic flavours of Japanese cuisine and an essential ingredient.

There must be as many misos as there are households in Japan. My friends all made it from tried and tested recipes handed down to them by their mothers and grandmothers. In the big thatched houses in the mountainous regions of Gifu, the miso-making seasons are in March, before the rice planting begins and when the air is still cool, and again in November, when fresh soya beans and rice are at their best. Every home has a carefully labelled store of several years' miso, in big pottery jars with wooden lids weighted with stones, kept in the cool larder area under the kitchen floor, or, if the family is large and wealthy enough, in big windowless earthen barns with the family crest over the door.

Cold fresh mountain air is best for miso making. In Takayama, a beautiful old town up in the mountains, you had to get up early to catch the country women in their indigo bonnets who brought their homemade misos and pickles to the morning market to sell. They would spread out their tubs of golden, brown or red miso along the riverside, and I would stroll along, stopping to chat and sample. Every miso was different, sweet, salty, smooth or chewy, full of barley, kombu seaweed, ginger or morsels of pickled vegetable. These and other misos from all over Japan are sold in the big department stores in the cities; in the food section down in the basement you will find an array of gleaming, dark-red, lacquered barrels, holding an astonishing variety of misos. Unfortunately most of these are not available in England; we are limited to a choice of white, red or sometimes dark barley miso. Generally speaking, white miso, made from rice, is sweeter and lighter and more suitable for summer, while red miso, made from barley, is saltier and stronger, and is used more in winter cooking. The amount of miso to be used in any particular recipe depends on the type being used.

Miso is made either from cooked soya beans or from cooked soya beans mixed with rice or barley, to which a yeast-like mould is added; it takes at least six months, and, for the best miso, up to three years, to mature. Mature miso should be stored in a cool place or refrigerated. The living enzymes in the miso are believed to be very good for the digestion; miso should never be boiled, since this alters the flavour and destroys the enzymes.

Simply dissolved in hot water, miso makes a warming and savoury soup, to which a variety of different vegetables, seaweed or tofu are added, depending on the season. It is also used as a dressing for vegetables, a pickling medium and as the basis for a variety of sauces. It is even used to make a particularly delicious filling for the tiny cakes that accompany the tea ceremony.

Making Miso

Many Japanese women still prefer to make their own miso, just as we enjoy bottling fruit and making jam in the autumn. Homemade miso, like everything homemade, of course tastes better, and the basic recipe can be varied in many ways to suit your taste. I have never had two homemade misos that taste the same.

Miso can be made very simply using ready-made rice or barley koji as the fermenting agent; this is available in some health-food and oriental shops, and is the way that most Japanese women make miso. Making koji from koji spores and cooked rice or barley is quite a delicate operation; like yogurt or yeast, the fermenting koji needs to be kept at body temperature for 45 hours. A little of the fresh koji is dried and stored to use as culture for future batches. Miso makers use the same koji culture for generations, so that each shop or household produces miso with a distinctive flavour.

Miso is made from roughly equal weights of uncooked soya beans and rice or barley koji, plus about half the weight of salt. It will need at the very least 3 months to ferment, and usually 12–18 months, stored in a large earthenware jar with a lid. You will also need a drop lid or plate which fits inside the jar, and some clean stones as weights.

1 lb 2 oz (500 g) uncooked soya beans
4 pts (1·2 l) water
8 oz (225 g) sea salt
1 lb 2 oz (500 g) dried rice or barley koji

Wash the soya beans very thoroughly, removing floating husks and discoloured beans. Drain well, then put in a pressure cooker or large saucepan with the measured water, and leave to soak overnight.

If you are using a pressure cooker, cook at high pressure over a very low flame for 25 minutes; allow the pressure to return to normal, and check that the soya beans are very soft. Alternatively, cook in a large saucepan for 1½–2 hours until the beans are very soft. Drain thoroughly, reserving the cooking liquid. Mash the beans in several batches in a suribachi, or put into a large bowl and mash with a potato masher; mash all the beans for smooth miso, and leave some whole for chunky miso.

With a wooden spoon, mix 7½ oz (212 g) salt into the mashed soya beans. Add the dried rice or barley koji. Measure out 8 fl oz (230 ml) of the reserved soya bean cooking liquid, and add little by little to the mixture, mixing and kneading well, until the consistency is like mature miso.

Wash a large container, such as an earthenware jar, very thoroughly and rinse with boiling water. Dry the container and rub a little of the reserved salt over the sides and base. Spoon the miso mixture into the jar, to fill it about two-thirds full. Smooth the surface of the miso and sprinkle with salt.

Lay 2 or 3 sheets of greaseproof paper smoothly over the top. Put a drop lid or plate directly on to the paper, and top with a weight no heavier than one-eighth of the total weight of the miso. Cover with cloth or paper to keep the miso clean, and label with the date and contents.

Store in a cool dry place to ferment for at least 1 year, and preferably 1½–2 years.

The proportions of soya beans, koji and salt may be varied to give different textures and tastes. A slightly larger proportion of koji gives a sweeter miso that requires less time to ferment. Miso made with less salt also ferments more quickly.

Making Koji

Koji is made from rice, barley or soya beans, cooked and mixed with koji spores, and left to ferment in a warm moist atmosphere for 45 hours. You will need a lidded container for the fermenting koji, and some means of keeping it warm and moist; it must also be kept very clean. In Japan fermenting koji is spread in large shallow wooden trays or on thin straw mats and left in a warm place such as above the steaming bath, which is kept full of water, or under the heated table (kotatsu).

10oz (285g) short-grain white or brown rice
¼ tsp seed koji (tane koji)

Brown rice must first be lightly ground and sieved to break up the grains. Wash the white or broken brown rice thoroughly and soak in water overnight. Rinse and put into a muslin-lined bamboo or flat metal steamer; set over boiling water and steam for about 1 hour until the rice is cooked. Each grain should be dry and fluffy; the rice should not be at all wet or sticky.

Spread out the rice and allow to cool to body temperature (115°F, 46°C). Sprinkle over the seed koji and mix in quickly with a wooden rice paddle or spoon. Either wrap the rice in a clean sheet or spread in a shallow container, wrap in blankets and put in a warm place such as the airing cupboard. Check frequently that the rice is warm, (75–95°F, 24–35°C); place for a short time near a heater if it becomes cool.

When the rice becomes slightly white, with a miso-like aroma, stir it and spread in a shallow container to a depth of about 1½in (4cm). This should occur after about 24 hours. Cover the container, wrap in blankets, and keep in a warm moist place, occasionally checking the temperature of the rice. Mix again after 4 hours; by now the temperature should have risen to 100°F (38°C). Cover and keep warm.

After 45 hours of fermentation the koji will be ready; the rice grains will be bound together with a delicate white mould. Stir and allow to cool to room temperature. Then mix with cooked soya beans as in the recipe above.

To make barley koji, replace the rice in this recipe with barley and proceed in the same way.

Miso Soup

For most Japanese the day begins with a warm and nourishing bowl of miso soup, and many a housewife is up at six in the morning preparing it for her husband and children, before waving them off to work or school. And the day ends with another bowlful, traditionally the last course of the meal. Miso soup is not merely an essential Japanese food; to most Japanese life is unimaginable without it, and Japanese shops in London stock instant packets (which are rather good) so that no one, however far from home, need be deprived.

The test of a good cook is said to be the quality of her miso soup. Every housewife makes a wide variety for the different seasons: light soups in which float a few tiny leaves and slivers of vegetable for summer, and thick broths full of vegetables for winter. Practically any vegetable may be used, usually in small quantities and very finely or decoratively sliced. Tofu, sea-weeds and yuba are added at the last minute, and need simply to be heated. The soup can therefore be prepared in only a few minutes. The miso itself is added last. A little hot stock is poured into a cup and the miso creamed until it is smooth. Do not boil the soup once the miso has been added, for this will spoil the taste of the miso as well as destroying the nutritious enzymes.

In Japan miso soup is served in lacquer bowls with lids which keep it very hot. The bowl is lightly squeezed to release the lid. Vegetables and tofu are picked out and eaten with chopsticks; and the soup is drunk direct from the bowl which is held in both hands. It is correct to slurp your soup.

Spring

MISO SOUP WITH BAMBOO SHOOTS AND WAKAME SEAWEED

The sudden appearance of fresh white bamboo shoots pushing their way up through the moss in the bamboo thickets is a sure sign of spring. Plucked out of the ground while still young and tender, they make a delicious and crunchy spring vegetable. Occasionally you may be able to find fresh bamboo shoots at Chinese grocery shops; otherwise you will have to make do with tinned ones.

1 oz (30 g) bamboo shoot
few strands dried wakame seaweed
1½ pts (900 ml) dashi (page 143)
2–3 tbsps white miso
1 spring onion or young leek, washed and trimmed

Rinse and dry the bamboo shoot and slice very finely. Cut the wakame into 1 in (2½ cm) pieces. Bring the dashi to the boil in a small saucepan; add the bamboo shoot and wakame and simmer for 2 minutes. Pour a little of the hot stock into a bowl and cream the miso in it. Pour the miso into the soup; heat until nearly boiling, but do not boil. Ladle into 4 bowls. Slice the spring onion or leek very finely and scatter over the soup.

MISO SOUP WITH SPINACH AND DEEP-FRIED TOFU

1 sheet deep-fried tofu
2 leaves spinach, washed
1½ pts (900 ml) dashi (page 143)
2–3 tbsps white miso
12 slivers lemon peel

Immerse the deep-fried tofu in boiling water to remove excess oil; drain and slice into julienne strips. Chop the spinach coarsely. Bring the dashi to the boil, add the spinach and deep-fried tofu and simmer for 1–2 minutes, until the spinach is just wilted. Dissolve the miso in a little of the hot stock and add to the soup. Ladle into 4 bowls, distributing the solid ingredients equally. Float a few slivers of lemon peel on each bowl and serve immediately.

Summer

MISO SOUP WITH AUBERGINE AND WAKAME SEAWEED

Aubergines are at their best during the summer and, like other rich foods, are said to provide energy to help one cope with the heat and humidity. Miso soup with aubergine is a popular breakfast dish.

4 oz (115 g) aubergine
1½ pts (900 ml) dashi (page 143)
few strands dried wakame seaweed
2–3 tbsps red miso

Quarter the aubergine lengthwise and slice across into very fine slices. Bring the dashi to the boil, add the aubergine, and simmer for 2–3 minutes until the aubergine is tender. Chop the wakame roughly and add; continue to simmer for another minute. Dissolve the miso in a little of the hot stock and add to the soup. Serve immediately.

MISO SOUP WITH FRENCH BEANS AND TOFU

This pale soup garnished with dark threads of nori seaweed is served in early summer. Delicate 'silken' tofu, rather than standard tofu, is delicious with it; it is available in England in long-life packs.

1 oz (30 g) French beans
1½ pts (900 ml) dashi (page 143)
4 oz (115 g) tofu
2–3 tbsps white miso
1 sheet nori seaweed

Top and tail the beans and slice diagonally into 2 in (5 cm) lengths. Bring the dashi to the boil, add the beans and simmer for 1–2 minutes, until the beans are just tender and bright green. Cut the tofu into small ½ in (1 cm) cubes, and gently add to the soup. Dissolve the miso in a little of the hot stock and return to the soup. Bring nearly to the boil, remove from heat and ladle into 4 soup bowls. Lightly toast the nori and cut with scissors into very thin strips. Scatter a few nori strips in the centre of each bowl of soup and serve immediately.

Autumn

MISO SOUP WITH DRIED MUSHROOMS, FRESH MUSHROOMS AND TOFU

Autumn is mushroom time in Japan, and in the morning you will often find clumps of tiny grey nameko mushrooms, even tinier yellow enokitake mushrooms or even Western button mushrooms floating in your miso soup.

4 dried mushrooms
1½ pts (900 ml) water
4 fresh mushrooms, wiped and trimmed
2 oz (60 g) tofu
3 tbsps red miso
4 sprigs coriander leaf or parsley, washed and patted dry

Soak the dried mushrooms overnight in the water. In the morning, drain, reserving the flavoured water. Remove the mushroom stems and slice the caps very finely. Return to the soaking water and simmer for 15 minutes. Slice the fresh mushrooms finely and cut the tofu into ½ in (1 cm) cubes. Add the mushrooms and tofu to the soup and return to the boil. Dissolve the miso in a little of the hot stock and add to the soup. Ladle into 4 bowls and garnish each bowl with a sprig of coriander or parsley.

MISO SOUP WITH CHINESE CABBAGE AND DEEP-FRIED TOFU

2 leaves Chinese cabbage, rinsed and patted dry
1 sheet deep-fried tofu
1½pts (900ml) dashi (page 143)
2–3 tbsps white miso
seven-spice pepper

Shred the Chinese cabbage. Immerse the deep-fried tofu in boiling water to remove excess oil; drain and slice into julienne strips. Bring the dashi to the boil, add the Chinese cabbage and deep-fried tofu and simmer for 1–2 minutes, until the Chinese cabbage is nearly tender but still a little crisp. Dissolve the miso in a little of the hot stock and add to the soup. Bring back nearly to the boil and ladle into 4 bowls. Sprinkle over a little seven-spice pepper and serve immediately.

Winter

MISO SOUP WITH TURNIPS AND TURNIP LEAVES

You will need turnips with a little of their green leafy stem still attached for this soup. If they are unobtainable you could substitute a couple of leaves of spinach.

2 small turnips (2–3oz, 60–85g each), with leaves attached
1½pts (900ml) dashi (page 143)
2–3 tbsps red miso
½ tsp English mustard, mixed with a little water

Trim the turnip roots; cut off the leaves just above the stem and set aside. Slice the turnips across into thin slices and cut the leaves into 1in (2½cm) lengths. Wash well.

Bring the dashi to the boil, add the turnips and simmer for 2–3 minutes. Add the leaves and cook for 1–2 minutes, until the turnips are tender and the leaves have wilted. Dissolve the miso in a little of the hot stock and add to the soup. Place a little mustard in each of 4 bowls, ladle over the soup and serve immediately.

MISO SOUP WITH LEEKS, TOFU AND WAKAME SEAWEED

This is the classic miso soup, served for breakfast in homes throughout the land. To complete your Japanese breakfast, serve one or two small portions of vegetables, perhaps a salad, some Japanese pickles, natto, rice, a raw egg, and small rectangles of lightly toasted nori seaweed. Wrap some of the rice in nori to eat; beat the raw egg into the remaining rice and season with soy sauce. Serve the miso soup in a lacquer bowl and finish the meal with green tea. This makes a delicious and nourishing start to the day.

1 young leek, washed and trimmed
1½pts (900ml) dashi (page 143)
few strands dried wakame seaweed
4oz (115g) tofu
2–3 tbsps red miso

Slice the leek finely. Bring the dashi to the boil, add the leeks and simmer for 2–3 minutes until they are tender. Break the wakame seaweed into small pieces, cut the tofu into ½in (1 cm) cubes, and add the wakame and tofu to the soup. Dissolve the miso in a little of the hot stock, return to the soup, and heat until nearly boiling. Ladle into 4 bowls, distributing the leek slices, wakame and tofu evenly.

MISO SOUP WITH DAIKON RADISH

2oz (60g) daikon radish
1 medium carrot
1½pts (900ml) dashi (page 143)
3 tbsps red miso
½oz (14g) dried yuba (optional)

Wash and trim the daikon and carrot and slice into very thin rounds. Bring the dashi to the boil, add the vegetables and simmer for 2–3 minutes until nearly tender. Dissolve the miso in a little of the hot stock and add to the soup together with the yuba, which will soften immediately. Bring back nearly to the boil and serve immediately.

Natto

Natto seems to be uniquely Japanese; the only other food I have encountered which is remotely like it is Indonesian tempeh. Natto's creation too seems to be peculiarly Japanese. Cooked soya beans, stored in rice straw, naturally ferment to become natto without any further assistance, a process brought about by the natto bacillus in the rice straw in combination with the humidity of the climate. Nowadays natto is commercially produced, although it is often packaged in rice straw, a reminder of its rustic origins.

Natto has a distinctive musty flavour and sticky texture, which, it must be confessed, is somewhat of an acquired taste, particularly to Westerners unused to sticky foods. It is used to make one of the most popular nori rolls, on sale in every sushi shop. When cooked natto is quite transformed. It loses its stickiness and becomes crisp and nutty, and makes a most delicious tempura. It is extremely nutritious, and contains all the protein of the soya bean in a very digestible form. Recently, with the growing interest in health foods in Japan, young people have been taking a second look at their own traditional foods. A recently published book called *The Nattow*, with an English title but Japanese recipes, contains recipes such as natto quiche, natto pizza, even natto cookies, experimenting with this traditional food in modern, Western-inspired ways.

Natto is imported frozen from Japan, and can be found in Japanese shops and some health-food shops. It is sold in 3½oz (100g) packets, complete with mustard, enough for 2 servings.

Making Natto

Once, you have acquired the taste for natto, you may want to try making your own. It is rather like making yogurt:

commercial natto can be used as a starter, and the temperature must be carefully regulated, for natto, like yogurt or yeast, is a living organism. Natto needs a warm and if possible humid environment to ferment. The ideal to aim for is a natto with moist beans and strong sticky threads. You will need 2–3 large ceramic or glass bowls, with large plates to serve as covers. The following recipe makes a very large quantity; halve or quarter the quantities as necessary.

2lbs (900g) soya beans
4pts (2·4l) water
1 packet natto (3½oz, 100ml)

Wash the soya beans thoroughly, removing floating husks and discoloured beans. Drain well, put in a large saucepan with water to cover and soak overnight.

Drain and cover with fresh water; bring to the boil and simmer for 10 minutes. Discard the water and add the measured water. Bring back to the boil and simmer for 1½–2 hours or until soft. Do not use a pressure cooker to cook the beans.

When the beans are soft and nearly dry, drain very well, and set aside to cool to 140°F (60°C). Prepare 2–3 large ceramic or glass bowls with covers, which will comfortably hold the beans, allowing a space of 1½in (4cm) between the beans and the cover. Warm the bowls by filling with hot water; drain and dry thoroughly.

Mix the natto into the cooled beans, stirring to distribute evenly. Put the mixture into the warmed bowls, filling them to 1½in (4cm) from the top. Cover with large plates, and place in a warm, preferably moist environment to ferment overnight.

The following day the natto should be fragrant and bound together with sticky threads. If the natto is not yet ready, leave for another day or at most another 2 days. Try to maintain the temperature at 140°F (60°C).

Natto may be eaten immediately, and will keep, frozen, for up to 2 months. Use homemade natto in place of commercial natto in any of the following recipes.

PLAIN NATTO

Natto is usually served very simply. The sticky beans, chopped or left whole, are put into a bowl, seasoned and whisked with chopsticks so that the natto coheres and becomes light and foamy. Sometimes raw egg or raw egg yolk is added to make it rich and creamy. Natto is traditionally a breakfast food, and a small bowl of it topped with a few shreds of leek appears at each place on tables across the land at breakfast time. You may prefer to serve natto for lunch or dinner. In any case, try eating natto, simply prepared as in the following recipe, on its own as the Japanese do.

2 packets natto (7 oz, 200 g)
½ tsp prepared English mustard
2 tsps soy sauce
1 young leek or spring onion
1 egg yolk (optional)
½ sheet nori seaweed

Natto may be used either whole or chopped. To chop, spread natto on a chopping board; resting the knife on the point, move the blade rapidly up and down to chop it roughly. Put into a small deep bowl, and add the mustard and soy sauce. Shred and rinse the leek or spring onion (see page 94), pat dry, and add to the natto, together with the egg yolk if used. With chopsticks, beat the natto; the texture will change, and the natto will quickly become pale and foamy. Continue to beat to make it as light as possible. Put into 4 small deep bowls for serving.

   Toast the nori and cut with scissors into thin strips. Scatter a few strips over each bowl.

NATTO WITH FRENCH BEANS

Plain natto is sometimes served combined with vegetables. Lightly cooked French beans provide a contrast of taste, texture and colour. Mangetout peas and okra are also often served with it.

6 oz (170 g) French beans
½ packet natto (1¾ oz, 50 g)

1 tsp soy sauce
½ tsp dry English mustard
1 tsp white sesame seeds, toasted

Top and tail the beans, plunge into lightly salted boiling water and parboil for 2–3 minutes until just tender. Drain and rinse in cold water. Pat dry and slice on the diagonal into very thin slices.

Chop the natto coarsely and beat together with the soy sauce and mustard until foamy. Stir the beans into the natto and arrange in mounds in 4 small deep bowls. Scatter with a few sesame seeds and serve.

MISO SOUP WITH NATTO

Natto is often added to miso soup, and gives it a distinctive flavour; the natto beans lose their stickiness when they are heated.

2 young leeks
4 oz (115 g) small fresh mushrooms
1½ pts (900 ml) dashi (page 143)
2 tbsps red miso
1 packet (3½ oz, 100 g) natto
seven-spice pepper

Wash and trim the leeks and slice finely on the diagonal. Wipe and trim the mushrooms and remove the stems; cut large caps in half and leave small caps whole.

Bring the dashi to the boil, add the leeks and mushrooms and simmer for 1–2 minutes. Dissolve the miso in a little of the hot stock and return to the soup. Add the natto, stir, and bring nearly to the boil.

Just before the soup boils, remove from heat and ladle into 4 warmed soup bowls. Sprinkle with a little seven-spice pepper and serve immediately.

NATTO OMELETTE

At lunch or dinner, natto is often served in an omelette. In Japan omelettes are usually served at room temperature in neat slices, carefully arranged on small plates.

1 packet natto (3½oz, 100g)
½ young leek or ½ spring onion or 4 small fresh mushrooms
½ tsp light soy sauce
4 eggs
2 tbsps dashi (page 143)
dash sake or mirin (optional)
¼ tsp salt
vegetable oil
sprigs of parsley or watercress

Chop the natto coarsely (see page 236). Shred and rinse the leek or spring onion or trim the mushrooms and chop finely. Whisk the natto with the leek or mushrooms and the soy sauce until foamy. Beat the eggs lightly with the dashi, sake or mirin if used and salt.

Brush a rectangular frying pan or small omelette pan with oil and heat over medium to high heat. Pour in half the egg mixture. As soon as the base of the omelette begins to set, spread half the natto mixture evenly over the omelette. Continue cooking until the eggs are just set. With chopsticks or a fish slice roll up the omelette firmly, and remove from the pan. It is helpful to roll the omelette in a bamboo rolling mat and leave it to cool to neaten the shape. Make a second omelette with the remaining ingredients in the same way.

When the omelettes are cool, cut with a sharp knife into 1 in (2½cm) slices and arrange a few on individual plates. Garnish with a little parsley or watercress.

NATTO TEMPURA

Natto tempura is a speciality of a little restaurant hidden behind a curtain of ropes and a heavy sliding door in Gifu's notorious bar district, Yanagasse. The sticky beans are quite transformed and lose their stickiness, making a crisp and nutty tempura.

2 packets natto (7oz, 200g)

batter
1 egg yolk
5 fl oz (150 ml) iced water
2oz (60g) flour (white or wholemeal)
pinch salt

vegetable oil for deep-frying
parsley to garnish

In a small saucepan heat the oil to a temperature of 340°F (170°C). While it is heating, prepare the batter, combining the ingredients very lightly and rapidly to make a rather lumpy batter.

Take a teaspoonful of natto. With the back of a second spoon, push the natto into the batter and roll it around quickly to coat it, keeping it in a neat ball. Take the natto from the batter with a spoon and slide it gently into the hot oil. Deep-fry for 1½-2 minutes, turning once or twice, until crisp and golden. The natto will burn if overcooked. Drain on absorbent paper. Continue in the same way until all the natto is used.

Arrange 2 or 3 pieces of natto tempura on each plate and garnish with parsley. Natto tempura is usually eaten plain; it could also be served with tempura dipping sauce (page 156), grated daikon radish and grated ginger.

NORI ROLLS WITH NATTO

Natto is a classic and particularly delicious filling for nori rolls. Fresh perilla leaves, if available, provide an interesting contrast of flavour and texture. If unavailable, simply omit them; or substitute a leafy salad vegetable such as lettuce, parsley, watercress or coriander leaves to give a similarly refreshing effect, although the taste is completely different.

sushi rice prepared from 10 oz (285 g) uncooked rice
1 packet natto (3½ oz, 100 g)
4 fresh perilla leaves (optional)
4 sheets nori seaweed
rice vinegar
soy sauce

Prepare the sushi rice (see page 260). Turn the natto on to a board and chop coarsely. Wash the perilla leaves, if using, pat dry and chop.

Toast the nori. Lay 1 sheet of nori on a bamboo rolling mat or working surface, and spread about 3 oz (85 g) prepared sushi rice over the front half of the nori. With wet hands press the rice firmly, smearing it to the sides of the nori. Spread a quarter of the natto in a thin line along the centre of the rice, and scatter over some chopped perilla leaf. Roll up firmly and carefully so that the rice encloses the filling, and seal the far edge with rice vinegar. Leave with the sealed edge downwards and prepare 3 more rolls in the same way.

Wet a sharp knife and cut each roll in half, then cut each half into 3 slices. Arrange in sets of 6 on individual plates and serve with soy sauce to dip.

NORI CONES WITH NATTO

In many sushi bars when you order nori rolls, the chef piles the filling on to a fresh perilla leaf, combines it with a neat ball of rice and twists a cone of nori around it, all in a second, then hands it across the bar with a flourish. Having received your nori cone, you have no option but to eat it; if you put it down it falls apart. I have not yet mastered the art of eating one elegantly. Any of the fillings for nori rolls may be used, but natto is a classic. I have suggested a small lettuce leaf as a substitute for perilla leaf, but if it can be found, the fresh taste of perilla is incomparable.

1 packet natto (3½oz, 100g)
2 sheets nori seaweed
6oz (170g) prepared sushi rice (page 260)
4 fresh perilla leaves or 4 small lettuce leaves
a little freshly made wasabi horseradish (optional)
rice vinegar
soy sauce

Chop the natto coarsely and divide into 4 portions. Toast the nori lightly and cut each sheet in half with scissors to make 4 long rectangular sheets. With moistened hands, take a quarter of the sushi rice and shape into an oval; repeat with the remaining rice to make 3 more ovals. Wash the perilla or lettuce leaves and pat dry.

Pile 1 portion of natto into the centre of a perilla or lettuce leaf, and fold the leaf to enclose the filling. With moistened hands take 1 ball of rice and dab with a little wasabi if you like; press it gently around the leaf, leaving the top of the leaf free. Wrap the nori firmly around the rice to form a cone and twist to close the bottom. Seal the edge with a dab of rice vinegar.

Serve immediately with a small dish of soy sauce for dipping.

Eggs

In Japan eggs are sold in tens, not in dozens or half dozens. As well as hens' eggs, shops and supermarkets sell tiny, speckled quails' eggs, about 1 in (2½ cm) long. Although dairy products are not part of the traditional Japanese diet, eggs are often used, in the Buddhist vegetarian cuisine of the temples as much as in the home. In some of the most basic and delicious dishes of the Japanese repertoire, eggs are transformed into golden threads, paper-thin omelettes to hold sushi rice, pale yellow rectangular blocks, or the lightest, most delicate savoury custard imaginable. They also appear in more robust dishes, as a savoury topping for rice or in thick, pancake-like omelettes. Like many Japanese dishes, egg dishes are often served at room temperature, so that the flavour emerges more clearly. Although this goes against the grain with Westerners, it is worth acquiring the habit; the taste of many Japanese egg dishes becomes stronger as they cool, and they remain delicate and not at all leathery.

At breakfast time in Japan you will find beside your plate an unbroken raw egg, and this is another Japanese taste worth persevering with. After eating some of your rice, you break the egg into the rest, add a little soy sauce, stir the mixture around with your chopsticks, and then raise the bowl to your lips to eat it.

The most important point to remember when cooking eggs the Japanese way is that they are rarely beaten to a froth: they are usually only lightly stirred to give a smooth texture.

When whole, hardboiled eggs are required, quails' eggs are often used in preference to hens' eggs; they may be threaded on to skewers and used in one-pot dishes, or coloured and shaped to make decorative garnishes. Fresh quails' eggs are sold in

Chinese and other specialist shops in England, and tinned
hardboiled eggs can sometimes be found in delicatessens.

ROLLED OMELETTE

In the rarefied world of the sushi shops, this light, slightly
sweet rolled omelette is said to be the test of a good chef, and
the connoisseur checks the quality of a new sushi shop by
tasting the rolled omelette. A Japanese rectangular omelette
pan is part of every cook's equipment: it ensures a neat
symmetrical roll and makes the rolling process easier. However, the omelette can also be made in a round omlette pan
and trimmed. A bamboo rolling mat helps to shape the roll.
Reduce the quantity of dashi to make the omelette easier to
roll.

4 eggs
4 fl oz (115 ml) dashi (page 143)
½ tsp salt
½ tsp sugar or honey
splash of sake or mirin (optional)
vegetable oil
2 tbsps grated daikon radish
soy sauce

Combine the eggs, dashi, salt, sugar or honey and sake or
mirin (if used) in a jug and mix together lightly so that the eggs
do not become frothy; if the eggs are overbeaten, the roll will
be heavy. These quantities will make 2 rolls.
   Heat a rectangular or small round omelette pan over medium
heat and brush with oil. Pour in just enough of the egg mixture
to coat the pan, tilting the pan so that the mixture forms an
even layer. The egg should cook quickly, but not burn or
bubble up. As soon as the mixture is set, roll the omelette
towards you with chopsticks or a spatula, to form a roll at the
front of the pan. Push the roll to the back of the pan, brush the
pan with oil, and pour in a little more of the egg mixture to
coat the pan. Lift the roll you have just made slightly so that the
egg mixture flows underneath it. As soon as this mixture has
set, roll the omelette towards you. enclosing the first roll inside
the second. Push the new, thicker roll to the back of the pan,

and continue in the same way until half the egg mixture is used, and you have a thick firm roll. Remove the omelette from the pan and roll in a bamboo rolling mat; press gently and leave to rest for 1 minute. Then remove from the mat and slice into ¾in (2cm) pieces. Make a second roll with the remaining mixture in the same way. Squeeze the grated daikon radish lightly to drain it, and flavour with a few drops of soy sauce. Arrange 2 or 3 slices of rolled omelette on each small plate, and garnish with daikon radish.

ROLLED OMELETTE WITH NORI

Nori seaweed is sometimes rolled up with the rolled omelette so that each slice has a dark-green spiral pattern.

ingredients for rolled omelette (page 243)
4 sheets nori

Toast the nori lightly and trim to fit your rectangular pan. Make the rolled omelette as on page 243; before you roll the egg the first time, lay a sheet of nori over it and roll with the omelette. Repeat with the second layer of egg. Complete the omelette as above and slice to reveal the spiral.

ROLLED OMELETTE WITH SPINACH

ingredients for rolled omelette (page 243)
12 leaves spinach

Steam the spinach leaves until wilted, and pat dry. Make the rolled omelette as on page 241, spreading 3 leaves of spinach over the egg before the first and second rollings, and rolling the spinach up with the omelette. Each slice will have a dark-green spiral of spinach.

ROLLED OMELETTE WITH VEGETABLES

Small or finely chopped vegetables are often incorporated into rolled omelettes to make an attractive contrast of colour and texture. This makes the rolling process a little more difficult.

½oz (15 g) of one of the following: peas, sweetcorn, small carrot
   cubes, green pepper cubes, or finely sliced French beans
ingredients for rolled omelette (page 243)

Parboil the vegetables, drain and pat dry. Combine the omelette ingredients and stir in the vegetables. Make the rolled omelette as on page 243, distributing the vegetables evenly and rolling each layer with care. Slice and serve.

EGG SUSHI

Slices of rolled omelette are pressed on to vinegared rice to make one of the most delicious sushis, a staple of the sushi shops.

2 prepared rolled omelettes (page 243)
1 sheet nori seaweed
1 lb (450 g) prepared sushi rice (see page 260)
a little rice vinegar
soy sauce

Prepare a rolled omelette as on page 243, roll in a bamboo

rolling mat and press gently to form a rectangle; leave for a few minutes to rest. Lightly toast the nori and cut with scissors into ¼–½in (¾–1 cm) strips. Remove the omelette from the mat and cut into ½in (1 cm) slices. Wrap a strip of nori around the middle of each slice, trimming the nori to fit and moistening the ends with vinegar to seal. Moisten your hands with a little vinegar, take a handful (about 1oz, 30g) of rice, and press firmly into a rectangle. Press a slice of omelette on to the rice. Continue in the same way until all the rice and omelette slices are used. Serve the egg sushis in pairs, sushi-shop style, with a little soy sauce in a tiny saucer to dip. Sushi is the one food that can be eaten with the hands in Japan.

EGG WRAPPERS

Egg wrappers are thin omelettes , rectangular or square, which are used like nori seaweed to roll or wrap rice and vegetables.

6 eggs
2 egg yolks
pinch potato starch (katakuriko) dissolved in a little water
½ tsp salt
a dash of sake and mirin (optional)
vegetable oil

Combine all the ingredients except the oil and stir together lightly; do not beat. Brush a rectangular or 8in (20 cm) round omelette pan with oil and heat. Over high heat, pour in just enough egg mixture to coat the surface, tilting the pan so that the egg mixture forms an even layer. When the edges begin to curl and the surface is dry, shake the pan to loosen the omelette and remove with a fish slice. Lay the omelette flat to cool, gently spreading it if necessary. Oil the pan again and continue until all the egg mixture is used; the quantities given will make about 8–10 omelettes. Cool the omelettes separately; do not stack. Trim round omelettes to form rectangles or squares according to the recipe.

EGG STRANDS

Egg strands are part of the repertoire of every Japanese cook. They make an attractive pale yellow garnish, and are much used as a salad ingredient and to top vinegared rice.

ingredients for egg wrappers as above

Prepare egg wrappers as above and allow to cool. Halve 3 or 4 sheets, stack, and slice finely to make strands. Or roll up single round omelettes and slice across into fine strands.

OKONOMIYAKI: THICK VEGETABLE PANCAKE

Kyoto is a city of contrasts: noise and bustle and silent Zen temples. On a winter evening, businessmen gather to unwind in the restaurants near Gion, the pleasure quarter. One of the most popular places to eat is the okonomiyaki restaurant. Outside, the river Kamo quietly flows and the hills surrounding Kyoto loom in the darkness. But within, all is noise, bustle and smoke, as beer bottles open and sake flows.

Okonomiyaki means 'bake to your taste', and the customers cook their own fat vegetable pancakes. Sitting with their feet tucked under low tables with a cast-iron surface heated from below, men who would never dream of entering the kitchen in their own homes lavishly slap a rather dubious-looking dark oil on to the cast-iron surface with a brush big enough to paint a wall. They then order their own selection of vegetables, which come in a bowl with a little flour, and a raw egg broken on top. They mix it all together with chopsticks, pour the mixture on

to the hot surface, and tend it lovingly, carefully patting, cutting and turning it to see if it is done, waiting until both sides are brown and crisp, and finally smothering it in thick, sweetened soy sauce and sprinkling over fish flakes, powdered nori seaweed or dried herbs. Finally they proudly eat the surprisingly delicious result of their efforts.

These thick vegetable pancakes may be prepared at home using a cast-iron frying pan. They are cooked over lower heat than an ordinary pancake or omelette.

4 oz (115 g) cabbage
1 carrot
1 leek
½ green pepper
4 oz (115 g) tofu, drained
3 eggs
2 oz (60 g) plain white or wholemeal flour
3 fl oz (90 ml) dashi (page 143)
2 tsps light soy sauce
vegetable oil

garnishes
sweetened soy sauce (see Vegetable Barbecue, page 154) or 4 fl oz (120 ml) dark soy sauce mixed with 1–2 fl oz (30–60 ml) sugar or honey
nori seaweed, toasted and crumbled
toasted sesame seeds
red pickled ginger

Wash, trim and shred the vegetables, and pat dry with absorbent paper. Cut the tofu into ½ in (1 cm) cubes. Prepare the garnishes. Over low heat brush a heavy frying pan with oil. Combine the vegetables and tofu with the eggs, flour, dashi and soy sauce in a bowl, and pour half the mixture into the frying pan. Smooth and spread it with a fish slice or wooden rice paddle. Cook for 5 minutes, then quarter the pancake and carefully flip over each quarter. Cook for another 5 minutes, until the pancake is browned on both sides. Make a second pancake with the remaining mixture. Serve portions of pancake on small individual plates, and arrange the garnishes on the table to be used freely.

Any firm vegetables, such as sweetcorn, peas and French beans, are delicious in this pancake.

CHAWAN MUSHI: STEAMED VEGETABLE CUSTARD

Whether you visit the humblest of homes or dine in style in a
Kyoto restaurant, you will probably be served a delicately
flavoured savoury custard with morsels of vegetable and
tofu in a small lidded cup. Chawan mushi, 'steamed dish in a
cup', is a classic Japanese dish. It is usually served piping hot towards the end of the meal, and should be left covered until you
are ready to eat (you replace the lid to show that you have
finished); it is one of the few Japanese dishes which is eaten
with a spoon instead of chopsticks. No Japanese kitchen would
be complete without a set of chawan mushi dishes, handleless
cups a little larger than a teacup with loosely fitting lids.
Although less aesthetically pleasing, chawan mushi may be
made in ordinary mugs or ramekins, tightly lidded with foil.
To cook them use either a steamer or a large saucepan filled
with enough water to come halfway up the cups: lay a cloth
under the saucepan lid before using. The vegetables used
depend on the season and on the cook; here is one version using
some favourite Japanese ingredients.

8 large flat mushrooms, wiped and trimmed
1 small carrot
1 young leek
8 mangetout peas
4 oz (115 g) tofu
4 gingko nuts (optional)

custard
1 pt (600 ml) dashi (page 143)
3 eggs
1 tbsp soy sauce

garnish
slivers of lemon peel
sprigs of watercress

Wash and trim the vegetables. Remove the mushroom stems
and halve the caps. Cut the carrot into plum blossoms (see page
64) and finely slice the leek. Top and tail the mangetout peas,
parboil and drain. Cut the tofu into ½ in (1 cm) cubes. Shell the
gingko nuts, if used, boil and skin. Divide the vegetables

between 4 cups or mugs, to fill not more than three-quarters of the cup.

Heat the dashi slightly; it should be warm but not hot. Mix the eggs very lightly so that they do not become frothy and stir in the warm dashi and soy sauce. Pour the egg mixture over the vegetables in the cups. Float a few watercress leaves and 2 slivers of lemon peel on each.

Cover each cup with a lid or foil and steam in a preheated steamer or large saucepan over medium heat for 13–15 minutes, until the custard is just set; it will still be very soft. Serve immediately.

MOUNT KOYA CHAWAN MUSHI

Shingon Buddhism, the most colourful as well as the largest Buddhist sect in Japan, is based on Mount Koya, a mountain covered with temples and vast temple complexes, some set aside to lodge and feed the vast numbers of pilgrims and students who arrive all year round. As might be expected with such a concentration of Buddhist monks, a distinctive vegetarian cuisine has developed. The rich chawan mushi made here uses tofu and mushrooms.

6oz (170g) tofu, lightly drained
1 tsp sake
1 tbsp light soy sauce
4 large flat mushrooms, wiped and trimmed
17 floz (500ml) dashi (page 143)
1 tsp sugar or honey
1 tsp sesame oil
4 leaves spinach or 4 sprigs watercress
4 eggs
½ tsp salt
slivered lemon peel

Cut the tofu into small (½in, 1cm) cubes and sprinkle with the sake and 1 tsp soy sauce. Set aside for a few minutes to marinate. Cut off and discard the mushroom stems, and cut a cross in the top of each mushroom cap. In a small saucepan, combine the remaining 2 tsps soy sauce, 1½ floz (50ml)dashi, sugar or honey and sesame oil. Add the mushroom caps and simmer for a few minutes, basting them with the stock. Remove from the heat and leave to cool in the stock. Cut the spinach into ½in (1 cm) strips or break the watercress into small sprigs; wash and pat dry.

Mix the eggs lightly so that they do not become frothy and stir in the remaining 15½ floz (450ml) dashi and the salt.

Divide the tofu between 4 cups. Remove the mushrooms from the stock with chopsticks or a slotted spoon and put 1 mushroom in each cup. Pour the egg mixture into the cups, place a little spinach or watercress in each, and spoon over a little of the mushroom stock.

Cover each cup with a loose lid or foil and place in a preheated steamer or large saucepan filled with boiling water to come halfway up the cups. Place a cloth under the steamer or saucepan lid. Steam over medium heat for 11–13 minutes, until the custard is just set. Add a few slivers lemon peel to each cup just before steaming finishes.

Serve covered; the custard will remain hot for quite a long time.

TAMAGO DOFU: EGG 'TOFU'

Gifu is set in a ring of mountains, and summer there is particularly hot and oppressive. Many a time, as we sat languidly fanning ourselves, our hostess would appear with a tray of small bowls containing pale yellow squares of egg 'tofu', surrounded with a little pale sauce and topped with a single tiny leaf. This delicate and very soft steamed egg custard resembles tofu in its shape and texture, but actually contains no tofu at all.

Making egg 'tofu' successfully requires a little care. The

Japanese use a small square pan with a removable base, also used for yokan (aduki bean jelly). This can be improvised by lining a straight-sided square or oblong pan such as a 1 lb loaf tin with foil, keeping it as smooth as possible. The custard needs to be cooked extremely slowly so that it does not puff up or bubble, and should be removed from the heat as soon as it is just set.

4 eggs
16 fl oz (450 ml) dashi (page 143) (see recipe)
¼ tsp salt
¼ tsp sugar or honey

sauce
4 fl oz (115 ml) dashi
1 tsp sugar or honey
1 tbsp sake or mirin (optional)
1½ tbsps light soy sauce

garnish
4 coriander leaves or 4 sprigs parsley

Break the eggs into a measuring jug and add exactly twice as much dashi by volume. Stir lightly, trying not to create any bubbles; add the salt and sugar or honey. Line the walls and base of a small, deep, straight-sided baking dish or 1 lb loaf tin with foil, as smoothly as possible. Pour in the egg mixture to a depth of 1½–2 in (4–5 cm), to fill the dish two-thirds full. Lightly cover the top of the dish with foil.

Place the baking dish in a preheated steamer or saucepan of water, setting a towel under the lid to absorb moisture. Steam at lowest possible heat for 20 minutes, until a toothpick comes out clean. The egg should be just set, and there will still be a little free water around the custard.

Remove from the steamer and place in cold water. Slide a knife around the edge of the dish and either remove sides of tin or gently lift the foil lining out of the tin. Place a plate over the egg 'tofu', and invert to turn it on to the plate. Ease away the tin base or foil and refrigerate to cool.

Combine the sauce ingredients in small saucepan and bring to the boil, stirring to dissolve the sugar or honey. Cool and refrigerate.

To serve, cut the egg 'tofu' into 2 in (5 cm) squares, and place

1 or 2 squares, with the top, smooth side uppermost, in small deep bowls. Spoon over a little sauce and top with a coriander leaf or tiny sprig of parsley. A little lemon rind or grated ginger may also be used as a garnish.

Part Three

GRAINS

Rice

At the end of every Japanese meal, be it breakfast, lunch or dinner, when everyone has had their fill of the rich and savoury dishes, the tiny plates and bowls are cleared away and the hostess brings in a lacquered wooden tub of steaming rice, which she scoops into delicate porcelain bowls with a wooden paddle. No matter how many side dishes there are, the meal will not be complete, or the diner feel satisfied, without at least one bowlful of rice. To the Japanese way of thinking, rice and food are one and the same, and the same word, 'gohan', is used for both. Rice provides the true sustenance, and all the dishes which precede it are seen almost as an extended *hors d'œuvre*. No food in the West holds the same central place; it is much more of a staple than bread or wheat is to us.

Every spare inch of land in the flat plain of central and southern Japan is used for rice cultivation. The path from the bus stop to the school where I taught in Gifu wound through paddy-fields, and there are even small paddy-fields overshadowed by skyscrapers in the suburbs of Tokyo. In spring I would pass women in boots standing knee-deep in water in the flooded fields, planting out rows of rice plants, which would shoot up during the hot and steamy rainy season. Even the smallest village has a rice shop, full of sacks of different varieties and qualities of rice, and a noisy machine for milling.

Rice is a precious food in Japan. The samurai used to receive their monthly stipend in rice; and every child learns that the very last grain in his or her bowl must be eaten. It is served alone, unmixed with other foods, so that the delicate flavour of each grain can be fully savoured. The connoisseur can identify the particular region of Japan that it comes from, and everyone can appreciate the flavour of 'new rice', freshly harvested, which appears in the autumn.

The rice which is used in Japan is short grained, not the long-grain rice used in Chinese and Indian cookery and more common in England. Most people still prefer white rice, although brown rice, traditionally the food of Zen monks, is often served in the restaurants in Zen temples, and is popular among young people and vegetarians. Rice is always cooked until it is very soft and clings together, so that it is easy to eat with chopsticks.

As well as being the most basic food, rice is also the most special food, for celebrations and festivals – the dishes which are the equivalent of our Christmas dinner are based on it. At any of the great annual festivals you will eat freshly pounded rice cakes. Rice, usually in the form of rice wine, sake, is the most acceptable offering to the Shinto deities, who are said to be perhaps a little too fond of it.

Short-grain white or brown rice is ideal for Japanese recipes. Japanese and some Chinese shops stock a variety of Japanese and American short-grain white rice specifically for Japanese cookery, under names such as Kotobuki Rice or Kokuho Rice; white pudding rice, which is widely available, is also suitable, and makes good sushi rice. If you have difficulty finding short-grain rice, serve any white rice or short-grain brown rice to accompany a Japanese meal.

COOKING WHITE RICE

To most Japanese, rice is white rice, pure and glistening, and not just any rice but Japanese rice. Sushi in Japan is invariably made with white rice. Most Japanese cooks use an electric rice cooker, which boils and steams, producing perfect rice every time, and keeping it hot and ready to eat all day long, saving time and hob space. Traditionally rice was cooked in a large cast-iron saucepan with a wooden lid and transferred to a wide, shallow wooden tub to serve. The crust at the bottom of the rice pot is said to be the most delicious part.

In Japan rice is always washed a good 30 minutes before cooking, and either soaked or left to drain in a colander. The lid of the pot should never be removed while the rice is cooking, and the rice should be left on the cooker with the heat off to steam in its own retained heat for 15 minutes before serving.

Japanese cooks allow 4 oz (115 g) rice per person, which gives very large portions. In the West we tend to eat less; 10 oz (285 g) is ample for 4 people. The exact amount of water required varies according to the type of rice and the season; as a rule of thumb, allow 1 part rice to 1¼ parts water by volume.

10 oz (285 g) short-grain white rice
17 fl oz (500 ml) water
pinch salt (optional)

Wash the rice well about 1 hour before cooking, stirring and rinsing several times until the rinsing water is clear. Either leave to drain in a colander or soak in the measured cooking water for 1 hour.

Combine the rice with the measured water and salt, if you like, in a heavy saucepan with a closely fitting lid. Put a clean tea towel under the lid to retain the steam, taking care to fold it so that its ends are away from the heat. Cover and bring to the boil over high heat. Simmer for 5 minutes over medium heat; then reduce the heat to very low and leave the rice for 15 minutes to steam. Finally turn off the heat but leave the rice tightly covered on the cooker for another 15 minutes; this makes it fluffy. Either stir and serve immediately or transfer into a large, preferably wooden container and cover with a damp clean cloth.

SUSHI RICE

Sushi seems to be a uniquely Japanese invention. Rice is lightly vinegared (perhaps originally to preserve it) and combined with vegetables to make a variety of stylish and colourful dishes, including thick and thin nori rolls, stuffed tofu pouches and rolled omelette on rice. Sushi is quick and simple to assemble and, as it is always served at room temperature, can be prepared well before the meal. In Japan sushi is one of the most popular party foods. For almost any celebration or special occasion, the hostess will prepare sushi or send to the local sushi shop for a large tray of colourful assorted sushi, which one of the apprentices will bring, wobbling precariously on his bicycle. Sushi may be served as a complete meal, as part of a meal, or as a snack; but it is always a rather special food.

To make standard sushi rice, vinegar sweetened with a little sugar is sprinkled on to freshly cooked white rice spread in a shallow wooden tub, and the rice is tossed and fanned at the same time, so that each grain remains separate and cools as quickly as possible to give a glossy sheen.

10 oz (285 g) short-grain white rice
15 fl oz (450 ml) water
2½–3 tbsps rice vinegar
1–2 tbsps sake or mirin (optional)
2–3 tbsps sugar
1½ tsps salt

Cook the rice in the water as described on page 259. Combine the vinegar, sake or mirin, sugar and salt in a small saucepan and heat to dissolve the sugar and salt; allow to cool to room temperature.

When the rice has rested, spread it out in a wide, shallow container. In Japan a special wooden tub is used, but any large bowl will do. Sprinkle the vinegar mixture over it, and quickly and lightly cut and toss with a wooden rice paddle or spoon, using a cutting movement and tossing the rice so that it cools quickly. Ideally you should fan the rice as you toss it. Cover the rice with a damp cloth and leave for 5–10 minutes to fluff before serving.

It is best to use sushi rice immediately; otherwise leave it covered with a damp cloth until you need it and use within a few hours.

COOKING BROWN RICE

If you are going to use brown rice, short grain is best for Japanese dishes, and should be cooked until it is quite soft and not too chewy. Soak the rice for at least 30 minutes, preferably longer and use soy sauce rather than salt to make it tastier. Brown rice is not as sensitive as white, and boiling water may be added during cooking if necessary.

10oz (285 g) short-grain brown rice
2 tsps soy sauce
15 fl oz (450 ml) water

Wash the rice in plenty of cold water; stir well, allow to settle, and wash away the floating husks. Wash several times more, until the rinsing water is clear. Put the rice evenly in a saucepan and add the measured water and soy sauce. Set aside to soak for at least 30 minutes.

Cover and bring to the boil over high heat. Turn the heat down very low and cook, covered, without stirring, for 40–50 minutes. To check the rice take a few grains from the centre without disturbing the rest; if they are not cooked and the water has all been absorbed, add a little more boiling water. When the rice is cooked, turn off the heat and leave the pan, tightly covered, for 5–10 minutes. Stir well and serve.

To serve at table, transfer the rice into a large, preferably wooden, container, and cover with a damp cloth.

SUSHI RICE USING BROWN RICE

In Japan sushi is always made with white rice, but I find that brown rice has the chewy quality that afficionados demand and makes a delicious and tasty sushi.

To make it you can either stir a little rice vinegar, honey, soy sauce (and maybe a dash of mirin or sake) into hot, freshly cooked rice or, more orthodoxly, follow the method below.

10oz (285g) short-grain brown rice
2 tsps soy sauce
15 fl oz (450ml) water
2½ tbsps rice vinegar
1½–2 tbsps sugar or honey
2 tsps soy sauce
a dash of sake or mirin (optional)

Cook the rice in soy sauce and water as described on page 261. Combine the vinegar, sugar or honey, soy sauce and sake or mirin in a small saucepan and heat to dissolve the sugar or honey. Cool to room temperature.

When the rice has rested, turn it into a wide shallow container. Sprinkle the vinegar mixture over the rice, and lightly mix in with a wooden rice paddle or spoon, using a cutting movement and tossing the rice so that it cools quickly. Ideally you should fan the rice as you toss it. Cover with a damp cloth and leave for 5–10 minutes to fluff before serving.

Use sushi rice immediately, or leave covered with the damp cloth until ready to use.

RICE BALLS

Japanese cooks always cook plenty of rice and after the meal, while the rice is still quite hot, make some of it into rice balls for the following day. Rice balls make a quick and wholesome snack for lunch at school or the office, and are a favourite picnic food. They are usually made with plain rice, but sushi rice can be used and is particularly tasty. There are two secrets to making rice balls: firstly, use soft, well-cooked rice, and make the balls while the rice is still hot; secondly, keep your hands wet to stop the rice sticking.

1 lb (450 g) cooked rice or prepared sushi rice
  (pages 259–62)
2 tbsps toasted sesame seeds
soy sauce

With wet hands, take a handful (about 2 oz, 60 g) of rice, and
press firmly and quickly with both hands to make a triangular
or oval shape. In Japan rice balls are usually triangular, and you
will find that a triangular shape seems to come most naturally
from the squeezing process. Squeeze the rice quite firmly to
make it hold together.

The rice balls may be rolled in toasted sesame seeds if you
wish; once you have acquired the Japanese taste for plain rice
you may prefer them as they are, with just a little soy sauce to
dip.

Wrapped in cling film and kept in a cool place, rice balls will
keep for 2–3 days.

TOASTED RICE BALLS

Make rice cakes as above, omitting the sesame seeds, and shape
into flattened ovals. Toast over high heat, turning once, until
the outside is brown and crunchy. Serve immediately with soy
sauce to dip for a quick lunch or snack.

STUFFED RICE BALLS

In Japan snacks tend to be savoury rather than sweet, and a
popular snack is a rice ball wrapped in seaweed with, right at
the centre, a pickled plum or a few shreds of chopped pickle.
The pickle gives a piquant flavour, and helps to preserve the
rice.

1 lb (450 g) cooked rice
4 sheets nori seaweed
4 pickled plums (umeboshi)
1 oz (30 g) Japanese pickle

Prepare the rice and keep it hot. Toast the nori seaweed and cut
each sheet in half to make 2 rectangles. Cut open the pickled
plums and remove the stones. Chop the Japanese pickle finely.

With wet hands, take a handful (about 2oz, 60g) of rice, put a plum or a little chopped pickle in the middle, and squeeze firmly to form a triangular shape. Wrap the rice ball in nori, and leave folded side down to cool. Make 7 more rice balls with the remaining ingredients.

The rice balls can also be made by simply laying a whole sheet of toasted nori on a working surface, and spooning 2–3 tbsps (2oz, 60g) of cooked rice into the centre of the sheet. Place a stoned plum or a little pickle in the middle of the rice and fold the nori firmly to enclose the rice in a triangular packet, tucking in the corners neatly.

Rice balls can be eaten immediately, or wrapped in cling film to keep for a few days.

Natto and dried perilla leaves are also popular fillings.

COLOURED RICE

Vegetables, beans or deep-fried tofu, chosen to reflect the season, are often cooked together with rice to colour and subtly flavour it. Rice cooked in this way is served instead of plain rice, often when entertaining guests or on special occasions. Aduki beans, chestnuts and mushrooms are particularly popular; see pages 74, 101, 182. The following recipe is known as Five Colour Rice; five ingredients are cooked with the rice, in richly flavoured dashi.

8oz (225g) short-grain white or brown rice
½ medium carrot
1oz (30g) bamboo shoot
¼ sheet thin deep-fried tofu
2 dried mushrooms, softened in water (see pages 95–6)
¼ cake konnyaku
10–12 floz (300–360ml) dashi (page 143)
1–2 tbsps soy sauce
1 tsp sugar or honey
1–2 tbsps mirin or sake

Wash the rice thoroughly, drain, and soak in fresh water for 1–2 hours. Scrape and dice the carrot. Quarter the bamboo shoot lengthwise and slice finely. Rinse the deep-fried tofu in boiling water to remove oil and cut into matchsticks. Cut off the mushroom stems and slice the caps finely. Cut the konnyaku into julienne strips.

Drain the rice and put into a heavy bottomed saucepan. Spread vegetables, tofu and konnyaku over the rice. Mix together the dashi, soy sauce, sugar or honey and mirin or sake and pour over. Cover with a heavy lid with a tea towel under it and set aside for 10 minutes to allow the flavours to marry.

Bring to the boil and simmer, covered, over very low heat for 20–25 minutes for white rice and 40–50 minutes for brown until the rice and vegetables are cooked. Check the rice towards the end of cooking and add a little more dashi if necessary. When cooked, leave tightly covered off the heat for 10 minutes to steam, then mix the vegetables into the rice before serving.

DOMBURI: TOFU AND EGGS ON RICE

Domburi is a dish from the streets and countryside of Japan, not from the temples. It is a hearty bowlful of rice topped with a rich soupy mixture of vegetables and eggs, whose juices seep into and flavour the rice. Small stalls all over Japan serve it up in big lidded bowls twice the size of a porcelain rice bowl, and many a mother produces a wholesome lunch from leftovers in this way. Different toppings can be served on rice; tendon (tempura domburi) is another favourite. Serve domburi in large deep cereal or soup bowls.

10 oz (285 g) short-grain white or brown rice
17 fl oz (500 ml) water
pinch salt (optional)
8 oz (225 g) tofu, drained for 30 minutes
4 tsps light soy sauce
1 small leek
2 small carrots
2 fresh mushrooms
6 fl oz (240 ml) dashi (page 143)
1 tsp sugar or honey
1 tbsp mirin
4 eggs
½ sheet nori seaweed, lightly toasted

Cook the rice with the water and salt as on pages 259 and 261.

Prepare the topping while the rice is cooking.

Cut the tofu into 1 in (2½ cm) cubes, sprinkle with 1 tsp soy sauce, and set aside to marinate. Wash and trim the vegetables. Cut the leek on the diagonal into 2 in (5 cm) slices. Cut the carrots into matchsticks and slice the mushrooms.

Combine the dashi, sugar or honey, mirin and remaining 3 tsps soy sauce in a small saucepan and bring to a simmer. Add the leeks and carrots, cover and simmer for 2–3 minutes, until the vegetables are nearly tender. Add the tofu and mushrooms, bring just to a simmer and cook for another minute.

Lightly mix the eggs with chopsticks and slowly pour over the vegetables. Do not stir. When the egg begins to set, stir once; the egg will still be slightly runny. Cover and remove from heat.

Warm 4 deep bowls and fill two-thirds full with the hot rice. Ladle the egg mixture over the rice. Cut the nori with scissors into thin strips and scatter a few strips over each bowl.

Served piping hot with Japanese tea and a clear soup or pickles, domburi is a meal in itself.

NORI ROLLS (NORIMAKI)

Many people's first experience of Japanese food is norimaki, for these little vegetable-filled rolls of sushi rice wrapped in nori seem to be particularly representative of Japanese food, and are often offered to Western guests. The typical Japanese meal served on Japan Airlines always includes a plate of nori rolls, either the thin cylindrical rolls with a single vegetable filling or the thick wheel-like rolls with a multi-coloured hub of different vegetables.

Nori rolls could be described as a Japanese alternative to the sandwich, although they are rather more nutritious and better tasting. Like the sandwich, the variety of possible fillings is practically endless; Californian sushi chefs have come up with all manner of outlandish combinations, some of which, like avocado and lettuce, are even becoming popular in Japan. And, like the sandwich, one makes a snack, a few make a side dish, and a variety of different nori rolls is a complete meal. Each part of Japan has its own typical nori rolls, square in the east and round in the west, small and tidy in the city and fat and filled with all manner of wondrous ingredients in the countryside.

Below I give general instructions for making nori rolls, followed by suggestions for fillings, to be used singly or in combination. I also give some classic Japanese combinations. However, for Westerners, who are less concerned than the Japanese with perpetuating culinary traditions, the range of fillings for nori rolls is limited only by our imagination. The following quantities will give enough nori rolls to serve 4 as part of a Japanese meal or 6 as a snack.

sushi rice prepared from 10 oz (285 g) uncooked rice
fillings: see pages 268–70
4 sheets nori seaweed
3 tbsps rice vinegar
sprigs of parsley or watercress
red pickled ginger
soy sauce

Cook the rice as described on pages 260, 262. While the rice is cooking, prepare a variety of fillings (see below). Prepare the sushi rice and cover with a damp cotton cloth to keep it warm. Toast the nori lightly to bring out the aroma; it should not change colour or become crisp.

Japanese cooks use a bamboo rolling mat for making nori rolls; this is helpful but not essential. Lay 1 sheet of nori on a rolling mat or on a working surface. With a wooden rice paddle or with moistened hands, spread a layer of rice over the nori: for country-style rolls use about 6 oz (170 g) rice to make a strip 4 in (10 cm) wide at the front edge; for thinner rolls, use 3 oz (85 g) to make a 2 in (5 cm) strip. Wet your hands again and pressing so that the grains of rice stick together, spread the rice right to the sides and front of the nori.

Lay the selected filling(s) in a line along the centre of the rice, trimming the ends neatly. Holding the ingredients in place with your fingers, firmly roll the rice and nori around the fillings, using your thumbs to roll. The bamboo mat will help to ensure a firm and even roll. After rolling, dab a little vinegar along the loose edge of the nori sheet and press the roll firmly down on the moistened edge to seal. If using a bamboo mat,

gently press the mat around the roll to shape it. Leave the roll
with sealed edge downwards while you make 3 more in the
same way.

Moisten a sharp knife and cut each roll into 6–8 slices; wet
the knife again between each slice. Cut either straight downwards or on the diagonal to emphasise the colour contrasts of
the green nori, the rice and the filling. The rolls may be
arranged on one large serving platter or in individual portions;
thin nori rolls are usually served in groups of 6. Garnish with
sprigs of fresh parsley or watercress and small mounds of red
pickled ginger, and serve with soy sauce to dip.

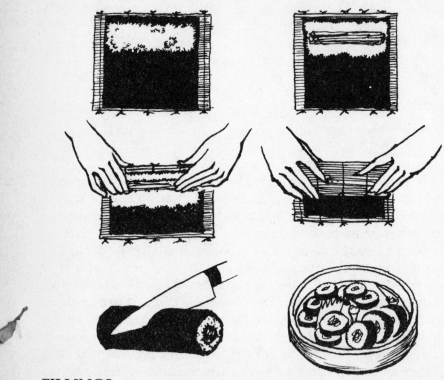

FILLINGS

To make authentic Japanese nori rolls, use 1 filling with 3 oz
(85 g) rice to make a thin, city-style nori roll, and precisely 5
fillings with 6 oz (170 g) rice to make a fat, country-style roll.
But of course you may use 2 or 3 if you wish. Complete recipes
for some nori rolls with classic vegetable fillings are included in
the vegetable section under the vegetable.

The following are the fillings which are traditionally used alone in thin nori rolls; they are also used in thick rolls.

1. Cucumber (page 84).
2. Natto (page 240).
3. Egg. Make 1 rolled omelette using 2 eggs (see page 243). Allow to cool and cut into long thin strips ⅜ × ⅜ in (1 × 1 cm) thick.
4. Strips of gourd ribbon (kampyo). ½ packet (⅔ oz, 20 g) is ample. Knead the gourd ribbon in a bowl with a little salt, adding a little water to make this easier. Then just cover with water and leave to soften for 30 minutes. Rinse well and squeeze gently. Simmer in enough dashi to cover (8–10 fl oz, 250–300 ml) (page 143) seasoned with 2½ tbsps dark soy sauce, 2 tsps sugar or honey and a little sake or mirin for 30 minutes. Leave to cool in the stock, then drain well and cut into 7 in (18 cm) lengths. This is a particularly delicious filling for nori rolls.
5. Japanese pickles. Shredded readymade or homemade Japanese-style pickles are a popular filling for nori rolls.
6. Red pickled ginger.

The following fillings are traditionally combined with 3 or 4 others to make thick nori rolls.

1. 4 large dried mushrooms. Soak for 30 minutes to reconstitute. Drain, remove the stems and slice the caps finely. Simmer in 4 fl oz (115 ml) dashi (page 143) seasoned with 1 tsp each of dark soy sauce, honey and with a dash of mirin or sake and sugar for 20 minutes, until the simmering stock is nearly all absorbed. Leave to cool in the cooking liquid, then drain.
2. 2 cakes dried tofu (koya dofu). Soak in warm water for a few minutes, then squeeze in water and rinse several times until the water is clear. Simmer in 7 fl oz (200 ml) dashi (page 143) seasoned with 1 tsp each of light soy sauce and sugar or honey and 1 tbsp sake or mirin for 20 minutes until most of the liquid is absorbed. Leave to cool in the cooking liquid, then drain and cut each cake into 6 strips.
3. 1 sheet deep-fried tofu. Rinse in boiling water to remove oil and slice into long thin strips. Simmer for 10 minutes in 7 fl oz (200 ml) dashi (page 143) seasoned with 2 tsps each of sugar or honey, light soy sauce, 1 tbsp sake or mirin and ¼ tsp salt. Leave to cool in the cooking liquid, then drain.

4. 4 oz (115 g) spinach or watercress. Separate into individual leaves and parboil for 1–2 minutes until wilted; plunge into cold water, then drain and pat lightly with absorbent paper.

5. 8–12 French beans. Top and tail, and cook as for spinach.

6. 1 medium carrot. Wash, trim and cut into long julienne strips. Parboil for 1–2 minutes until just tender, drain and pat dry with absorbent paper.

7. 4 oz (115 g) fresh mushrooms, trimmed, brushed with oil and lightly grilled or sautéed in sesame oil, and thinly sliced.

8. Raw vegetables, such as lettuce leaves in strips or bean sprouts, trimmed, washed and patted dry. Nori rolls with raw vegetables are known as 'salad maki', salad rolls.

Sometimes a little of one of the following seasonings is sprinkled over the filling before rolling:

pickled plum (umeboshi), stoned and finely chopped
fresh or dried perilla leaves, chopped
freshly made wasabi horseradish
sesame seeds, toasted and lightly ground
sweetened miso, 'natto miso' or 'kombu miso'
finely grated lemon peel

These are the traditional Japanese fillings. Some classic Japanese combinations for thick nori rolls are: egg, dried mushrooms, dried tofu and spinach; gourd ribbon, dried mushrooms, carrot, spinach and Japanese pickles; and egg, cucumber, natto, watercress and red pickled ginger.

MRS FUJII'S COUNTRY-STYLE NORI ROLLS

Mrs Fujii lives on a tiny island which feels centuries rather than just miles away from busy Tokyo. Most unusually for a Japanese woman, she has a full-time career as a professional potter: she is the only woman that Shoji Hamada, the great potter and friend of Bernard Leach, ever accepted as an apprentice, and she makes vigorous and beautiful pots. However, when it comes to cookery, she is as traditional as any Japanese woman; for her, cooking is almost a sacred tradition. The foods for each season and the methods of cooking each food have been handed down through her family for generations, and she would never dream of innovating. When she makes nori rolls she uses the following ingredients and no others; and, because she lives in western Japan, her rolls are always round, never flattened into a square shape. Here is not Mrs Fujii's but the Fujii household's centuries-old recipe for nori rolls.

sushi rice prepared from 10 oz (285 g) uncooked rice

fillings
½ packet (⅔ oz, 20 g) dried gourd ribbon (kampyo)
simmering stock for gourd ribbon:
   7 fl oz (200 ml) dashi (page 143)
   1 tbsp dark soy sauce
   2 tsps sugar or honey
   2 tsps mirin
1 medium carrot
simmering stock for carrot:
   7 fl oz (200 ml) dashi
   1 tsp each sugar or honey, soy sauce and mirin
8 stalks trefoil or young spinach leaves
½ cucumber
salt
1 rolled omelette made with 2 eggs (see page 243)

4 sheets nori seaweed
3 tbsps rice vinegar
soy sauce

Prepare the sushi rice (see pages 260, 262); prepare the fillings while the rice is cooking.

   Put the gourd ribbon into a bowl and knead with a little salt, adding a little water to make this easier. Cover with water and leave for 30 minutes to soften. Rinse well and squeeze gently. Put the gourd ribbon into a small saucepan with the simmering stock ingredients, bring to the boil and simmer for 20 minutes until very soft. Leave to cool in the stock, then drain well and cut into 7 in (18 cm) lengths. Scrape the carrot and cut it into long thin strips; simmer in its simmering stock until soft, and drain; pat dry. Parboil the trefoil or spinach in water for 1 minute, until wilted, and dip into cold water to stop further cooking. Pat dry with absorbent paper. Halve the cucumber lengthwise and scrape out the seeds; cut into long thin strips.

Soak in lightly salted water for 20 minutes; gently squeeze out excess moisture, rinse and pat dry. Prepare the rolled omelette; allow to cool and cut into long, narrow strips.

Lightly toast the nori. Lay 1 sheet on a bamboo rolling mat (or on a working surface). Spread 6 oz (170 g) prepared sushi rice over the front half of the sheet of nori and, with wet hands, press the rice down firmly, smearing it to the sides. Make a slight indentation along the centre of the rice. Using ¼ of the total fillings, lay the omelette and cucumber strips in a line along the rice, and lay the carrot, gourd ribbon and trefoil or spinach on top of them. Roll up firmly and carefully with your thumbs so that the rice encloses the filling, holding the filling in place with your fingers. Dab a little vinegar along the far edge of the nori and press the roll firmly down on the moistened edge to seal. Press the mat gently around the roll for a few seconds to shape it, then unroll and leave with sealed edge downwards while you make 3 more rolls in the same way.

Wet a sharp knife and cut each roll in half, then cut each half into 4 slices. Arrange on individual plates and serve with small dishes of soy sauce for dipping.

EGG-WRAPPED SUSHI

Opposite the Kabuki theatre in Tokyo is a rather smart sushi shop where the audience can buy boxed lunches to sustain them during the 5 or 6 hours of the performance. This sushi shop, like others in Tokyo's fashionable Ginza district, sells not only nori rolls but sushi wrapped in paper-thin omelette squares, neatly tied around the rice like a silk handkerchief.

sushi rice prepared from 10 oz (285 g) uncooked rice
4 large dried mushrooms, soaked

simmering stock
4 fl oz (115 ml) dashi (page 143)
1 tsp each dark soy sauce and sugar or honey
1 tbsp sake or mirin

2 oz (60 g) peas, mangetout peas or French beans
salt
½ oz (15 g) red pickled ginger

egg wrappers
6 eggs
2 egg yolks
pinch potato starch (katakuriko) dissolved in a little water
½ tsp each salt, sugar or honey and light soy sauce
a little mirin or sake

vegetable oil
1 sheet nori seaweed

Prepare the rice (see pages 260, 262). While the rice is cooking, prepare the mushrooms, peas or beans and ginger.

Cut off the mushroom stems. Combine the caps with the simmering stock ingredients and bring to the boil in a small saucepan; simmer for 20 minutes, until most of the stock is absorbed. Leave to cool in the cooking liquid, then drain, reserving the cooking liquid, and dice. Wash and trim the peas, mangetout peas or beans, and parboil in lightly salted boiling water for 2–3 minutes until just tender and bright green. Drain; if using mangetout peas or beans, slice finely on the diagonal. Cut the pickled ginger into threads.

Lightly mix the vegetables into the cooled sushi rice, moistening with a little of the reserved mushroom cooking liquid.

Make 8–10 egg wrappers with the ingredients above, following the instructions on page 246.

With wet hands take a handful (about 3oz, 85g) of the flavoured sushi rice, and squeeze it gently but firmly to form a ball with a flattened base. Place in the centre of one omelette, and neatly fold the omelette around it like a parcel. Lightly toast the nori and cut with scissors into long narrow strips. Use a few strips of nori as a garnish to 'tie' the parcel. Continue in the same way with the remaining ingredients.

SUSHI PARTY

Prepare-your-own-sushi makes the perfect party food. The rice, wrappers and fillings can be prepared well in advance, providing a rest for the host or hostess; and the guests enjoy creating their own sushi. All the different ingredients make an appetising display spread on an array of attractive plates and platters, on a large table. Complement the meal with an endless supply of green tea and a little Japanese music in the background to make a memorable evening. The following quantities will be ample for 6; adjust the quantities to suit the number of guests.

sushi rice prepared from 15oz (425g) uncooked rice
8–10 sheets nori seaweed
10–12 egg wrappers prepared from 6 eggs
8–12 leaves crisp red lettuce or small round lettuce (optional)
6–8 different nori roll fillings (pages 268–70)
nori roll seasonings (page 270)
soy sauce
red pickled ginger

Prepare the rice (see pages 260, 262). Transfer to a large, wide, shallow wooden tub or a large serving bowl, and cover with a damp white cotton cloth. Provide a wooden rice paddle or spoon for serving.

Lightly toast the sheets of nori and halve with scissors to make long rectangular sheets. Prepare the egg wrappers (see page 246), and allow to cool; then stack and cut with a sharp knife to make half moons. Wash the lettuce leaves (if using) and pat dry. Arrange the nori, egg wrappers and lettuce separately on 3 large plates.

Prepare a selection of different fillings and seasonings and arrange in attractive bowls. Provide saucers or small bowls of soy sauce for dipping and small dishes of red pickled ginger.

The guests spoon a little rice on to a sheet of nori, an egg wrapper or a lettuce leaf, add 1 or more fillings, sprinkle on a little seasoning, and finally roll it all up to make their own sushi.

CHIRASHI ZUSHI: SCATTERED VEGETABLE SUSHI

Chirashi zushi, sushi rice topped with a colourful mixture of vegetables, can be simply and quickly assembled, and is often prepared at home. The rice is sometimes packed into fine lacquered wooden boxes, in which the vegetable toppings are artistically arranged, transforming it into a much more stylish dish. Any of the filling ingredients for nori rolls (pages 268–70) may be slivered and used to top chirashi zushi; select them to give a variety of colour and balance of textures and tastes. The rice and vegetable mixture for egg-wrapped sushi may be substituted for the rice mixture in this recipe.

sushi rice prepared from 10 oz (285 g) uncooked rice
8 dried mushrooms, softened in water
1 medium carrot, washed and trimmed

simmering stock
8 fl oz (230 ml) dashi (page 143)
1 tbsp dark soy sauce
1 tsp sugar or honey
1 tsp mirin

2 oz (60 g) mangetout peas, French beans or spinach
egg strands made with 1 egg and 1 yolk
1 sheet nori seaweed
½ oz (14 g) red pickled ginger

Prepare the sushi rice (see pages 260, 262). While the rice is cooking, prepare the toppings.

Drain the dried mushrooms and remove the stems; slice the

caps finely. Cut the carrot into long thin strips. Simmer the
mushrooms in the stock for 10 minutes, and leave to cool in it.
Drain, reserving the stock. Simmer the carrots in water till
soft, then drain. Wash and trim the peas, beans or spinach; cut
the peas or beans into thin strips; chop the spinach coarsely.
Parboil for 2–3 minutes until just tender, and dip into cold
water to stop further cooking. Prepare the egg strands (see
page 247), cutting the strands very finely into threads. Toast
the nori and cut with scissors into thin strips. Cut the red
pickled ginger into threads.

Put aside half the mushroom slices, choosing the longest
slices to use as topping. Chop the remaining slices and lightly
mix into the cooled sushi rice, moistening the rice with a little
of the reserved simmering stock. Spread the rice in a large bowl
or in individual wooden or ceramic containers and scatter over
the remaining ingredients or arrange them artistically.

Mochi: Rice Cakes

When a Japanese child looks at the moon he sees not a man but a hare, busy pounding rice to make rice cakes. Rice cakes are one of the most familiar and dearly loved Japanese foods, eaten as a daily food, as a snack, or given to children as a special treat. At festivals you can watch as two men with heavy mallets alternately pound a tubful of sticky cooked rice while a third man quickly folds it between each blow. In a few minutes the hot rice forms almost magically into a cohesive ball, which is torn into pieces, shaped into small balls and distributed amongst the expectant crowd. Rice cakes are particularly associated with the New Year festival, and in the old days the whole family used to help with the pounding. One of the characteristic New Year's decorations, the equivalent of a Christmas tree, is still a large rice cake topped with a smaller rice cake and a tangerine, which is set in the entrance hall of every Japanese home; after two weeks, the rice cakes are actually eaten.

Rice cakes are made from glutinous rice, in itself an essential ingredient of festive cooking, and are usually made in bulk, most being set aside to dry. Modern Japanese women make rice cakes with a machine, which cooks the rice to just the right consistency and then twists and kneads it into a big ball. While the rice is still very hot it is quickly formed into smaller balls or flattened into a big sheet and cut into squares; rice balls are made in western Japan while in the east rice cake always comes in squares. Freshly made rice cakes may be eaten immediately, perhaps rolled in roasted soy flour with a drop of soy sauce.

Ready-made dried rice cakes in packages of six 2 × 1½ in (5 × 4 cm) squares are sold in Japanese shops and some health-food and Chinese shops in England. Well-cooked rice can be kneaded and pounded to make a close approximation of rice cakes, although to be authentic you should use glutinous rice. Rice cake is perhaps an acquired taste, although once acquired it is hard to lose. To my taste brown rice cake is more delicious than white. Dried rice cake is usually grilled to make it crisp outside and soft and sticky inside, and used in a variety of dishes.

OZONI: NEW YEAR'S SOUP, TOKYO-STYLE

On New Year's morning, after everyone has drunk sake and exchanged congratulations, the traditional breakfast is a big bowl of vegetable soup with a soft sticky rice cake at the bottom. The soup is prepared with appropriate care, in theory with fresh spring water drawn at break of dawn, and the vegetables are cut into auspicious shapes laid down by tradition. Daikon radish is cut into hexagons like the shell of a tortoise, a symbol of longevity. This thick and filling soup is actually delicious at any time of year.

2 oz (60 g) daikon radish
1 medium carrot
1 small leek
12 small fresh mushrooms
1¾ pts (1 l) dashi (page 143)
dash of sake (optional)
4 rice cakes
1 tbsp light soy sauce
12 slivers lemon peel

Wash and trim the vegetables. Pare the sides of the daikon to form a long hexagonal block, and cut off hexagonal slices ¼ in (½ cm) thick. Cut the carrot into flowers (see page 64) ¼ in (½ cm) thick and slice the leek diagonally into fine slices. Wipe, trim and halve the mushrooms.

Bring the dashi to the boil, add the daikon, carrot and leek slices, and simmer for 2–3 minutes until the vegetables are just tender. Add the mushrooms and simmer for another minute.

Grill the rice cakes under a preheated hot grill for 2–3 minutes on each side, so that they soften and swell. Cut them into quarters to make them easier to eat with chopsticks and put four quarters in the bottom of each of 4 deep soup bowls. With chopsticks or a slotted spoon, remove the vegetables from the stock and distribute between the bowls. Season the dashi with soy sauce and sake if used, tasting to check the seasoning. Bring back to the boil and ladle over the vegetables and rice cakes. Float a few slivers of lemon peel on each bowl and serve immediately.

NEW YEAR'S SOUP, KYOTO-STYLE

In Kyoto and western Japan, New Year's soup is made with sweet white miso. Here is the soup that Ryoko, from Kyushu in the far south-west of Japan, makes for her family every year.

4 dried mushrooms, softened in water
1½ pts (900 ml) dashi (page 143)
4 stalks watercress or 4 small spinach leaves
4 rice cakes
2 eggs, hardboiled
2 tbsps sweet white miso
12 slivers lemon peel

Trim off the mushroom stems and cut the mushroom caps into quarters. Simmer in the dashi for 20 minutes; remove with chopsticks or a slotted spoon and set aside. Parboil the watercress or spinach in the dashi for 30 seconds, just until it wilts, remove and rinse in cold water. Grill the rice cakes under a preheated hot grill for 2–3 minutes on each side so that they soften and swell; cut into quarters. Quarter the hardboiled eggs and cut the quarters into halves.

Warm 4 deep soup bowls, and put 4 rice-cake quarters in each bowl. Divide the vegetables and hardboiled eggs between the bowls. Cream the miso in a little of the dashi; return to the pan and stir into the rest of the dashi. Bring the dashi just to the boil, and ladle into the 4 soup bowls. Float a few slivers of lemon peel on each bowl and serve immediately.

DEEP-FRIED RICE CAKES

Deep-fried rice cakes, crisp outside and soft and chewy inside, are often served in seasoned dashi with a little daikon radish.

4 rice cakes
12 fl oz (360 ml) dashi (page 143)
3 tbsps soy sauce
1 tbsp sake or mirin
1 tsp sugar or honey
2 tbsps grated daikon radish
1 young leek or spring onion
vegetable oil

Cut the rice cakes into quarters. Combine the dashi, soy sauce, sake or mirin and sugar or honey in a small saucepan and bring to the boil; keep warm. Prepare and squeeze the grated daikon and shred and rinse the leek or spring onion (see page 94).

Heat 2–3 ins (5–7 cm) oil in a small saucepan to 320°F (160°C). Deep-fry the rice cake quarters, a few at a time, for 4 minutes, until they become crisp and golden and float to the surface. Drain on absorbent paper.

Divide the rice-cake quarters between 4 small deep bowls; ladle over the hot dashi. Put a mound of grated daikon in each bowl and sprinkle over a few shreds of leek or spring onion.

STUFFED RICE CAKES IN NORI

Rice cakes demand to be stuffed. When they are grilled they swell up dramatically and the inside begins to burst out, forming a pocket, while the outside becomes crisp and golden. They are usually stuffed with flavoured misos such as walnut miso (page 83) or sesame miso (see below). Stuffed rice cakes can be prepared in a few minutes, making a quick, delicious and nutritious snack.

4 rice cakes
4 sheets nori seaweed
1 oz (30 g) sesame seeds or 2 tbsps sesame paste
1 tbsp red or white miso
1 tsp sugar or honey
1 tsp fresh lemon juice

Grill the rice cakes under a preheated hot grill for 3–5 minutes
on each side until they swell up, the inside begins to burst out,
and the outside is crisp and brown. Toast the nori lightly so
that it becomes fragrant but not brittle. Toast the sesame seeds
and grind in a suribachi until pasty; or use ready-made sesame
paste. Blend the sesame with the miso, honey and lemon juice.

With a very sharp knife, cut open the toasted rice cakes and
fill with the sesame mixture. Fold the rice cake to enclose the
filling, and wrap in a sheet of nori, folding in the sides to make
a package. Serve immediately. It is quite difficult to eat stuffed
rice cakes elegantly; if you want to make them more elegant,
omit the nori.

SWEET RICE CAKES

Some of the most traditional Japanese sweets are rice rather
than sugar based, and actually not very sweet. Sweet rice cakes
are particularly popular and very quick to make. Freshly made
rice cakes, shaped into balls and simply rolled in roasted soya
flour, are considered to be quite a delicacy. Here are a few
simple traditional sweets made with dried rice cakes.

2 fl oz dark soy sauce
1 tbsp sugar or honey
2 oz (60 g) roasted soya flour
salt
1 oz (30 g) sesame seeds
12 rice cakes

Combine the soy sauce with the sugar or honey in a small
saucepan and heat to dissolve the sugar or honey. Pour into a

saucer. Season the soya flour with a little salt in a small bowl. Toast the sesame seeds and grind lightly in a suribachi or simply crush with a rolling pin; spread in a saucer. Put some hot water into a soup bowl. Arrange the 4 bowls or saucers conveniently and prepare 4 small plates.

Grill the rice cakes under a preheated hot grill for 2–3 minutes on each side so that they soften and swell. Quickly dip 4 cakes in the hot water and roll in soya flour. Brush the remaining 8 cakes with the soy sauce and honey mixture. Roll 4 of the cakes in soya flour and roll the remaining 4 in sesame seeds.

Arrange 1 of each type of sweet cake on each plate, and serve with a tiny fork, to eat as a snack with tea.

Soba (Buckwheat Noodles)

Soba are narrow, flat, greyish brown noodles made of buckwheat flour. Served with plenty of vegetables in hot broth in winter and chilled in summer, they make a simple, nourishing and tasty meal loved by all Japanese. The businessman rushing from one engagement to another will pause in a station noodle shop to down a quick bowlful; noodle stands in the temple precincts provide steaming bowls to succour weary pilgrims and tourists; and children of course always demand soba for supper. Noodles are very much a part of the folk cuisine of Japan, and are never included in a formal meal. The simple but delicate taste of soba reminds everyone of a childhood spent among thatched farmhouses in green paddy-fields; and the first meal of every year is a bowl of soba, eaten at midnight on New Year's Eve, to ensure good luck throughout the coming year. Soba noodles are most popular in Tokyo and northern Japan. Like all Japanese foods, they have their connoisseurs, who prefer to eat them as simply as possible with only a little dipping sauce or stock, so as to savour the subtle taste of the noodles themselves. Noodles are always served in a broth, hot in winter and cold in summer, and it is a sign of enjoyment to slurp one's noodles, particularly if they are hot. The participants in a Zen retreat are allowed to break their silence only when they eat noodles, for it is said to be impossible to eat them quietly.

Cooking Soba

Soba is always eaten *al dente*, cooked through to the centre but still quite firm. The traditional way of cooking them is to add cold water whenever the noodles come to the boil; this should be done 2 or 3 times for perfect noodles. In noodle shops they are cooked in huge batches, and reheated as needed; the chef puts a portion of noodles into a deep bamboo colander and vigorously dunks it in boiling water before serving.

Allow 3–4oz (85–115g) buckwheat noodles per person.

Bring plenty of unsalted water to a rolling boil in a large saucepan and gradually add the noodles, stirring a little to stop them from sticking. Over high heat bring the water back to the boil and add half a cup (5 floz, 150ml) cold water. Bring back to the boil and repeat. When the water boils a third time, taste 1 noodle; if it is not cooked, simmer for 2–3 minutes. The noodles should be just cooked and still firm.

Drain the noodles when cooked. Reserve the cooking water, which can be used in the noodle broth or for soup. Immerse the noodles in cold water, rubbing to separate the strands and remove starch.

Just before serving, place the noodles in a strainer and immerse in boiling water for a few seconds to reheat.

HOMEMADE BUCKWHEAT NOODLES

There is always an audience of children outside one of Gifu's soba shops, pressing their noses against the window to watch the soba maker. In a few seconds he rolls out a ball of soba dough into a huge flat sheet, folds it, makes a few lightning strokes of the knife, and as he lifts the sheet of soba on a long chopstick it separates into thousands of strands. Most Japanese women leave soba making to the soba maker, and buy it readymade. However, one day my flower arrangement teacher, Mrs Misono, invited me to lunch, and proceeded to roll up her kimono sleeves and set about making soba in a big bowl, rolling it out on a wooden board on the floor and deftly slicing it.

It is not difficult to make your own soba. Buckwheat flour is low in gluten and needs to be mixed with strong wheat flour, traditionally in the proportions 4 parts buckwheat flour to 1 part wheat flour; you may find it easier to increase the proportion of wheat flour up to half to make a more manageable dough. The dough should be vigorously kneaded to activate the gluten and left to rest, preferably for several hours.

1 lb (450 g) buckwheat flour
4 oz (115 g) strong white flour
1 tsp salt
1 egg, beaten (optional)
8–12 fl oz (240–360 ml) warm water

Combine the flours and salt in a large mixing bowl; make a well in the centre and pour in the egg, if used, and 8 fl oz (240 ml) warm water. Gradually draw the liquid ingredients into the dry, adding enough of the remaining water to make a stiff dough. Knead vigorously until the dough is smooth and pliable. Cover with a damp cloth and leave in a warm place for at least 2 hours to rest.

Dust a tabletop or large board with buckwheat flour and roll out the dough into a large even rectangle, about ⅛ in (½ cm) thick; or cut the dough in half and roll out 2 smaller rectangles. Dust the dough evenly with buckwheat flour. Fold the rectangle of dough in half; then fold each half back on itself so that the dough is quartered lengthwise. With a sharp knife slice across the folds into thin strips about ⅛ in (½ cm) wide. Japanese cooks slide a chopstick into the centre fold, lift the noodles and shake them out. If this is difficult, simply shake the noodles gently to separate them.

Homemade noodles are cooked in the same way as dried noodles. The noodles are best eaten immediately, but will keep for up to 2 days in the refrigerator.

SUMMER SOBA

Iced soba refreshes the humid days of summer in Japan. The diners sit outside on low wooden benches under huge red parasols, delicately lifting noodles from amidst ice cubes in a big glass bowl, or sometimes from a small clear stream of water which flows before them, ice cubes tinkling. Less romantically, they may be served in slatted bamboo containers. The noodles are dipped into a small glass of dipping sauce spiced with a touch of fresh ginger and hot wasabi horseradish and scattered with shreds of spring onions and nori.

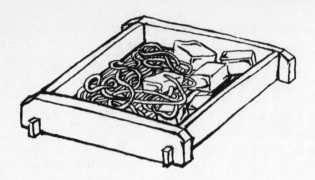

14 oz (400 g) buckwheat noodles

dipping sauce
1 pt (600 ml) dashi (page 143)
3½ fl oz (100 ml) dark soy sauce
2 tsps sugar or honey
2 tbsps mirin

1 sheet nori seaweed
4 spring onions
1 tbsp freshly grated root ginger
1 tsp freshly made wasabi horseradish

Cook the noodles (see pages 283–4) and set aside. Combine the dipping sauce ingredients and bring to the boil, stirring to dissolve the sugar or honey; allow to cool and divide between 4 glasses or glass bowls. Toast the nori and cut with scissors into thin strips. Slice the white part of the spring onions very finely and rinse in cold water; wring gently and drain. Arrange the nori, ginger, wasabi and spring onions in 3 small bowls in the centre of the table, or provide a small portion of each for each diner. Put the noodles in 1 large or 4 small glass bowls with plenty of ice cubes, or use 4 bamboo containers.

Each diner is provided with a glass or bowl of dipping sauce into which he or she mixes ginger, wasabi, spring onions and nori to taste; the noodles are dipped in the dipping sauce before eating.

FIVE-COLOUR SOBA

This refreshing summer dish combines beige soba noodles
with yellow egg strands, green cucumber, brown mushroom
and white daikon radish.

10 oz (285 g) buckwheat noodles
4 dried mushrooms, softened in water

simmering stock for mushrooms
7 fl oz (200 ml) dashi (page 143)
1 tsp soy sauce
½ tsp honey
1 tbsp sake or mirin

½ small cucumber
2 oz (60 g) daikon radish
egg strands made from 1 egg (page 247)

dipping sauce
1 pt (600 ml) dashi (page 143)
3½ fl oz (100 ml) soy sauce
2 tsps honey
1 tbsp sake or mirin

4 spring onions
2 tbsps sesame seeds, toasted
1 tbsp freshly grated root ginger

Cook the noodles (see pages 283–4) chill. Remove the
mushroom stems and slice the caps very finely. Combine with
the simmering stock ingredients and simmer for 20 minutes;
set aside to cool in the stock; drain and squeeze lightly. Cut the
cucumber and daikon radish into fine julienne strips. Soak in
lightly salted water for 20 minutes, squeeze lightly, rinse and
drain. Prepare the egg strands. Combine the dipping sauce
ingredients and bring to the boil, stirring to dissolve the honey;
set aside to cool. Rinse and finely slice the white part of the
spring onions (see page 94).

Put the chilled noodles into 4 individual glass bowls.
Arrange the mushrooms, egg strands, cucumber and daikon
radish attractively on the noodles. Pour the dipping sauce over
all, sprinkle with spring onions, sesame seeds and grated ginger
and serve.

WINTER SOBA

A big bowlful of steaming soba in hot broth makes a warming and nourishing winter meal. In this dish the noodles are served quite simply so that the delicate taste of the soba itself can be appreciated.

14 oz (400 g) buckwheat noodles

noodle broth
1½ pts (900 ml) dashi (page 143)
3 tbsps dark soy sauce
1 tbsp sugar or honey
1 tsp salt
1 tbsp mirin

2 young leeks or spring onions
seven-spice pepper

Cook the noodles (see pages 283–4) and set aside. Combine the noodle broth ingredients and bring to the boil; keep at a simmer. Slice the white part of the leeks and spring onions very finely and rinse in cold water; wring gently and drain.

Warm 4 deep bowls. Put the noodles in a strainer or colander and immerse in boiling water for a few seconds to reheat. Divide the noodles between the 4 bowls, and ladle over the hot broth. Top each bowlful with a mound of finely sliced leek or spring onion and serve immediately. Pass seven-spice pepper separately.

WINTER SOBA WITH VEGETABLES

This is good hearty fare for winter nights, a big steaming bowl of noodles each, topped with vegetables, in a warming soup. Traditionally this dish is prepared and served in individual earthenware casseroles. If necessary it could be prepared in one large lidded flameproof casserole.

14 oz (400 g) buckwheat noodles
1 medium carrot, scraped
4 leeks
4 large dried mushrooms, softened in water

simmering stock for mushrooms
7 fl oz (200 ml) dashi (page 143)
1 tsp dark soy sauce
½ tsp sugar or honey
1 tbsp sake or mirin

noodle broth
1½ pts (900 ml) dashi
3 tbsps dark soy sauce
1 tbsp sugar or honey
1 tsp salt
1 tbsp mirin

8 spinach leaves, washed and trimmed
4 eggs

Cook the noodles (see pages 283–4) and set aside. Cut the carrot into flowers (see page 64) about ¼ in (½ cm) thick and parboil till nearly cooked. Slice the leeks on the diagonal into 1½ in (4 cm) lengths, wash and parboil till nearly cooked. Remove the mushroom stems and cut a decorative cross in the top of each mushroom cap. Combine the mushrooms with the simmering stock ingredients and simmer for 20 minutes. Combine the noodle broth ingredients and bring to the boil; turn the heat low and keep at a simmer.

Put the noodles into 4 small flameproof casseroles with lids. Drain the mushrooms and divide together with the carrots and leeks between the 4 casseroles. Tear the spinach leaves into 3 or 4 pieces and add to the casseroles. Ladle over the noodle broth, cover the casseroles, bring to the boil and simmer for 1–2 minutes. With the back of a spoon make a small hollow in the noodles in each casserole and break an egg into the hollow. Immediately cover the casseroles and turn off the heat so that the egg half cooks; or simmer for a few minutes until the white is cooked but the yolk is still soft. Serve immediately.

FOX NOODLES (KITSUNE SOBA)

As you approach a great Shinto shrine through avenues of ancient towering cryptomeria trees, you will more than likely find two stone foxes guarding the entrance. The wily fox is a powerful creature in Japanese folklore, and its favourite food is said to be deep-fried tofu.

14 oz (400 g) buckwheat noodles
2 sheets deep-fried tofu

simmering stock
7 fl oz (200 ml) dashi (page 143)
2 tbsps light soy sauce
1 tsp sugar or honey
1 tbsp mirin

2 young leeks or spring onions

noodle broth
1½ pts (900 ml) dashi
3 tbsps dark soy sauce
1 tbsp sugar or honey
1 tsp salt
1 tbsp mirin

Cook the noodles (see pages 283–4) and set aside. Rinse the deep-fried tofu with boiling water to remove oil; drain. Combine the simmering stock ingredients in a small saucepan, add the deep-fried tofu and bring to the boil. Simmer uncovered for 10 minutes until the liquid is nearly absorbed and the tofu well flavoured. Drain and halve each sheet of tofu to make 4 squares. Slice the leeks or spring onions very finely and rinse in cold water; wring gently and drain. Combine the noodle broth ingredients and bring to the boil.

Warm 4 deep bowls. Put the noodles in a strainer or colander and immerse in boiling water for a few seconds to reheat. Put the noodles in the 4 bowls and put a square of deep-fried tofu and some leek or spring onion on each bowl. Ladle the boiling broth over the noodles and serve immediately.

TEMPURA SOBA

Tempura soba combines two favourite Japanese foods and is one of those dishes that no one ever tires of. It can be made using practically any vegetable tempura, or even with reheated tempura left over from the previous night. Freshly made tempura is of course the most delicious, as in the following recipe.

14 oz (400 g) buckwheat noodles

noodle broth
1½ pts (900 ml) dashi (page 143)
3 tbsps dark soy sauce
1 tbsp sugar or honey
1 tsp salt
1 tbsp mirin

2 leeks, trimmed
8 fresh mushrooms, wiped and trimmed
½ sheet nori seaweed
1 medium carrot
1 small onion, peeled
tempura batter (page 156)
vegetable oil for deep-frying
½ tsp (2½ ml) finely chopped root ginger
slivers of lemon peel to garnish
seven-spice pepper

Cook the noodles (see pages 283–4) and set aside. Combine the noodle broth ingredients, bring to the boil, and simmer over low heat.

Cut the leeks diagonally into 1 in (2½ cm) slices and wash. Remove the mushroom stems and cut a neat cross in the top of each mushroom cap. Cut the nori with scissors into 1 × 2 in (2½ × 5 cm) rectangles. Chop the carrot and onion very finely. Pat all the vegetables dry with absorbent paper. Heat 3 in (7 cm) oil to 340°F (170°C), and mix the tempura batter while the oil is heating. One by one dip the mushrooms and leeks into batter and deep-fry until golden; drain on absorbent paper. Dip the bottom half of each rectangle of nori into batter and deep-fry for only a few seconds to set the coating. Mix the carrot, onion and ginger and stir in just enough batter to coat all the ingredients. Slide by spoonsful into the hot oil and deep-fry until golden. Drain on absorbent paper.

Warm 4 deep bowls. Reheat the noodles in boiling water, drain well and distribute between the bowls. Put a few pieces of each type of tempura in each bowl, and ladle over the hot broth. Garnish with slivers of lemon peel and pass the seven-spice pepper separately.

'MOON-VIEWING' NOODLES (TSUKIMI SOBA)

Ever since the days of Prince Genji, admiring the full moon in August has been a Japanese tradition. In this dish the yellow egg yolk floating on each bowl of noodles resembles a perfect full moon.

14oz (400g) buckwheat noodles

noodle broth
1½pts (900ml) dashi (page 143)
3 tbsps dark soy sauce
1 tbsp sugar or honey
1 tsp salt
1 tbsp mirin

4 spring onions or small leeks
½ sheet nori seaweed
4 eggs

Cook the noodles (see pages 283–4) and set aside. Combine the noodle broth ingredients and bring to the boil; turn the heat low and keep at a simmer. Slice the green part of the leeks or spring onions on the diagonal into 2 in (5 cm) slices and wash. Toast the nori seaweed and cut with scissors into 1 × 2 in (2½ × 5 cm) rectangles.

Warm 4 deep bowls. Put the noodles in a strainer or colander and immerse in boiling water for a few seconds to reheat. Divide between the 4 bowls and top with slices of leek or spring onion. With the back of a spoon make a small hollow in the noodles in each bowl and gently break an egg into the hollow, taking care not to break the yolk. Immediately ladle the hot broth over the noodles, garnish with nori seaweed, and serve.

Japanese Food Suppliers in the United Kingdom

Many ingredients for the recipes in this book can be found in ordinary grocers and greengrocers; health-food shops and Chinese shops stock some of the more esoteric ingredients. The shops listed below have a particularly wide selection of specifically Japanese ingredients. While Japanese shops stock standard, traditional Japanese ingredients, wholefood shops stock Japanese wholefoods, that is foods produced from whole grains without additives, such as brown rice cakes and organic miso.

Outside London

ABERDEEN

Ambrosia Wholefoods
160 King Street
Aberdeen
tel 0224 639096

Stocks a wide range of Japanese wholefoods including mirin, koji and nigari; also Japanese utensils.

BATH

Harvest Wholefoods
37 Walcot Street
Bath
Avon
tel 0225 65519

Japanese wholefoods, including nigari; also stocks suribachis.

BERKHAMSTED

Cook's Delight
360–2 High Street
Berkhamsted
Herts HP4 1HU
tel 04427 3584

A wide range of Japanese wholefoods, including mirin, rice vinegar, rice cakes, nigari and sometimes koji; also teas, sake and a wide range of utensils.

BIRMINGHAM

Wing Yip Supermarket
96–8 Coventry Street
Birmingham
tel 021 643 2851

Basic Japanese ingredients.

BRIGHTON

Infinity Foods
25 North Road
Brighton BN1 1YA
tel 0273 603563

The basic range of Japanese
wholefoods, including nigari and
koji; a wide range of utensils.

BRISTOL

Wild Oats
11 Lower Redland Road
Redland
Bristol
tel 0272 731967

All the basic Japanese
wholefoods, including koji and
nigari; some utensils.

CARDIFF

Nam Kiu Supermarket
32–4 Tudor Street
Cardiff
tel 0222 45487

Some Japanese ingredients.

CLEVELAND

Open Sesame
2 High Street
Sedgefield
Cleveland TS21 2AU
tel 0740 20456

Basic Japanese wholefoods,
including tofu, miso and
seaweeds; some utensils.

EDINBURGH

Edinburgh Chinese Company
26 Dublin Street
Edinburgh
tel 031 556 2304

Basic Japanese ingredients.

GLASGOW

Chung Ying Supermarket
63 Cambridge Street
Glasgow
tel 041 336 4404

Basic Japanese ingredients.

KINGSTON

Miura Foods
40 Coombe Road
Norbiton
Kingston
Surrey
tel 01 549 8076

Japanese food shop.

LEEDS

Wing Lee Hong
Hereford House
6 Edward Street
Leeds LS2 7NN
tel 0532 457203

Basic Japanese ingredients, fresh
tofu, oriental vegetables.

LINCOLN

Pulse
25 Corporation Street
Lincoln
tel 0522 28666

Japanese wholefoods, including nigari; some utensils.

MAIDENHEAD

New Morning Wholefoods
King Street Market
Maidenhead
Berks
tel 0628 25592

Open: Fridays and Saturdays. Most Japanese wholefoods, including dried yuba; some utensils.

MANCHESTER

On the Eighth Day
111 Oxford Road
Manchester M1 7DU
tel 061 273 4878

Japanese wholefoods, including nigari; also does utensils.

NEWCASTLE-UPON-TYNE

Wing Hong Company
45–51 Stowell Street
Newcastle-upon-Tyne
tel 091 612630

Some Japanese foods, including seaweeds, Japanese tea and tinned burdock root.

Mandala Wholefoods Ltd
43 Manor House Road
Newcastle-upon-Tyne
tel 091 281 0045

Basic Japanese wholefoods, including long-life tofu and seaweeds.

NOTTINGHAM

Ouroboros
37A Mansfield Road
Nottingham
tel 0602 419016

Basic Japanese wholefoods and utensils.

RICHMOND

All-Manna
179 Sheen Road
Richmond
Surrey
tel 01 948 3633

Japanese wholefoods, including Paul's tofu; a few utensils.

TRURO

Carley & Co
35–6 St Austell Street
Truro
Cornwall TR1 1SE
tel 0872 77686

Japanese wholefoods, including nigari; utensils.

TWICKENHAM

Gaia Wholefoods
123 St Margaret Road
Twickenham
Middlesex TW1 2LH

tel 01 892 2262

Limited range of Japanese
wholefoods, including fresh tofu
and seitan; suribachis.

WEST WICKHAM

J.A. Centre
70 Coney Hall
West Wickham
Kent

tel 01 462 3404

A Japanese shop, branch of
London J.A. Centre.

WOODBRIDGE

Loaves and Fishes
52 Thoroughfare
Woodbridge
Suffolk

tel 0394 35650

Basic Japanese wholefoods; a few
utensils.

London

Clearspring Natural Grocer
196 Old Street EC1

tel 01 250 1708

A large macrobiotic centre,
supplying wholefood shops
throughout the country; an
extremely wide range of
wholefood Japanese ingredients,
including brown rice cakes, a
variety of misos, koji, nigari,
organic sake, Japanese snacks
and utensils. Also has a mail
order service: send three first-
class stamps for catalogue.

Earth Exchange
213 Archway Road N6

tel 01 340 6407

Seaweeds, Japanese wholefoods.

Furusato Foods
67A Camden High Street NW1
tel 01 388 4381/3979

Open: Tuesday–Sunday, 9.00–
5.00. A very wide selection of all
Japanese foods, including fresh
tofu and bean sprouts; also does
mail order.

Habitat
All branches. Japanese utensils:
tempura pans and suribachis.

J.A. Centre
348–56 Regent's Park Road
Finchley Central N3

tel 01 346 1042

Open: Tuesday–Sunday, 10.00–
6.00. A very large Japanese
supermarket with a wide
selection of Japanese foods,
utensils and crockery. Bulk mail
order.

J.A. Centre
250 Upper Richmond Road
Putney SW15
tel 01 789 3980

Open: Sunday–Monday, 11.00–
5.00; Tuesday–Friday, 10.00–
5.00; Saturday, 10.00–6.00. A
large Japanese supermarket.

Japanese Centre
66–8 Brewer Street W1
tel 01 437 4480

Open: Monday–Friday, 10.00–
6.00; Saturday, 9.30–6.30;
Sunday, 10.30–6.30. Has dried,
frozen and preserved foods,
including pickles; also utensils,
crockery and Japanese books.

Loon Fung Supermarket
31 Gerrard Street W1
tel 01 437 1922

The biggest London Chinese
supermarket, with Japanese food
as well. Fresh tofu and exotic
vegetables; also Chinese dried
beancurd skin, dried
mushrooms, Japanese sauces and
vinegar.

Mitsukiku
Several branches, including
Regent Street, W1. Japanese
crockery and utensils.

Neal Street East
Neal Street WC2
tel 01 240 0135

Japanese utensils and crockery.

N.F.C. Mikado-ya
193 Upper Richmond Road
Putney SW15
tel 01 788 3905 and 4259

Open: Monday–Friday, 11.00–
4.00; Saturday, 10.00–6.00.

Ninjin
140 Brent Street NW4
tel 01 202 5971

Open: Tuesday–Sunday, 10.00–
7.00.

Ninjin
244 Great Portland Street W1
tel 01 486 9841/5 & 388 2511

Open: Tuesday–Sunday, 10.30–
7.00. A large Japanese
supermarket with a very wide
range of Japanese foods,
including fresh tofu.

Tokyo-ya
20 North End Road
Golders Green NW11
tel 01 485 8333

Open: Monday–Saturday,
10.00–6.00; Sunday, 11.00–
5.00. A small Japanese shop with
all the basic foods.

Yamato-ya
55–7 Church Street NW4
tel 01 203 4773

Open: Tuesday–Friday, 9.30–
6.00; Saturday–Sunday, 9.30–
6.30. A large Japanese shop with
plenty of choice.

Japanese Food Suppliers in Australia

ADELAIDE

Asian Kitchen
34A and 40 Gouger Street
Adelaide
ph 51–2021

Boomerang Supermarket
Shop 8
161 The Parade
Norwood
ph 31–6056

BRISBANE

Japanese Shop
Queens Arcade
77 Queen Street
Brisbane
ph 229–3069

CANBERRA

Japanese Grocer Asakusa
Green Square
Jardine Street
Kingston
ph 95–3608

HOBART

Bellerive Chinese Emporium
Bellerive Quay
Shop 12
29 Cambridge Street
Bellerive
ph 44–4625

MELBOURNE

Japan Mart
568 Malvern Road
Prahran
ph 51–9344
and
66 Batman Road
West Melbourne
ph 329–0827

Miyajima Food Centre
2 Sanicki Court
Bentleigh East
ph 570–3321

Spiral Foods
17 Morey Street
Armadale
ph 429–8425

Suzaran-Shoten Grocers
159 Union Road
Surrey Hills
ph 890–3950

Tokyo Mart
584 Glenhuntly Road
Elsternwick
ph 523–6200

Wing Wah Trading Company
896 Canterbury Road
Box Hill South
ph 890–7598

PERTH

Japanese Food Centre
113 Murray Street
Perth
ph 325–3929

SYDNEY

Anegawa Trading Company
16A Deepwater Road
Castle Cove
ph 406–5452

Ichibankan Japanese Grocery
36 Nurses Walk
The Rocks
ph 27–2667

Sakura Shokai
100 Edinburgh Road
Castlecrag
ph 95–1947

Tokyo Mart
27 Northbridge Plaza
Northbridge
ph 95–6860

Index

Note: page numbers referring to recipes are in *italic*.

Aburage: *see* Tofu, deep-fried
Aduki bean paste, *183–4*
  Deep-fried Chestnut Cakes, *78–9*
  Ohagi, *185–6*
  Potato Chestnuts, *115*
  Steamed Chestnut Cakes, *77*
  Yokan, *184–5*
Aduki beans, 21
  Red Rice, *182–3*
Agar, 21–2, 140
  Yokan, *184–5*
Apricots, dried:
  Autumn Salad, *103–4*
  Marinated Turnip Rolls, *138–9*
Arum root: *see* Konnyaku
Aubergine(s), 45–52
  Fans, *45–6*
  Grilled, *46–7*
  Grilled, with Peanut Sauce, *111–12*
  Miso Pickles, *173–4*
  Miso Soup with Wakame, *230*
  pickled, 172
  Quick Pickles, *174*
  Sesame, after Sen no Rikyu, 49
  Simmered, whole, *47*
  Stuffed with Sesame, *51–2*
  Stuffed, Tempura, *50–1*
  with Sweet Miso, *48–9*
  Tempura, *156–7*
  Vegetable Dengaku, *152–3*
Autumn dishes, 73
  Autumn Salad, *103–4*
  Chestnut Rice, *74*
  Chrysanthemum Turnips, *136–8*
  Miso Soups, *231–2*
  Mushroom Rice, *101–2*
  Ohagi, *185–6*
  Turnips Simmered in Dashi, *134*
Autumn Salad, *103–4*

Bamboo rolling mat, 34
Bamboo shoots, 22
  Casserole of Tofu and Vegetables, *161–2*
  Coloured Rice, *264–5*
  Miso Soup with Wakame Seaweed, *228–9*
  Vegetables Sautéed and Simmered in Kuzu
    Sauce, *150–1*

Barbecue, Vegetable, *154–5*
Barley koji, *228*
  Miso, *226–7*
Barley tea, 12–13
Batter:
  for Aubergine Tempura, *50–1*
  for Chinese-style Stuffed Yuba Tempura,
    218–19
  for Deep-fried Carrot Cakes, *67–8*
  for Mrs Misono's Special Tempura, *159*
  for Pumpkin Tempura, *118–19*
  for Tempura, *156–7*
Bean curd sheets/skin, 33, 211, 215, 218
  Chinese-style Stuffed Yuba Tempura, *218–19*
  Clear Soup with, *220–1*
  Dried Yuba, Deep-fried and Simmered,
    215
Beans, 179–86. *See also* Aduki beans; Black
  beans; French beans; Soya beans
Bean sprouts:
  Casserole of Tofu and Vegetables, *161–2*
  Nori Rolls, *270*
Black beans:
  Black Bean Rice, *180*
  Sweet-simmered, *182*
Breakfast, 233, 236
  sample menu, 18
Broccoli, 53–6
  Clear Soup with, *56*
  with Golden Dressing, *54–5*
  Sautéed with Sesame, *54*
  with Sesame dressing, *121*
  Tempura, *157*
  with Tofu, *55*
Buckwheat flour:
  Homemade Buckwheat Noodles, *284–5*
Buckwheat noodles: *see* Soba
Burdock, 22
  Kimpira, *66*
  Kombu Rolls, *144–5*
  Tempura, *158*
  Winter Carrot Mix, *68*

Cabbage, 57–63
  Fritters, *158*
  Gyozu 'Pancakes', *61–2*

Japanese Salad, *52–3*
Okonomiyaki, *248*
and Spinach Rolls, *60–1*
Vegetables Sautéed and Simmered in Kuzu
    Sauce, *150–1*
See also Chinese cabbage
Cabbage and Spinach Rolls:*60–1*
    Oden, *167–9*
Cakes/sweetmeats: *see* Sweet dishes
Carrot(s), 64–70
    Barbecued, *154–5*
    Cakes, Deep-fried, *67–8*
    Casserole of Tofu and Vegetables, *161–2*
    Chawan Mushi, *249–50*
    Coloured Rice, *264–5*
    flowers, *64–5*
    Fritters, *158*
    Grilled with Peanut Sauce, *111–12*
    Kimpira, *66*
    Kombu Rolls, *144–5*
    Miso Pickles, *173–4*
    Miso River-bank Casserole, *166–7*
    Miso Soup with Daikon Radish,
        233
    Mrs Fujii's Nori Rolls, *270–2*
    Nori Rolls, *270*
    Okonomiyaki, *248*
    One-pot Dish with Noodles, *164–6*
    Ozoni, *278–9*
    Red and White Salad, *90–1*
    Salad Nori Rolls, *146*
    Simmered in Dashi, *65–6*
    Snow Country Winter Casserole, *162–4*
    Tempura, *156–7*
    Tempura Soba, *291–2*
    Three-colour Salad, *83*
    added to Tofu, 192
    Tofu Treasure Balls, *199–200*
    Vegetables Sautéed and Simmered in Kuzu
        Sauce, *150–1*
    White Salad with Tofu dressing, *69–70*
    Winter Mix, *68–9*
    Winter Soba with Vegetables, *288–9*
Casserole dishes: *see* One-pot dishes
Casseroles, earthenware, 36, 160
Cast-iron pans, 34
Cauliflower, 71–2
    and French Beans with Sesame Dressing,
        72
    Sautéed with Miso, *71–2*
    Tempura, *157*
Celery:
    Miso Pickle, *175*
Charcoal grilling, 40, 152, 154
Chawan Mushi, *249–50*
    Mount Koya, *250–1*
    Turnip, *134–5*
Chawan Mushi cups, 34–5, 249
Chestnut(s), 73–9
    in Burrs, *75–7*
    Deep-fried Cakes, *78*
    Kuri Kinton, *75*

Mrs Misono's Special Tempura,
    158–9
peeling, 73
Potato, *114*
Rice, 74
Steamed Cakes, 77
Chillies, dried:
    Red Maple Radish, *88*
Chinese cabbage, 57
    Casserole of Tofu and Vegetables, *161–2*
    and Deep-fried Tofu, *58*
    Miso Soup with Deep-fried Tofu, *232*
    One-pot dish with Noodles, *164–6*
    pickles, 172
    Salt Pickled, *172–3*
    Shinoda Rolls, *58–60*
    Snow Country Winter Casserole, *162–4*
    and Spinach Rolls, *60–1, 167–9*
Chinese-style Stuffed Yuba Tempura,
    218–19
Chirashi Zushi: Scattered Vegetable Sushi,
    275–6
Chopsticks, 35
Chrysanthemum leaves, 22
    Miso River-bank Casserole, *166–7*
    One-pot Dish with Noodles, *164–6*
    Snow Country Winter Casserole, *162–4*
Coloured Rice, *264–5*
Cooking methods, 15, *39–41*
Corn on the cob: *see* Sweetcorn
Cotton tofu, 187–8, 192
Cucumber(s), 80–5
    Autumn Salad, *103–4*
    Clear Soup with, *81*
    Egg-drop Soup with, *81–2*
    Five-colour Soba, *287*
    Kappa Rolls, *84–5*
    Miso Pickles, *173–4*
    Mrs Fujii's Country-style Nori Rolls, *270–2*
    Nori Rolls, *84–5, 269*
    pickled, 172
    Salt Pickled, *172–3*
    slicing, 80
    Three-colour Salad, *83–4*
    and Tofu Salad, *82*
    and Wakame Salad, *147–8*
    with Walnut Miso, *82–3*
Custard, savoury vegetable: *see* Chawan
    Mushi

Daikon pickle, 86–7, 172
Daikon radish, 22–3, *86–92*
    Clear Soup with Deep-fried Tofu, *88*
    Dashi, *143*
    Five-colour Soba, *287*
    Grated, *87*
    Miso Oden, *169–70*
    Miso Pickles, *173–4*
    Miso River-bank Casserole, *166–7*
    Miso Soup with, *233*
    Oden, *167–9*
    One-pot Dish with Noodles, *164–6*

Daikon radish–*cont.*
  Ozoni, *278–9*
  Red Maple Radish, *88*
  Red and White Salad, *90–1*
  Rounds with Hot Sesame Sauce,
    89–90
  Salad with Kombu and Orange, *92*
  Salt Pickled, *172–3*
  Simmered Winter Vegetables, *89*
  slicing, 87
Dashi, 23, 143
  Kombu, *143–4*
Deep-fried dishes, 40–1
  Carrot Cakes, *67–8*
  Chestnuts in Burrs, *75–7*
  Chestnut Cakes, *78–9*
  Chinese-style Stuffed Yuba Tempura,
    218–19
  Mock Eel, *200–1*
  Mrs Misono's Special Tempura, *158–9*
  Natto Tempura, *238–9*
  Potatoes, *112–13*
  Pumpkin Tempura, *118–19*
  Rice Cakes, *280*
  Stuffed Aubergine Tempura, *50–1*
  Stuffed Green and Red Pepper Boats,
    108–9
  Stuffed Potatoes, *113–14*
  Stuffed Yuba, *217*
  Temple Tofu, *198*
  Tempura, *155–8*
  Tofu Treasure Balls, *199–200*
  Turnip Puffs, *135–6*
  Vegetable Fritters, *158*
  Yuba Rolls, *214*
  Yuba Tempura, *213*
Dessert, 16. *See also* Sweet dishes
dipping sauces: *see* Sauces
Dobin Mushi, *98–9*
Domburi: Tofu and Eggs on Rice, *265–6*
Dough:
  for Steamed Spinach Buns, *124–5*
Dressing(s):
  Golden, for Broccoli, *54–5*
  Lemon Soy, *106*
  miso, for Flower Peppers, *109*
    hot, for Leek Salad, *94*
  tofu, for Autumn Salad, 103–4
    for Broccoli, *55*
    for Japanese Cabbage Salad, *63*
    for spinach, *123–4*
    for White Salad, *69–70*
  vinegared, for Chrysanthemum Turnips,
    136–8
    for Cucumber and Tofu Salad, *82*
    for Marinated Turnip and Apricot Rolls,
      138–9
    for Red and White Salad, *91*
    for Turnip and Mushroom Salad, *139*
    for Wakame and Cucumber Salad,
      147–8
  walnut, *103–4, 126*

Drop lid, 35

Eggs, 242–53
  Casserole of Tofu and Vegetables, *161–2*
  Chawan Mushi, *249–50*
  Clear Soup with Spinach and, *125–6*
  Domburi, *265–6*
  Egg-drop Soup with Cucumber, *81–2*
  in Golden Dressing, *54–5*
  hardboiled, 242–3
  Moon-viewing Noodles, *292–3*
  Mount Koya Chawan Mushi, *250–1*
  Natto Omelette, *238*
  New Year's Soup, *279*
  Nori Rolls, *269*
  Quails, 28, 242–3
  Rolled Omelette, *243–6*
  Sushi, *245–6*
  Tamago Dofu, *251–3*
  Winter Soba with Vegetables, *288–9*
Egg Strands, *206–7, 247*
  Five-colour Soba, *287*
Egg Wrappers, *246, 273–4*
  for Sushi Party, *274–5*
Etiquette, Japanese, 2–6

Five-colour Soba, *287*
Five-colour Soya Beans, *181*
Five-colour Tofu Pouches, *206–7*
Fox Noodles, *290*
French Beans:
  and Cauliflower with Sesame Dressing, *72*
  Clear Soup with Wakame and Mangetout
    Peas, *148–9*
  Miso Soup with Tofu, *230–1*
    with Natto, *236–7*
  Nori Rolls, *270*
  Okonomiyaki, *248*
  Tempura, *156–7*
  in Vegetable Fritters, *158*
Fried dishes: *see* Grilled/fried dishes
Fritters, Vegetable, *158*
Fu: *see* Gluten

Garnishes, 94
Ginger, 23
Ginger, pickled red, 23
  Nori Rolls, *269*
Ginger root:
  Pumpkin Tempura, *118–19*
Gingko leaves, potatoes cut as, *112*
Gingko nuts, 23
  Barbecued, *155*
  Chawan Mushi, *249–50*
  in Chestnut Rice, *74*
  Mrs Misono's Special Tempura,
    158–9
  Snow Country Winter Casserole, *162–4*
  added to Tofu, *192*
  Tofu Treasure Balls, *199–200*
Ginnan: *see* Gingko nuts
Gluten, 33

One-pot Dish with Noodles, *164–6*
Gobo: *see* Burdock
Goma: *see* Sesame seeds
Goma abra: *see* Sesame oil
Gourd ribbon, 24
　Mrs Fujii's Country-style Nori Rolls,
　　270–2
　Nori Rolls, *269*
　Winter Carrot Mix, *68–9*
Grater, Japanese, 36
Grilled/fried dishes, 40
　Aubergine, Grilled, *46–7*
　Aubergines with Sweet Miso, *48*
　Flower Peppers, *109*
　Marinated Tofu Tatsuta Style, *195–6*
　Potatoes with Peanut Sauce, *111–12*
　Roasted Corn on the Cob, *127*
　Stuffed Rice Cakes, *280–1*
　Sweet Potatoes, *130*
　Tofu Dengaku, *196–7*
　Vegetable Barbecue, *154–5*
　Vegetable Dengaku, *152–3*
Gushi: *see* Skewers
Gyozu: *61–2*

Harusame noodles, 24
　Tempura, *156–7*
Hashi: *see* Chopsticks
Hijiki, 24, 140, 141–2
　Rich Simmered, with Tofu, *141–2*
　with Sesame Seeds, *142*
　with Sweet Potatoes, *132*
　Winter Carrot Mix, *68–9*
Horseradish, 33
Hospitality, traditions of, 4–6

Inari Sushi, *204–6*
Ingredients:
　suppliers, 295–301
　variety, 16

Japanese Cabbage Salad, *62–3*
Japanese Pickles:
　Nori Rolls, *269*
　Stuffed Rice Balls, *263–4*

Kaminari Jiru, *193–4*
Kampyo: *see* Gourd ribbon
Kanten: *see* Agar
Kappa Rolls, *84–5*
Katakuriko, 24
Kimpira, *66*
Kinako: *see* Soya flour, roasted
Kinusaya: *see* Mangetout peas
Kitsune Soba, *290*
Knives, 36
Koji, 24, 227–8
　in miso making, 226–7
Kombu, 9, 24, 140, 142–5
　in Daikon Salad with Orange, *92*
　Dashi, *143–4*
　Miso River-bank Casserole, *166–7*

Pickled, 173
　Rolls, *144–5*
　added to Tofu, 192
　Tofu Treasure Balls, *199–200*
Kombu rolls: *144–5*
　Oden, *167–9*
Konnyaku, 25
　Coloured Rice, *264–5*
　Kimpira, *66*
Miso Oden, *169–70*
　Oden, *167–9*
　Snow Country Winter Casserole, *162–4*
　Unohana, *223*
　Vegetable Dengaku, *152–3*
Koya Dofu: *see* Tofu, dried
Kuri Kinton, *75*
Kuzu, 25, 105
　Sauce, with Sautéed and Simmered
　　Vegetables, *151*
　Sesame Tofu, *202–3*

Laver, 145
Leek(s), 25, 93–4, 105
　Barbecued, *154–5*
　Casserole of Tofu and Vegetables, *161–2*
　Chawan Mushi, *249–50*
　Miso River-bank Casserole, *166–7*
　Miso Soup with Natto, *237*
　Miso Soup with Tofu and Wakame, *233*
　Okonomiyaki, *248*
　One-pot Dish with Noodles, *164–6*
　Ozoni, *278–9*
　Salad with Hot Miso Dressing, *94*
　Snow Country Winter Casserole, *162–4*
　Tempura, *156–7*
　Tempura Soba, *291–2*
　Vegetable Dengaku, *152–3*
　in Vegetable Fritters, *158*
　Vegetables Sautéed and Simmered in Kuzu
　　Sauce, *150–1*
　Winter Soba with Vegetables, *288–9*
Lemon(s):
　Soy dipping sauce, *161–2*
　in Tofu making, *190–2*
　Twists, *221*
Lettuce:
　Nori Cones with Natto, *240–1*
　Nori Rolls, *270*
　Salad Nori Rolls, *146*
　for Sushi Party, *274–5*
Lotus root, 25–6
　Barbecued, *155*
　Kimpira, *66*
　Tempura, *157*

Makiyaki Nabe, 37
Mangetout peas, 26
　Casserole of Tofu and Vegetables, *161–2*
　Chawan Mushi, *249–50*
　Clear Soup with Wakame, *148–9*
　　with Natto, *236–7*
　Tempura, *157*

Marinated Tofu Tatsuta Style, *195–6*
Marinated Turnip and Apricot Rolls, *138–9*
Matsutake mushrooms, 95, 98
Menus, planning, 15–18
  sample, *18–20*
Mirin, 26
Miso, 9, 26, 224–33
Miso, flavoured, *152–3, 196–7, 214*
  Deep-fried Yuba Rolls, *214*
  with Grilled Sweet Potatoes, *130*
  Miso Oden, *169–70*
  Tofu Dengaku, *196–7*
  with Vegetable Dengaku, *152–3*
Miso Oden, *169–70*
Miso, pickling with, 172, *173–4*
Miso, red, 225
  Celery Pickle, *175*
  Deep-fried Yuba Rolls, *214*
  Miso Soup: with Aubergine and Wakame,
    230
    with Daikon Radish, *233*
    with Dried Mushrooms, Fresh
      Mushrooms and Tofu, *231*
    with Leeks, Tofu and Wakame, *233*
    with Natto, *237*
    with Turnips, *232*
  for pickles, *173–4*
  in Salad Nori Rolls, *146*
  Tofu Pickled in, *201–2*
  Vegetable Dengaku, *152–3*
Miso 'River-bank', *166–7*
Miso River-bank Casserole, *166–7*
Miso, sesame:
  in Stuffed Rice Cakes in Nori, *280*
Miso soups: see Soups, miso/thick
Miso, sweet, *48–9*
  with Aubergines, *48–9*
  Aubergines Stuffed with Sesame,
    51–2
  New Year's Soup, *279*
Miso, walnut:
  with Cucumber, *82–3*
  Stuffed Rice Cakes in Nori, *280–1*
Miso, white, 225
  Aubergine Pickles, *174*
  Deep-fried Yuba Rolls, *214*
  Dressing for Flower Peppers, *109*
  Miso Soup: with Bamboo Shoots and
    Wakame, *228–9*
    with Chinese Cabbage and Deep-fried
      Tofu, *232*
    with French Beans and Tofu, *230–1*
    with Spinach and Deep-fried Tofu, *229*
  Pumpkin Simmered with, *117–18*
  Salad Nori Rolls, *146*
  with Sautéed Cauliflower, *71–2*
  with Sweet Potato, *130–1*
  Vegetable Dengaku, *152–3*
  Walnut Miso, *83*
Mixed vegetable dishes, 150–70
Mochi: see Rice cakes
Mock Eel, *200–1*

'Moon-Viewing' Noodles, *292–3*
Mount Koya Chawan Mushi, *250–1*
Mrs Fujii's Country-style Nori Rolls, *270–2*
Mrs Misono's Special Tempura, *158–9*
Mushiki: see Steamer
Mushroom(s), 26–7, 95–104
Mushrooms, dried, 95–6
  Autumn Salad, *103–4*
  Coloured Rice, *264–5*
  Dashi, *143*
  Dobin Mushi, *98–9*
  Five-colour Soba, *287*
  Miso River-bank Casserole, *166–7*
  Miso Soup with Fresh Mushrooms and
    Tofu, *231*
  New Year's Soup, *279*
  Nori Rolls, *269*
  Rice, *101–2*
  Simmered Whole Shiitake, *96–7*
  Snow Country Winter Casserole, *162–4*
  Stuffed with Tofu, *100–1*
  Stuffing for Aubergine, *50*
  Sweetcorn Soup, *128*
  added to Tofu, *192*
  with Tofu and Deep-fried Walnuts, *99–
    100*
  Tofu Treasure Balls, *199–200*
  Whole Shiitake Sautéed and Simmered,
    97–8
  Winter Soba with Vegetables, *288–9*
Mushrooms, Fresh:
  Barbecued, *154–5*
  Casserole of Tofu and Vegetables, *161–2*
  Chawan Mushi, *249–50*
  Miso Soup with Dried Mushrooms, Fresh
    Mushrooms and Tofu, *231*
  Miso Soup with Natto, *237*
  Mount Koya Chawan Mushi, *250–1*
  Nori Rolls, *270*
  One-pot Dish with Noodles, *164–6*
  Ozoni, *278–9*
  Salad with Walnut Dressing, *102–3*
  Tempura, *156–7*
  Tempura Soba, *291–2*
  with Tofu and Deep-fried Walnuts, *99–
    100*
  and Turnip Salad, *139*
  in Vegetable Dengaku, *152–3*

Nabe: see One-pot dishes
Natto, 27, 234–41
  with French Beans, *236–7*
  Miso Soup with, *237*
  Nori Cones with, *240–1*
  Nori Rolls with, *240, 269*
  Omelette, *238*
  Plain, *236*
  Tempura, *238–9*
Negi: see Leeks
New Year dishes, 133, 277
  Five-colour Soya Beans, *181*
  Kombu Rolls, *144–5*

Kuri Kinton, 75
Marinated Turnip and Apricot Rolls,
    138–9
New Year's Soup, Kyoto-style, 279
Ozoni, 278–9
Potato Chestnuts, 114–15
Red and White Salad, 90–1
sample menu, 20
Soba, 283–4
Sweet-simmered Soya Beans, 182
Nigari, 27, 190
Noodle broth, 288
Noodle dishes: see Harusame noodles;
    Shirataki; Soba
Nori, 27, 140, 145–6
Mrs Misono's Special Tempura, 158–9
Rolled Omelette with, 244
Stuffed Rice Balls, 263–4
Stuffed Rice Cakes in, 280–1
Sushi Party, 274–5
Tempura Soba, 291–2
toasting, 145
Nori Cones with Natto, 240–1
Norimaki, 266–70
Nori Rolls, 234, 266, 267–70
Kappa Rolls, 84–5
Mrs Fujii's Country-style, 270–2
with Natto, 240
Salad, 146

Oden (Japanese Winter Stew), 167–9
Ohagi: Rice and Aduki Bean Balls, 185–6
Oils, 27, 40. See also Sesame oil
Okara, 27, 189, 191, 212, 222–3
Unohana, 223
Okome: see Rice
Okonomiyaki, 57, 247–8
Okra, with Natto, 236–7
Omelette pan, rectangular, 37
Omelettes:
Egg Wrappers, 246, 273–4
Natto, 238
Omelettes, rolled, 243–4
Egg Sushi, 245–6
Mrs Fujii's Nori Rolls, 270–2
with Nori, 244
Snow Country Winter Casserole, 162–4
with Spinach, 245
with Vegetables, 245
One-pot dishes, 57, 133, 159–60, 207
Casserole of Tofu and Vegetables, 161–2
earthenware casserole for, 36, 160
eggs in, 242
equipment, 160
Miso River-bank Casserole, 166–7
with Noodles, 164–6
Snow Country Winter Casserole, 162–4
Spinach and Cabbage Rolls, 60–1
Yudofu, 194–5
Onion(s), 105–6
Barbecued, 154–5
Pumpkin Simmered with Miso, 117–18

Salad with Lemon Soy Dressing, 106
Simmered Yoshino-style, 105–6
Tempura, 156–7
Tempura Soba, 291–2
Vegetables Simmered and Sautéed in Kuzu
    Sauce, 150–1
Oroshi gane: see Grater, Japanese
Otoshi buta: see Drop lid
Ozoni: New Year's Soup, Tokyo-style, 29,
    278–9

Pancakes:
Gyozu, 61–2
Okonomiyaki, 247–8
Parboiling, 39
Parsley:
Mrs Misono's Special Tempura,
    158–9
Pumpkin Tempura, 118–19
Party dishes:
Sushi Party, 274–5
Peanuts:
Sauce, 111–12
Spinach Rolls, 122–3
Tofu, 103
Peas:
Okonomiyaki, 248
Peppers, 107–9
Barbecued, 154–5
Flower Peppers, 109
Okonomiyaki, 248
Stuffed Green and Red Pepper Boats,
    108–9
Tempura, 156–7
Vegetable Dengaku, 152–3
Vegetables Sautéed and Simmered in Kuzu
    Sauce, 150–1
Perilla, 27–8
Mrs Misono's Special Tempura,
    158–9
Nori Cones with Natto, 240–1
Salad Nori Rolls, 146
Umeboshi, 175–6
Persimmons, dried:
Autumn Salad, 103–4
Marinated Turnip Rolls, 138–9
Pickles, 28, 57, 171–6
Celery in Miso, 175
Japanese: see Japanese pickles
Miso Pickled Vegetables, 173–4
Plums (Umeboshi), 32, 175–6
Quick Aubergine, 174
Salt Pickled Vegetables, 172–3
Tofu, in Miso, 201–2
Plum blossoms: see Carrots, flowers
Plums, pickled, 32, 175–6
Stuffed Rice Balls, 263–4
Poppy seeds, 28
Porphyra, 145
Potato(es), 110–15
Barbecued, 154–5
Chestnuts, 114–15

Potato(es)—*cont*.
    decorative, 112
    Deep-fried, *112–13*
    Deep-fried Stuffed, *113–14*
    Grilled with Peanut Sauce, *112–13*
    Simmered with Wakame, *110–11*
    Snow Country Winter Casserole, *162–4*
    Tempura, *157–8*
Potato starch: *see* Katakuriko
Presentation, 17–18, 133
Pumpkin, 116–19
    Simmered with Miso, *117–18*
    Sweet Simmered, *116–17*
    Tempura, *118–19*

Quails' eggs, 28, 242–3
    Barbecued, *155*
Quantities, 41

Red Maple Radish, *88*
Red Rice, *182–3*
Red and White Salad, *90–1*
Renkon: *see* Lotus root
Rice, 28, 78, 257–82
    Brown, *261*
    Brown Sushi, *262*
    Koji, *227–8*
        in miso making, 226–8
    with Pickles, 171
    Sushi: *see* Sushi rice
    White, *259*
Rice bran, 172
Rice cakes, 29, 258, 277–8
    Deep-fried, *280*
    Miso River-bank Casserole, *166–7*
    New Year's Soup, *279*
    One-pot Dish with Noodles, *164–6*
    Ozoni, *278–9*
    Stuffed, in Nori, *280–1*
    Sweet, *281–2*
    Sweetcorn Soup, *128*
    Zenzai, *186*
Rice dishes:
    Chestnut Rice, *74*
    Coloured Rice, *264–5*
    Domburi, *265–6*
    Egg Sushi, *245–6*
    Five-colour Tofu Pouches, *206–7*
    Inari Sushi, *204–6*
    Kappa Rolls, *84–5*
    Mrs Fujii's Country-style Nori Rolls,
        270–2
    Mushroom Rice, *101–2*
    Nori Cones with Natto, *240–1*
    Nori Rolls, *267–72*
    Nori Rolls with Natto, *240*
    Ohagi, *185–6*
    Red Rice, *182–3*
    Rice Balls, *262–3*
    Soya Bean, *179–80*
    Stuffed Rice Balls, *263–4*

Toasted Rice Balls, *263*
    See also Sushi rice
Rice paddle, 37
Rice vinegar, 32, 172
    Sushi Rice, *260–1*, 262
    Tofu, *190–2*
Rice wine: *see* Sake

Sakata Kimpira, 66
Sake, 13–14, 29
Salad Nori Rolls, 146
Salads:
    parboiling for, 39
Salads, dressed:
    Autumn Salad, *103–4*
    Broccoli with Golden Dressing, *54–5*
    Broccoli with Tofu, *55*
    Cauliflower and French Beans, *72*
    Cucumber with Walnut Miso, *82–3*
    Fresh Mushroom with Walnut Dressing,
        102–3
    Japanese Cabbage, *62–3*
    Leek with Hot Miso Dressing, *94*
    Natto with French Beans, *236–7*
    Onion, with Lemon Soy Dressing, *106*
    Spinach with Rich Tofu Dressing, *123–4*
    Spinach with Sesame Dressing, *121*
    White Salad with Tofu Dressing,
        69–70
Salads, Vinegared:
    Chrysanthemum Turnips, *136–8*
    Cucumber and Tofu, *82*
    Cucumber and Wakame, *147–8*
    Daikon with Kombu and Orange, *92*
    Marinated Turnip and Apricot Rolls,
        138–9
    Red and White, *90–1*
    Three-colour, *83–4*
    Turnip and Mushroom, *139*
Salt Pickled Vegetables, *172–3*
Salt, pickling, *172*
Saucepan, cast-iron, 34
Sauces:
    Hot Sesame, *90*
    Kuzu, *151*
    Peanut, *111–12*
    Sesame, for Casserole of Tofu and
        Vegetables, *161–2*
    for Temple Tofu, *198*
    for Tofu Treasure Balls, *199–200*
    Vegetable Barbecue, *154–5*
Sauces, dipping:
    for Aubergine Tempura, *50–1*
    Lemon Soy, *161–2*
    for Stuffed Green and Red Pepper Boats,
        108–9
    for Tempura, *156–7*
    for Yudofu, *194–5*
Scissor frying, 50–1
Seasons:
    in menu planning, 16
    sample menus, 19

Seaweeds, 8–9, 140–9
Seitan, 29
  Green and Red Pepper Boats, 108–9
Sesame miso:
  Stuffed Rice Cakes in Nori, 280–1
Sesame oil, 27, 29
Sesame paste, 30
Sesame seeds, 29–30
  Broccoli Sautéed with, 54
  Dressing for Cauliflower and French
    Beans, 72
  Dressing for Spinach, 121
  with Hijiki, 142
  Sauce for Tofu Casserole, 161–2
  in Spinach Rolls, 122–3
  Sweet Rice Cakes, 281–2
  toasting, 30
  Tofu, 202–3
  Vegetable Dengaku, 152–3
Sesame Tofu, 202–3
  Aubergines Stuffed with Sesame,
    51–2
Seven-spice pepper, 30
Shamoji: see Rice paddle
Shichimi togarashi: see Seven-spice pepper
Shinoda Rolls, 58–60
  Oden, 167–9
Shirataki noodles, 30
  Casserole of Tofu and Vegetables, 161–2
  Three-colour Salad, 83
Shiso: see Perilla
Shoga: see Ginger
Shoyu: see Soy sauce
Shungiku: see Chrysanthemum leaves
Silken tofu, 188, 192, 194, 230
Simmered dishes, 39–40
  Aubergines, 47
  Carrots in Dashi, 65–6
  Chinese Cabbage and Deep-fried Tofu, 58
  Chinese Cabbage Shinoda Rolls, 58–60
  Daikon Rounds with Hot Sesame Sauce,
    89–90
  Deep-fried Yuba Rolls, 215–16
  Dried Yuba, Deep-fried, 215
  Five-colour Soya Beans, 180–1
  Grilled Tofy Purses, 208–9
  Hijiki with Sesame, 142
  Kimpira, 66
  Kombu Rolls, 144–5
  Kuri Kinton, 75
  Mushrooms with Tofu and Deep-fried
    Walnuts, 99–100
  Onions, Yoshino-style, 105–6
  Potatoes, with Wakame, 110–11
  Pumpkin, with Miso, 117–18
  Rich Simmered Hijiki with Tofu, 141–2
  Sesame Aubergine, 49
  Sweet Potatoes with Hijiki, 132
  Sweet Pumpkin, 116–17
  Sweet-simmered Soya Beans, 182
  Tofu Purses, 207–8
  Turnips in Dashi, 134

Unohana, 223
Vegetables in Kuzu Sauce, 150–1
Whole Shiitake Mushrooms, 96–7
Whole Shiitake Mushrooms Sautéed and
  Simmered, 97–8
Winter Carrot Mix, 68–9
Winter Vegetables, 89
Skewers, 37
Snow Country Winter Casserole, 162–4
Soba, 283–93
  Five-colour, 287
  Fox Noodles, 290
  Homemade, 284–5
  Moon-viewing Noodles, 292–3
  One-pot Dish with, 164–6
  Summer, 285–6
  Tempura, 291–2
  Winter, 288
  Winter with Vegetables, 288–9
Social customs, 2–6
Somen, 31
  Chestnuts in Burrs, 75–7
Soups, clear:
  with Broccoli, 56
  with Cucumber, 81
  with Daikon and Deep-fried Tofu, 88
  Dashi, 143
  Egg-drop with Cucumber, 81–2
  with Spinach and Egg, 125–6
  Wakame and Mangetout Peas, 148–9
  with Yuba, 220–1
Soups, miso/thick: 26, 225, 228
  with Aubergine and Wakame, 230–1
  with Bamboo Shoots and Wakame, 228–9
  with Chinese Cabbage and Deep-fried
    Tofu, 232
  Classic, 233
  with Daikon Radish, 233
  Dobin Mushi, 98–9
  with Dried Mushrooms, Fresh
    Mushrooms and Tofu, 231
  with French Beans and Tofu, 230–1
  Kaminari Jiru, 193–4
  with Leeks, Tofu and Wakame, 233
  with Natto, 237
  New Year's Soup, Kyoto-style, 279
  Ozoni, 278–9
  with Spinach and Deep-fried Tofu, 229
  Sweetcorn, 128
  with Turnips and Turnip Leaves, 232
Soups, sweet:
  Zenzai, 186
Soya bean curd: see Tofu
Soya bean husks: see Okara
Soya bean products, 9, 189–90
Soya beans:
  Five-colour, 181
  Miso, 226–7
  Natto, 235
  Rice, 179–80
  Sweet-simmered, 182
  Tofu, 190–2

Soya flour, roasted, 31
  Ohagi, *185–6*
  Sweet Rice Cakes, *281–2*
Soya milk, 212
Soya milk whey, 189–90, 191–2
Soy sauce, 31
Special dinner menu, 20
Spinach, 120–6
  and Cabbage Rolls, *60–1*
  Casserole of Tofu and Vegetables, *161–2*
  Clear Soup with Egg, *125–6*
  Miso River-bank Casserole, *166–7*
  Miso Soup with Deep-fried Tofu, 229
  Mrs Fujii's Nori Rolls, *270–2*
  New Year's Soup, 279
  Nori Rolls, 270
  One-pot Dish with Noodles, *164–6*
  Rolled Omelette with, *245*
  Rolls, *122–3*
  Roots, 126
  Salad with Rich Tofu Dressing, *123–4*
  with Sesame Dressing, *121*
  Snow Country Winter Casserole, *162–4*
  Steamed Buns, *124–5*
  Winter Soba with Vegetables, *288–9*
Spring dishes:
  Deep-fried Turnip Puffs, *135–6*
  Miso Soups, *228–9*
Spring onions, 94, 105
  added to Tofu, 192
Standard tofu: *see* Cotton tofu
Steamed dishes, 40
  Chawan Mushi, *249–50*
  Chestnut Cakes, 77
  Dobin Mushi, *98–9*
  Mount Koya Chawan Mushi, *250–1*
  Mushrooms Stuffed with Tofu, *100–1*
  Spinach Buns, *124–5*
  Tamago Dofu, *251–3*
  Turnip Chawan Mushi, *134–5*
Steamer, 37
Stock:
  Dashi, 23, *143–4*
  Mushroom, *96*
  Simmering, for One-pot dishes, *163–4*
Stuffed dishes:
  Aubergine Tempura, *50–1*
  Chinese Cabbage Shinoda Rolls, *59–60*
  Chinese-style Yuba Tempura, *218–19*
  Deep-fried Potatoes, *113–14*
  Green and Red Pepper Boats,
    108–9
  Gyozu Pancakes, *61–2*
  Mushrooms, *100–1*
  Sweet Potatoes, *130–1*
  for Yuba, *217*
Su: *see* Vinegar
Sudare: *see* Bamboo rolling mat
Summer dishes:
  Aubergine, grilled, *46–7*
  Aubergine, Simmered Whole, *47*
  Clear Soup with Cucumber, *81*

Five-colour Soba, *287*
Miso Soups, *230–1*
Mock Eel, *200–1*
Soba, *285–6*
Summer Tofu, *192–3*
Tamago Dofu, *251–3*
Three-colour Salad, *83*
Summer Tofu, *192–3*
Suribachi, 30, 38
Sushi rice, 259–60, *260–1*
  Brown, 262
Sushi dishes:
  Chirashi Zushi, *275–6*
  Egg Sushi, *245–6*
  Egg-wrapped, *272–4*
  Five-colour Tofu Pouches, *206–7*
  Inari Sushi, *204–6*
  Kappa Rolls, *84*
  Mrs Fujii's Country-style Nori Rolls,
    270–2
  Nori Cones with Natto, *240–1*
  Nori Rolls, *267–8*
  Nori Rolls with Natto, 240
  Party, *274–5*
  in Rice Balls, *262–3*
Sweetcorn, *127–8*
  Okonomiyaki, *248*
  Roasted Corn on the Cob, *127*
  Soup, 128
Sweet dishes, 129, 183
  Deep-fried Carrot Cakes, *67–8*
  Deep-fried Chestnut Cakes, *78–9*
  Ohagi, *185–6*
  Potato Chestnuts, *114–15*
  Rice Cakes, *281–2*
  Steamed Chestnut Cakes, 77
  Sweet Potato Stuffed with Miso,
    130–1
  Yokan, *184–5*
  Zenzai, *186*
Sweet potatoes, 129–32
  Baked, *129–30*
  Grilled, *130*
  Kuri Kinton, 75, 129
  Simmered with Hijiki, *132*
  Stuffed with Miso, *130–1*
  Tempura, *156–7*
Sweet-Simmered Soya Beans, *182*

Tahini: *see* Sesame paste
Takenoko: *see* Bamboo shoots
Takuan: *see* Daikon pickle
Tamago Dofu: Egg 'Tofu', *251–3*
Tamari, 31
Taste, variety of, 17
Tea, 11–13
  flavouring for Potato Chestnuts, *115*
Tea ceremony, 12, 73, 129
Techniques, cooking, 39–41
Temple cuisine, 3–4, 10, 73, 75–6, 99, 196,
  198, 202
Temple Tofu, *198*

Tempura, 150, *155–8*
  Chinese-style Stuffed Yuba, *218–19*
  Mrs Misono's Special, *158–9*
  Natto, *238–9*
  Soba, *291–2*
  Yuba, *213*
Tetsu nabe: *see* Saucepan, cast iron
Texture, 16
Three-colour Salad, *83–4*
Tofu, 9, 31, 187–203
  Casserole with Vegetables, *161–2*
  Chawan Mushi, *249–50*
  Clear Soup with Spinach and Egg, *125–6*
  and Cucumber Salad, *82*
  Dengaku, *196–7*
  Domburi, *265–6*
  draining, 189
  dressing: for Autumn Salad, *103–4*
    for Broccoli, *55*
    for Japanese Cabbage Salad, *63*
    for Spinach Salad, *123–4*
    for White Salad, *69–70*
  dried, 32
  Kaminari Jiru, *193–4*
  Marinated, Tatsuta-style, *195–6*
  Miso Oden, *169–70*
  Miso River-bank Casserole, *166–7*
  Miso Soup: with Dried Mushrooms and
      Fresh Mushrooms, *231*
    with French Beans, *230–1*
    with Leeks and Wakame, *233*
  Mount Koya Chawan Mushi, *250–1*
  Mrs Misono's Special Tempura,
    158–9
  with Mushrooms and Deep-fried Walnuts,
    99–100
  Okonomiyaki, *248*
  pickled, 173
  Pickled in Miso, *201–2*
  pressing box, 38, 190
  with Rich Simmered Hijiki, *141–2*
  shops, 187, 189, 204
  storing, 189
  Stuffing: for Aubergine, *50*
    for Mushrooms, *100–1*
  Summer, *192–3*
  Temple, *198*
  Treasure Balls, *199–200*
  varieties, 187–8
  Yudofu, *194–5*
Tofu, deep-fried, 32, 204–9
  Barbecued, *155*
  with Chinese Cabbage, *58*
  Chinese Cabbage Shinoda Rolls, *58–60*
  Clear Soup with Daikon, *88*
  Coloured Rice, *264–5*
  Inari Sushi, *204–6*
  Kitsune Soba, *290*
  in Leek Salad, *94*
  Miso Soup with Chinese Cabbage, *232*
  Miso Soup with Spinach, *229*
  Nori Rolls, *269*

Oden, *167–9*
One-pot Dish with Noodles, *164–6*
Pouches, 204
Pouches, Five-colour, *206–7*
Pouches, Stuffed (Inari Sushi), *204–6*
Purses, *207–8*
Purses, Grilled, *208–9*
Purses, in Oden, *167–9*
Simmered Winter Vegetables, *89*
Turnip Chawan Mushi, *134–5*
Unohana, *223*
Winter Carrot Mix, *68–9*
Tofu, dried, 32
  in nori rolls, *269*
Tofu, grilled:
  Miso River-bank Casserole, *166–7*
Tofu pouches: *see* Tofu, deep-fried
Tofu, sesame: *see* Sesame tofu
Trefoil:
  Mrs Fujii's Country-style Nori Rolls,
    270–2
Tsukemono, 28. *See also* Japanese pickles
Tsukimi Soba, *292–3*
Turnips, 133–9
  Chawan Mushi, *134–5*
  Chrysanthemum, *136–8*
  Daikon Rounds with Hot Sesame Sauce,
    89–90
  decorative cutting, 132, 133
  Deep-fried Puffs, *135–6*
  Grilled with Peanut Sauce, *111–12*
  Marinated Rolls with Apricots, *138–9*
  Miso Soup, *232*
  and Mushroom Salad, *139*
  pickled, 172
  Simmered in Dashi, *134*

Umeboshi, 32, *175–6*
  Stuffed Rice Balls, *263–4*
Umeboshi juice:
  in tofu making, *190–2*
Unohana: Okara Simmered with Vegetables,
    222, *223*
Usuage: *see* Tofu, deep-fried
Utensils, 34–8
Uzura no tamago: *see* Quails' eggs

Variety in food, 16–17
Vegetable Barbecue, *154–5*
Vegetable Dengaku, *152–3*
Vegetable Fritters, *158*
Vegetables, variety of, *7–9*
Vegetables Sautéed and Simmered in Kuzu
    Sauce, *150–1*
Vinegar, 32
Visual effect, 17–18

Wakame, 32, 140, 147–9
  Clear Soup with Mangetout Peas, *148–9*
  and Cucumber Salad, *147–8*
  in Leek Salad, *94*
  Miso Soup: with Aubergine, *230*

Wakame – *cont.*
  Miso soup: with Bamboo Shoots, *228–9*
    with Leeks and Tofu, *233*
  Potatoes Simmered with, *110–11*
  preparation, 147
Walnut(s):
  Cucumber with Walnut Miso, *82–3*
  Dressings: for Mushroom Salad,
    102–3
    for Spinach Roots, *126*
  Filling for Sweet Potato, *130–1*
  with Mushrooms and Tofu, *99–100*
  Tofu, *203*
Wasabi horseradish, 33
Watercress:
  Miso River-bank Casserole, *166–7*
  New Year's Soup, *279*
  Nori Rolls, *270*
  One-pot Dish with Noodles, *164–6*
White Salad(s), *69–70*
  Autumn Salad, *103–4*
  Broccoli, *55*
  Japanese Cabbage Salad, *62–3*
  Spinach, *123–4*
Wholefood ingredients, 9
Winter dishes, *159–60*
  Carrot Mix, *68–9*
  Clear Soup with Daikon and Deep-fried
    Tofu, *88*
  Kaminari Jiru, *193–4*

Miso Oden, *169–70*
Miso Soups, *232–3*
Oden, *167–9*
Simmered Vegetables, *89*
Snow Country Casserole, *162–4*
Soba, *288*
Soba with Vegetables, *288–9*
Turnips Simmered in Dashi, *134*
Women, role of, *2–3*, 5

Yokan: Aduki Bean Jelly, *184–5*
Yuba, 33, *210–11*
  Chinese-style Stuffed Tempura,
    218–19
  Clear Soup with, *220–1*
  Crisps, *215*
  Deep-fried Rolls, *214*
  Dried, *213*
  Dried, Deep-fried and Simmered,
    215
  Making, *211–13*
  One-pot Dish with Noodles, *164–6*
  Simmered Deep-fried Rolls, *215–16*
  Stuffed, *217*
  Tempura, *213*
  Turnip Chawan Mushi, *134–5*
Yudofu: Simmering Tofu, *194–5*

Zenzai: Aduki Bean Soup with Rice Cakes,
  186